HARD-FIGHTING
SOLDIERS

HARD-FIGHTING SOLDIERS

A History of African American Churches of Christ

EDWARD J. ROBINSON

THE UNIVERSITY OF TENNESSEE PRESS | KNOXVILLE

Copyright © 2019 by The University of Tennessee Press / Knoxville.

All Rights Reserved.
Manufactured in the United States of America.
Cloth: 1st printing, 2019.
Paper: 1st printing, 2021.

Library of Congress Cataloging-in-Publication Data

Names: Robinson, Edward J., 1967– author.

Title: Hard-fighting soldiers : a history of African American Churches of Christ / Edward J. Robinson.

Description: First [edition]. | Knoxville : The University of Tennessee Press, 2019. | Includes bibliographical references and index.

Identifiers: LCCN 2019007773 | ISBN 9781621904908 (hardcover) | ISBN 9781621907190 (paperback)

Subjects: LCSH: Churches of Christ—United States—History. | African American churches—History. | United States—Church history.

Classification: LCC BX7075 .R63 2019 | DDC 286.6/3—dc23

LC record available at https://lccn.loc.gov/2019007773

"Lord, you establish peace for us;
all that we have accomplished you have done for us."
—Isaiah 26:12 (NIV)

To:
Jack Evans Sr. and Patricia Officer Evans (1941–2019)
"hard fighting soldiers for the Lord."

CONTENTS

Acknowledgments xiii

A Chronology of African American
Churches of Christ xv

PROLOGUE
The Pilgrimage of F. F. Carson,
Spiritual Warrior xxi

PART ONE
From Slavery to Freedom:
Enslaved Africans and
the Stone-Campbell Movement,
1816–1899

CHAPTER 1
Brothers in Black:
Enslaved Africans in
the Stone-Campbell Movement
3

CHAPTER 2
Mother Churches:
The Emergence of African American
Churches of Christ
13

CHAPTER 3
Founding Fathers:
Pathfinders in African American
Churches of Christ
21

PART TWO

African American Churches of Christ and
the "Race Problem" in America,
1900–1930

CHAPTER 4

"Making Love to Our Daughters":
The Racial Thought of White Churches of Christ

33

CHAPTER 5

"In a Class by Himself":
S. R. Cassius and the "Race Problem"
in Churches of Christ

45

PART THREE

The Age of Marshall Keeble,
1931–1968

CHAPTER 6

Setting the House on Fire:
Marshall Keeble and the "Hard" Theology
of African American Churches of Christ

57

CHAPTER 7

Warhorses:
G. P. Bowser, the "Big Four," and the Structuring
of African American Churches of Christ

73

CHAPTER 8

"Nonviolent Gadflies":
African American Churches of Christ
and the Quest for Civil Rights

93

PART FOUR
Finding Their Own Way,
1969–2008

CHAPTER 9
Making Something Out of Nothing:
Annie C. Tuggle, Thelma M. Holt, and the Women's
Movement in African American Churches of Christ
117

CHAPTER 10
"I'm Coming Up Lord":
The Hymnody of African American Churches of Christ
133

CHAPTER 11
"The Magic of Education":
African American Churches of Christ
and the Pursuit of Knowledge
147

CHAPTER 12
Brothers in Arms:
African American Churches of Christ
in the Global Experience
161

EPILOGUE
From the Outhouse to the White House:
The Paradox of Black Churches of Christ
During the Obama Presidency
173

Notes 181

Bibliography 209

Index 217

ILLUSTRATIONS

David Lipscomb (1831–1917) 59

North Tenneha Church of Christ in Tyler, Texas, in 1935 63

Marshall Keeble (1878–1968) 65

The Higby Street Church of Christ in Jackson, Michigan 76

First Annual Lectureship for African Americans in Churches of Christ, 1945 81

The Thirty-Ninth Annual National Lectureship 82

Thirty-Eighth Ministers' Institute Conference, 2014 83

J. S. Winston (1906–2002) 84

R. N. Hogan (1902–1997) 88

Carl Spain 89

Reunion Photograph of Leaders of the First Annual National Youth Conference, 1952 94

Patricia Jenkins 97

Mary Carr and Her Daughter, Ethel, 1957 99

Kelly K. Mitchell (1928–1998) 103

Annie C. Tuggle (1890–1976) 123

Women Attending Annual National Lectureship, 1967 127

Women Attending the Thirty-Eighth Annual National Lectureship 128

A. Hugh Graham (1922–1980) 141

G. P. Bowser (1874–1950) and His Wife, Fannie 151

Jack Evans Sr., James Maxwell, J. S. Winston, and R. N. Hogan 153

Loyd Clay Harris 157

Roosevelt Sams (1923–2003) in Military Uniform 162

Obama Family 177

ACKNOWLEDGMENTS

Cicero once said: "If you have a garden and a library, you have everything you need." I don't have a green thumb, but I love libraries. Indeed, libraries and librarians are historians' greatest allies. This has certainly been true for me in constructing this book. I am deeply indebted to librarians at following places: Abilene Christian University in Abilene, Texas; Harding School of Theology in Memphis, Tennessee; Jarvis Christian College in Hawkins, Texas; Lipscomb University in Nashville, Tennessee; Oklahoma Christian University in Edmond, Oklahoma; Pepperdine University in Malibu, California; Southwestern Christian College in Terrell, Texas; Texas College in Tyler, Texas; and the Terrell Public Library in Terrell, Texas. All of these librarians answered my questions and provided invaluable assistance as I sought to track down various documents and sources.

Over the years, I have acquired many debts and have received much encouragement and inspiration from many people when pursuing this work, including: Leonard Allen, Fred Bailey, Carrisse Berryhill, Lawrence A. Q. Burnley, Craig Churchill, Ben Foster, Doug Foster, Don Haymes, Richard T. Hughes, Rick Hunter, James Maxwell, Don Meredith, Tom Olbricht, John Robinson, Jerry Rushford, Ervin D. Seamster, Scott Seay, Jerry Taylor, the late Dwayne VanRheenen, and D. Newell Williams. The late Calvin Bowers, R. Vernon Boyd, Michael Casey, Earl I. West, and Robert Woods—all inspired me early on when I first embarked on this journey as a graduate and postgraduate student.

Many thanks to Scot Danforth and the editorial staff at the University of Tennessee Press for believing in this work from its inception. Special thanks to Don and Kay Williams, who generously funded a couple of research trips for me; and to John L. Robinson, a former colleague and mentor at Abilene Christian University, who helped me produce a polished manuscript.

I am most grateful for my wife, Toni, and our daughters, Clarice, Ashley, and Erika, who have lived with this project for almost three decades. Their love and patience sustained me and inspired to complete this project.

I respectfully dedicate this volume to Jack Evans Sr. who has touched the lives of countless people through his preaching and teaching for more than five decades. As a renowned evangelist, dedicated educator, and fierce foe of racial discrimination, Evans has exerted a profound and enduring impact on the history of African American Churches of Christ.

A CHRONOLOGY OF AFRICAN AMERICAN CHURCHES OF CHRIST

1816	Formation of the Free Hills Church of Christ in Celina, TN
1832	Alexander Campbell preaches in a black Baptist Church in GA
1838 (ca.)	Birth of George Ricks, black leader in AL
1846	Birth of Levi Kennedy Sr., black leader in TN
1849	Birth of Preston Taylor, black leader in TN
1851	Birth of S. W. Womack, black leader in TN
1853	Birth of S. R. Cassius, black leader in OK
1855	Founding of the *Gospel Advocate*
1862	Birth of Alexander Campbell, black leader in TN
1863	Emancipation Proclamation issued by Abraham Lincoln
1865	Formation of the Antioch Church of Christ in Midway, TX
1874	Birth of G. P. Bowser, black leader in TN
1878	Birth of Marshall Keeble, black leader in TN
1879	Ordination of Levi Kennedy Sr. to the preaching ministry
1880	Preston Taylor begins writing for the *Christian Standard*
1882	Formation of the Mt. Zion Church of Christ in Thyatira, MS
1883	Conversion of S. R. Cassius in Brazil, IN
1885	Ordination of S. R. Cassius to the preaching ministry
1889	Birth of A. L. Cassius, black leader in CA
1890	Birth of Annie C. Tuggle, a black leader in TN

1893 Preston Taylor baptizes Marshall Keeble into the Gay Street Christian Church in Nashville, TN

1897 S. R. Cassius starts *The Industrial Christian*

G. P. Bowser converts from Methodism to the Stone-Campbell Movement

1899 S. R. Cassius forms the Tohee Industrial School in Tohee, Oklahoma Territory

Levi Kennedy Jr. born

1900 Establishment of the Jackson Street Church of Christ in Nashville, TN

1902 G. P. Bowser begins publishing the *Christian Echo*

Birth of Thelma M. Holt, black leader in TN

Birth of R. N. Hogan, black leader in CA

1904 Birth of Luke Miller, black leader in TX

1906 Birth of J. S. Winston, black leader in TX

Birth of G. E. Steward, black leader in TX

1907 G. P. Bowser organizes a school at the Jackson Street Church of Christ in Nashville, TN

1908 Death of George Ricks, black leader in AL

1909 G. P. Bowser relocates the Silver Point Christian Institute to Silver Point, TN

Birth of F. F. Carson, black leader in CA

1911 Death of Levi Kennedy Sr.

1914 Closure of the Silver Point Christian Institute

Marshall Keeble commits to full-time evangelism

1915 Birth of Orum Trone, black leader in MI

1918 Marshall Keeble plants his first congregation, the Oak Grove Church of Christ in Henderson, TN

1920	Southern Practical Institute opens and closes in Nashville, TN
	S. R. Cassius publishes first edition of *The Third Birth of a Nation*
	Death of S. W. Womack
1923	Annie C. Tuggle earns bachelor's degree from Walden University in Nashville, TN
	Birth of G. P. Holt, black leader in IN
1925	S. R. Cassius publishes second edition of *The Third Birth of a Nation*
1930	Death of Alexander "Aleck" Campbell
1930	Birth of Fred Gray, black leader in AL
1931	Death of Preston Taylor
	Death of S. R. Cassius
	Marshall Keeble baptizes 166 people in Valdosta, GA
1932	Birth of Jack Evans, black leader in TX
1938	G. P. Bowser forms the Bowser Christian Institute in Fort Smith, AR
	R. N. Hogan forms the first choral group for African American Churches of Christ in southern CA
1939	Formation of the Nashville Christian Institute
1945	Formation of the annual National Lectureship in Oklahoma City, OK
	Annie C. Tuggle publishes *Our Ministers and Song Leaders of the Church of Christ*
1946	Closure of the Bowser Christian Institute in Fort Smith, AR
1948	Formation of the Southern Bible Institute in Fort Worth, TX
1949	The Southern Bible Institute becomes Southwestern Christian College in Terrell, TX
1950	Death of G. P. Bowser

1952　Orum Trone Sr. establishes the National Youth Conference

1954　First graduating class from Southwestern Christian College

1955　Fred Gray works with Rosa Parks and Martin Luther King Jr. in AL

1961　Larry Bonner and Billy Curl enroll at Abilene Christian College in TX

1961　F. F. Carson and Richmond Church of Christ (CA) sends out white missionary, Myles T. Tune, to Hong Kong

1967　Jack Evans Sr. appointed president of Southwestern Christian College

　　　Southwestern Christian College chorus travels to and sings in Europe

1968　Death of Martin Luther King Jr.

　　　Death of Marshall Keeble

　　　Closure of the Nashville Christian Institute

1970　Death of Levi Kennedy Jr.

1973　Southwestern Christian College becomes fully accredited

1976　Death of Annie C. Tuggle

1979　Daniel Harrison forms the National Crusade for Christ

　　　Death of G. E. Steward

　　　Floyd Rose publishes *Beyond the Thicket*

　　　Jack Evans Sr. publishes *Before the Thicket*

1982　Death of A. L. Cassius

　　　Southwestern Christian College begins awarding bachelor's degrees in Bible and Religious Education

1985　Sylvia Rose writes: "Holy Spirit," "Restore My Soul," "Mansion, Robe, and Crown"

1986　Death of Thelma M. (Bowser) Holt

1997 Death of R. N. Hogan

2000 Jerry Taylor launches New Wineskins Movement

2002 Death of J. S. Winston

2005 Rick Hunter presents position paper on "Grace" in California

2008 Death of Orum Trone Sr.

Election of Barack Obama

2012 Reelection of Barack Obama

2017 H. Clay Williams launches the National Church of Christ Lectureship in DeSoto, TX

PROLOGUE

The Pilgrimage of F. F. Carson, Spiritual Warrior

> "Well, son, I'll tell you:
> Life for me ain't been no crystal stair,
> It's had tacks in it,
> And splinters,
> And boards torn up,
> And places with no carpet on the floor—
> Bare ... And sometimes goin' in the dark
> Where there ain't been no light.
> So boy, don't you turn back;
> Don't you set down on the steps,
> 'Cause you find it's kinder hard;
> Don't you fall now—
> For I'se still goin,' honey,
> I'se still climbin,'
> And life for me ain't been no crystal stair."
> —Langston Hughes, "Mother to Son"

In 1922, poet Langston Hughes poignantly captured the struggles of black people who transitioned from the dark night of chattel enslavement to the somber shadows of de jure segregation. Hughes' portrayal of the "climbin'" of black Americans vividly and appropriately describes the spiritual journey of African American Churches of Christ,[1] a religious fellowship who scratched and clawed to claim their humanity and dignity in a virulently racist[2] society. African American Churches of Christ, like black churches of other faith traditions, learned to praise God in "bare" circumstances with "tacks," "splinters," broken "boards," "no carpet," and "no light." In short, black believers survived and thrived on the discarded "scraps" of America, forging their own identity, fashioning their own lofty ecclesiology and "hard" theology, and creating their own papers, lectureships, liturgy, and congregations.

F. F. Carson's career embodies the message of the Hughes' poem, which serves as a microcosm for African American Churches of Christ, and furnishes the thesis for this book. Born in 1909 in Midway, Texas, to Perry and Sarah, descendants of enslaved Africans, Francis Frank Carson grew up in the dark shadow of the violent era of legalized segregation. A year after Hughes published his poem "Mother to Son," Carson received baptism at the hands of evangelist Billy Childress. Carson experienced the first of many hardships when his father died in 1925, the same year F. F. completed high school.[3]

The following year, Carson enrolled at Jarvis Christian College (JCC), a school established for blacks in the Disciples of Christ branch of the Stone-Campbell movement in Hawkins, Texas, in 1914.[4] The death of his father left the Carson family with scarce resources; it also meant that Francis had to juggle "odd jobs such as relocating out-door toilets, waiting tables for parties, and working in the campus kitchen." When one of his socks wore out, he embarrassed himself by wearing mismatched socks.[5] Even though he had limited resources, Carson possessed natural athletic ability and excelled in baseball, basketball, and football at JCC. His blazing speed earned him the nicknames "Smokey" and "Streak." A football injury, however, ended his athletic career and left him with a permanent limp. Notwithstanding this handicap, Carson completed his studies at JCC in 1930.[6]

In 1935, amid the throes of the Great Depression and New Deal Era, Carson came under the influence of black minister K. C. Thomas, who nudged him into the preaching ministry.[7] Three years later, Carson met and married Wilma E. Lyons. In 1939, Carson began preaching for a black Church of Christ in Ferris, Texas; he stayed there one year as he was "just a little poorer than the poverty stricken of the era." The next year, Carson ministered to a congregation in Atoka, Oklahoma, where his first daughter, Carol, was born. After the birth of his daughter, Carson considered abandoning the preaching ministry, since "preachers were paid very little, and Black preachers were mostly dependent" on financial support from white Christians. Carson recalled being on the "verge of starvation" and surviving on "food chits we had accumulated" over time.[8]

Despite severe monetary struggles, two people sustained him: his wife and his mother. Carson wrote that his wife "stuck by me, and she encouraged me to continue preaching. Had she not given me this support, the chances are very unlikely that I would have continued in the ministry." Then, shortly before her death, Carson's mother, Sarah, requested, "Francis, don't stay where people don't want you; and don't beg for money." This mother-to-son advice convinced Carson to be intolerant of rejection and to pursue an independent course. Carson would acknowledge that his mother's counsel had an enduring influence on his preaching ministry. "Little did I realize at that time that those words would have a significant impact on all that I was to do from that day forward."[9]

From Atoka, Oklahoma, Carson and his growing family moved to Ennis, Texas, in 1941. World War II changed the nation; and it lured Carson to Wichita, Kansas, where he preached for a black congregation and where he worked for the Boeing Aircraft Company, in a defense plant producing B-29 bombers. Carson detested moving "from congregation to congregation" to stave off starvation. More significantly, he resented the racist animus that separated black Churches of Christ from those of whites. In the Jim Crow era, Carson explained that "it was popular for congregations among whites to spend large sums of monies to establish churches for blacks, as well as support their minister—often inadequately. This was done to keep from having to deal with the problem of having blacks come to their doors for worship." Carson deemed these "racist times" and racist practices "sinful" because God never intended for blacks and whites "to live separately," basing his contention on the New Testament Book of Acts 17:26: "For out of one blood did He form all nations of the earth."[10]

But Carson's primary focus was not to stamp out racism in Churches of Christ; it was rather to lead lost souls to Christ. In 1943, while working for the Aircraft Company in Wichita, Kansas, he met a young coworker named Leroy R. Durley, an avid pianist in a Baptist Church. Carson and Durley developed a friendship which led to frequent Bible discussions. The former impressed Durley with his biblical knowledge and swayed him to be baptized in "an unheated pool" in the winter of 1944. Carson then encouraged Durley to enter the preaching ministry, which led Durley to serve black Churches of Christ in Denver, Colorado, and Milwaukee, Wisconsin.[11]

In 1949, Carson relocated to Berkeley, California, to work with a small congregation there. The Carsons lived in a converted basement where the "rats were so big and bold, it was all that we could do just to keep them at bay." The rodents' fur and droppings caused his wife to contract tuberculosis which confined her to a "sanitarium for many months." Later that year, Carson moved to nearby North Richmond, where he became minister for a congregation that met in a shack with a leaking roof and rotten floors. Armed with determination, diligence, and an unshakeable faith, Carson—over a forty-year period—guided the transformation of this small impoverished congregation in its dilapidated chapel into a thriving prosperous, and productive body of believers. The North Richmond church grew so strong that it began supporting white missionaries at a time when many black preachers still relied on support from white Christians. Indeed, in 1962, Carson took his first trip to Nigeria, traveling to evangelize the souls of black people.[12]

The evangelistic excursions of F. F. Carson mirror the origins, growth, development, and expansion of African American Churches of Christ. As Carson was born to descendants of enslaved Africans, most of the early black leaders of the Stone-Campbell Movement emerged from the shackles of chattel enslavement. Impoverished and intolerant of racism, Carson survived economic oppression as a minister in large measure because his wife encouraged him to stay the course. Similarly, many African American Churches of Christ gained strength from the leadership of black women such as Annie C. Tuggle.

Tuggle, who read scripture in public worship while illiterate men were present, also answered biblical questions that befuddled preachers. She at times counseled both black and white leaders in a male-dominated and racist-saturated fellowship. Many other strong black women made similar contributions such as Carson's mother, who urged him to live independently. Both women and men in African American Churches of Christ nourished a sense of black pride, preferring their own resources and their own institutions rather than depending on their white brethren in the faith.

But the Second World War changed so very many things for African Americans. The promise of economic advancement pulled Carson out of the South to the Midwest and on to the West Coast. World War II translated into economic mobility, social progress, political gains, and congregational growth for blacks in Churches of Christ. In the second half of the twentieth century, African Americans increased numerically, grew economically, and expanded their geographic reach as well.

Carson's experience reflected all these changes. He spent much of his life fighting racism in Churches of Christ. Black Churches of Christ in general adamantly opposed racial discrimination. Barred from white churches and schools, African American Churches of Christ charted their own course, forming their own paper, school, lectureships, youth conference, and congregations. Carson surely possessed what scholar W. E. B. Du Bois called a "double consciousness." The black man in America, wrote Du Bois, "ever feels his two-ness—an American, a Negro; two souls, two thoughts, two unreconciled strivings; two warring ideals in one dark body, whose dogged strength alone keeps it from being torn asunder."[13]

On the one hand, Carson expressed concern for the political and social plight of African Americans. On the other hand, he committed himself to addressing the spiritual needs of his people. Carson expressed it: "We believed then, and still believe, that winning souls is more important than erecting buildings."[14] Carson spoke generally for African American Churches of Christ, who while concerned about economic and civil rights for black people, devoted their lives to evangelizing the unsaved of their race.

When asked how he succeeded in strengthening congregations in Texas, Kansas, California, and eventually Africa, Carson explained that it was "a matter of faith." Carson's statement essentially captures the thesis of this book. African American Churches of Christ, soldiering their way through racial discrimination and economic oppression and battling what they perceived to be religious error, forged their own unique theological identity through diligent labor, the vigorous toil of devoted women, and an unwavering faith in God.

Several historians have composed books on the history of Churches of Christ in the United States. The works chiefly focused on white believers with perhaps a chapter or two devoted to African Americans, often highlighting the pivotal and contrasting work of Marshall Keeble and G. P. Bowser.[15] Other books have treated individual black evangelists in Churches of Christ[16] or African American Churches of Christ in a particular state.[17] This volume builds on this earlier work. In 1947, black evangelist J. S. Winston wrote an article entitled "Work among the Colored People in the U. S."[18] In 1973, aforementioned Annie C. Tuggle, an educator and historian in African American Churches of Christ, composed her autobiography and chronicled important historical events in her faith tradition.[19] Recently, researcher and minister James Maxwell wrote a book exploring the "black presence" in the Restoration Movement.[20] In 2014, W. W. Morrison, a black preacher in Churches of Christ in Texas, collected several discussions on race, highlighted the Keeble-Bowser polarity, and published *The Shaping of a Brotherhood: Historical Reflections*.[21] The same year, minister Leroy Butler Jr. composed a useful book, *A New Citizenry in an Old South: The Story of the First Black Church of Christ in Georgia*, chronicling the origins and development of the first African American Church of Christ in Valdosta.[22] Building on what others have done, the present work stands apart as the first academic, full-length study of African American Churches of Christ. Additionally, unlike previous studies it reaches beyond the Keeble-Bowser dichotomy and relates the stories of lesser known figures (such as F. F. Carson), who left indelible, yet often unexamined imprints on the history of African American Churches of Christ.

I have constructed this historical narrative in four parts with twelve chapters. Part one, consisting of three chapters, chronicles the encounters enslaved Africans had with white leaders in the Stone-Campbell Movement, traces the rise of black congregations in the antebellum and postbellum eras, and highlights African American leaders who shaped these fledgling churches. Part two examines the racial views of white leaders and members of Churches of Christ, while assessing S. R. Cassius's responses to racist perspectives. Part three compares and contrasts the life and labor of Marshall Keeble and G. P. Bowser and notes the varied contributions their disciples made to the destruction of Jim Crow. Part four details the role black women played in strengthening, guiding, and solidifying their congregations as mothers, wives, teachers, nurturers, and missionaries. This section also appraises the lofty place education and music have played in African American Churches of Christ, before noting the work of black leaders in global missions.

The title "Hard Fighting Soldiers" is drawn from a song by that title, a song that the Sensational Nightingales, a black traditional gospel group, popularized in the 1950s. More importantly, the book's title is fitting because black leaders in this faith tradition consistently viewed themselves as militant fighters. Like many of their white counterparts, black leaders and members in Churches of Christ imbibed a "hard and graceless style"[23] and theology that often alienated their black neighbors in other religious groups. In addition, S. W. Womack in 1904 encouraged his fellow ministers by affirming: "If we will only remember that we must have some hard times mixed with our good times, we will not become discouraged, but will learn to 'endure hardness, as a good soldier.'"[24] The verse in 2 Timothy 2:3 also struck a chord with church planter Marshall Keeble, who echoed Womack's exhortation thirteen years later, adding: "No one knows the hardships of an evangelist but one who has engaged in the work."[25]

In the 1940s, Russell H. Moore, a preacher in Dallas, Texas, lauded fellow ministers O. L. Aker, D. M. English, and T. W. Fitzhugh, declaring that "these are all wonderful soldiers for Christ."[26] R. H. Harrison, a reporter for a black congregation in Oklahoma City, referred to J. S. Winston, G. E. Steward, and R. N. Hogan as "faithful and zealous soldiers of the Cross in our midst...." Similarly, reporters in the *Christian Echo* used metaphors of combat to describe their subjects. Joe Cryer, a black Christian from Arkansas, commented: "I am happy to say that we are still fighting the good fight and keeping the faith,"[27] and Truly Cathey, an African American Christian from Mississippi, reported that G. B. Hervey "shot the gospel gun."[28] In 1947, after converting a black Baptist Church in Hopewell, Virginia, into a Church of Christ, John R. Vaughner, a gifted preacher from Florida, informed *Christian Echo* readers that he was "still fighting for that true and living Way."[29] By the same token, Leroy R. Durley, who came under the influence of F. F. Carson, confessed that his mentor was "more than a child in God's family, he was also a soldier in God's army."[30] These statements attest that African American Churches of Christ were indeed "hard fighting soldiers," struggling to stamp out the sins of racism and sectarianism; yet while fighting against others, they often fought amongst themselves.

PART ONE

From Slavery to Freedom

*Enslaved Africans and
the Stone-Campbell Movement,
1816–1899*

—1—

Brothers in Black

Enslaved Africans in the Stone-Campbell Movement

"I love the pure, peaceable, and impartial Christianity of Christ:
I therefore hate the corrupt, slaveholding, women-whipping, cradle-
plundering, partial and hypocritical Christianity of this land."
—Frederick Douglass, *Narrative of the Life of Frederick Douglass*

Enslaved Africans and Barton W. Stone

In the summer of 1801, flames of revivalism blazed across the Kentucky frontier as perhaps ten to twenty thousand people gathered before Barton W. Stone and other ardent white preachers to hear from God. "Bodily agitations" (including jerking, dancing, barking, laughing, running, and singing) emanated from the fervent prayers, melodious songs, and passionate sermons uttered by Stone and his cohorts in Cane Ridge, Kentucky. Such religious "exercises," Stone recalled, were "seen and acknowledged in every neighborhood, and among the different sects it silenced contention, and promoted unity for awhile...."[1]

Unlike the First Great Awakening which was heavily influenced by Calvinism, Arminianism dominated the mindset of the Cane Ridge revivalists. Stone urged his listeners to "believe *now* and receive salvation," proclaiming that "Jesus died for all."[2] Cutting against the grain of Calvinism, Cane Ridge preachers not only advocated human effort and responsibility, but they also proclaimed impartial and unlimited salvation for all human beings who responded to God's calling.

This theological posture, moreover, bore racial and social implications in that African Americans could find a place in God's fold as easily as could whites. Indeed, Stone himself, deeply moved by the fervor of revivalism, emancipated his own slaves. "This revival cut the bonds of many poor slaves," Stone testified, "and this argument speaks volumes in favor of the work. For of what avail is a religion of decency and order, without righteousness?"[3]

As enslaved Africans had been eager participants in the First Great Awakening,[4] black seekers similarly imbibed the enthusiasm of the Second Awakening. Because Baptists and Methodists presented an emotional message, deemphasized formal education, and welcomed black exhorters into their pulpits, enslaved Africans joined those two groups in large numbers.[5] Yet many black bondspeople also found a spiritual home in the movement led by white leaders Barton W. Stone and Alexander Campbell.

Charles Spencer, a black man described as "without hypocrisy," came under the influence of Barton W. Stone and aligned himself with the Cane Ridge Church of Christ, making him one of its seventy-two members of African descent. Spencer brought a measure of emotionalism to his local congregation. Endowed with an unusually high-pitched voice, Spencer sang "but one note, and that of the highest key, and in every song that not was sounded most thrillingly, electrifying those unaccustomed to the unearthly shriek, and during the balance of the song his body would sway to and fro like the rhythmic swinging of a great pendulum." The black worshiper's rhythmic melody and swaying motion proved to be "something overwhelming" to the children in the audience.[6]

Alexander Campbell, a black man unrelated to the white church leader and a Stone convert, also worshiped at the Cane Ridge congregation. In the early 1830s, concerned white Christians, recognizing his potential as a preacher, pooled their resources and purchased his freedom for $1,000. Campbell soon emerged as a noteworthy evangelist in Midway, Kentucky, where he expanded the church's membership to three hundred. He and his wife, Rosa, gave two sons to the preaching ministry: Stafford and Alexander Jr.[7] Details of the elder Campbell's life and death remain nebulous, yet his evangelistic efforts attest to the important presence of black leaders in the Stone-Campbell Movement in pre-Civil War America.

Inspired by a spirit of social justice and Presbyterian spirituality, Stone reached out to his sable neighbors. Under his leadership, the body of Samuel January, another enslaved African who worshiped at Cane Ridge, was interred at the church's cemetery, a sacred plot formerly reserved for whites only. Stone himself, a staunch opponent of chattel enslavement, served as president of the American Colonization Society, an organization formed in 1816 to repatriate free blacks to Africa. In addition, Stone became president of the ACS's local branch in Georgetown, Kentucky.[8]

Enslaved Africans and Thomas Campbell

In 1819, when the Missouri Territory applied for admission into the Union, James Tallmadge Jr., a New York congressman, introduced a pivotal amendment prohibiting the entry of slavery into the proposed state. The Tallmadge resolution ignited a storm of controversy with southerners generally opposing the measure and northerners generally supporting it. The Missouri Controversy so disturbed the new nation that Thomas Jefferson wrote: "But this momentous question, like a firebell in the night, awakened and filled me with terror. I considered it at once the knell of the Union."[9] This intense political and racial conflict between the North and the South, known as sectionalism, intensified through the next three decades, sowed the seeds for secession, and helped to tear the country apart.

In the same year, Thomas Campbell, an 1807 European immigrant and a Presbyterian clergyman, felt the sting of sectionalism firsthand. When conducting a popular school for white students in Burlington, Kentucky, Campbell enjoyed cordial relations with his neighbors until he reached out to enslaved Africans. One Sunday afternoon, the white instructor invited them "all to come into his school-room, read the Bible to them, and joined them in singing hymns with their sweet melodious voices." The following day, however, a concerned neighbor told Campbell that he had violated Kentucky laws which prohibited whites from instructing black people except when other white observers were present. A "thunderstruck" Campbell confessed to ignorance of the law and wondered: "Can the Word of God be thus bound and the proclamation of the gospel be thus fettered in a Christian land? Is it possible for me to remain in a place, where, under any circumstances, I am forbidden to preach a crucified Savior to my perishing fellow-beings?"[10] Thomas Campbell's commitment to teaching scripture to all people—white or black—superseded his compliance to the Old South's mores. Furthermore, Campbell, unlike many of his contemporaries, viewed enslaved Africans as human beings. Hence, the good news about Jesus was for them as well as for whites. Deeply disturbed that his Kentucky neighbors opposed his teaching efforts toward African Americans, Campbell departed the state abruptly and went north where he could labor without racial or religious restrictions.

Enslaved Africans and Alexander Campbell

A decade after the Missouri Controversy, a free black man, David Walker from North Carolina, published an inflammatory document known as *Walker's Appeal*. Walker summoned enslaved Africans to rise up and throw off the shackles of chattel enslavement. "I do declare it," raged Walker, "that one good black man can put to death six white men; and I give it as a fact, let twelve black men get well armed for battle, and they will kill and put to flight fifty whites. The reason is, the blacks, once you get them started, they glory in death." Walker disseminated his fiery anti-slavery message from Wilmington, North Carolina, to Boston, Massachusetts, challenging fellow African Americans to rise up in rebellion, galvanizing proslavery advocates and influencing northern abolitionists to take the fight against of slavery to higher moral ground.[11]

While Walker sought to dissolve chains for black bondsmen, the white Alexander Campbell, son of Thomas Campbell and himself a preacher and educator, found himself ensnared in a vortex of religious turmoil. The Beaver Baptist Church in Pennsylvania issued an "anathema" denouncing Campbell for his insistence on baptism "for the remission of sins" as well as his contention of no direct operation of the Holy Spirit before baptism. The Beaver "Anathema" prompted Campbell's break from the Baptists. Shortly thereafter, he launched a new journal, *Millennial Harbinger*, and stirred a new movement: the Reformers or Disciples.[12] Campbell without question regretted his discord with and his separation from the Baptists because of his commitment to unity, but he felt he had no other choice.

Campbell detested not only religious discord, but he also hated black chattel enslavement. He referred to it as "that largest and blackest blot," "that many-headed monster, that Pandora's box, that bitter root, that blasting curse under which so fair and so large a portion of our country groans."[13] Yet despite his public denunciation of the practice of owning humans, Campbell, echoing in his person the divisiveness of the system, purchased two bondsmen, eighteen-year-old James and twenty-year-old Charley Pool, from a Methodist cleric. He freed both men at age twenty-eight, yet they stayed and worked for the Campbells after their manumission. The Campbell family owned another enslaved African, Mary, who possessed such a "bad disposition and strong will" that Selina Campbell, Alexander's wife, was happy when her husband made her a "present to her father, who lived in Pennsylvania." Unlike Mary who was reportedly abrasive and assertive, Ben, another black bondsman, was compliant, obedient, and a "wonderful musical talent." Selina Campbell noted that he often charmed visitors with the "sweetness and pathos of his voice."[14]

Historians have convincingly shown that the personalities of enslaved Africans were varied and complex but that stereotypes were entrenched. Scholar John W. Blassingame has delineated three slave personalities on most plantations in the South: "Sambo," "Jack," and "Nat." Sambo was faithful and obedient; Jack was compliant as long as his owners treated him right; Nat was a bloodthirsty rebel.[15] Historian Deborah Gray White has similarly found divergent stereotypes among female enslaved people: "Jezebel" and "Mammy," the former abrasive and naturally promiscuous, the latter faithful and submissive.[16] These varied personalities and stereotypes existed in the Campbell household: Jim, Charley, and Ben apparently fit the "Sambo" stereotype, while Mary seemed to the Campbell family to be clearly a "Jezebel." Therefore, Mrs. Campbell rejoiced to see her depart.

Of course, enslaved people were more than perceived personalities, but black rebels actually lived on some plantations in the South. In the summer of 1831, Nat Turner (from whom Blassingame drew his example) and his armed black posse roamed across Southampton County, Virginia, killing fifty white residents. Inspired by his interpretation of biblical teachings, Turner led the most violent slave rebellion in American history, jolting white southerners out of their comfort zone. "In one desperate blow," observed historian Stephen B. Oates, "Nat Turner had smashed the prevailing stereo-type of master-slave relations in the Old South, forcing whites to confront a grim and dreaded reality—that all was not sweetness and sunshine in their slave world, that their own Nats and Harks might be capable of hatred and rebellion."[17] In the religious sphere, Turner's fierce rebellion also shook Campbell and his followers. Campbell's biographer, Robert Richardson, attested that the rebels' murderous acts created a "feeling of alarm and insecurity" across the Southampton community. "The subject of slavery," he explained, "previously referred to only in the most guarded manner, was now everywhere freely and unreservedly canvassed, and various plans were proposed for its removal...."[18]

Notwithstanding the brutality of the Nat Turner revolt, Alexander Campbell believed that the Gospel was for all men. In 1832, the white preacher embarked on a tour across the Deep South, where he met a black Baptist cleric, Andrew Marshall, in Savannah, Georgia. A gifted and energetic exhorter, Marshall had garnered a following of almost 2,500 members. After the black pastor welcomed Campbell into his pulpit, Marshall drew the ire of the Sunbury Baptist Association, which denounced the white preacher's "new doctrines" and ousted the black minister for "holding sentiments avowed by Alexander Campbell."[19]

In 1839, Campbell again visited Savannah and expressed admiration for "brother Andrew Marshall, a man of color." Campbell interviewed the black minister and offered the following sketch: After first purchasing his wife and children out of chattel enslavement, Marshall then secured his own freedom for six hundred dollars. Eighty-one-year-old Marshall, Campbell noted, was worth twenty thousand dollars and led a congregation of eighteen hundred members. The white visitor called Marshall "the ablest and best preacher in Savannah," and admitted that the black cleric had been "shamefully persecuted" because of his association with "Campbellism." The white admirer concluded: "Take him all in all, he is an honor to the race to which he belongs."[20]

In spite of his laudatory remarks about Andrew Marshall, Alexander Campbell espoused complex and contradictory views about enslaved Africans. Like his father Thomas Campbell, the younger Campbell prioritized the proclaiming of the Gospel to all men. Even after Nat Turner's bloody uprising, Alexander felt no misgivings about interviewing a black pastor and preaching to his large flock. Yet at the same time, the white editor openly defended the practice of chattel enslavement, arguing that scripture did not condemn it and that it should not be made a test of fellowship.[21] Moreover, Campbell unquestionably absorbed a great deal of the racism of his era, inexplicably concluding: "Much as I may sympathize with a black man, I love a white man more."[22]

Campbell issued this racist statement in 1845, the same year John L. O'Sullivan, a New York journalist, coined the phrase: "Manifest Destiny." For O'Sullivan, Campbell, and other nineteenth-century whites, it was God's will for white men to expand across the North American landscape. Consequently, white leaders claimed divine sanction for the removal of Native Americans to Oklahoma, the overthrow of Mexicans in Texas and other regions, and the subjugation of black people across the South and beyond.[23]

Frederick Douglass, the most prominent black man in nineteenth-century America, contested the racist views of Manifest Destiny's supporters. Born into chattel enslavement in Maryland as Frederick Augustus Washington Bailey, Douglass escaped from bondage in 1837, changed his name, and published his autobiography eight years later. Douglass delineated two strands of American Christianity: The Christianity of the nation and the Christianity of Christ. "I love the pure, peaceable, and impartial Christianity of Christ," emphasized Douglass. "I therefore hate the corrupt, slaveholding, women-whipping, cradle-plundering, partial and hypocritical Christianity of this land." Douglass never mentioned Alexander Campbell directly; still he had in mind all white ministers who led "Christian churches" but lived "in union with slaveholders."[24]

The 1850s proved to be a decade of divisiveness. Religious polarization dissolved the ties of the three largest religious bodies—Baptists, Methodists, and Presbyterians—over the issue of chattel enslavement.[25] Literary polarization followed religious polarization after the release of Harriet Beecher Stowe's *Uncle Tom's Cabin* in 1852. Political polarization permeated the 1850s with the passage of the Fugitive Slave Law of 1850, the Gadsden Purchase of 1853, the Kansas-Nebraska Act of 1854, the Brooks-Sumner Affair of 1856, and the Dred Scott Case in 1857. Emotional polarization also shook the nation in 1859 when zealous abolitionist John Brown raided the federal arsenal at Harpers Ferry, Virginia, intending to incite a rebellion of enslaved Africans across the South.[26]

All of these volatile events touched and shaped the Stone-Campbell Movement in some way, for the polarization of the 1850s concerned the plight and future of the 3.2 million enslaved humans living on American soil. Members of the Stone-Campbell Movement owned 101,000 black people.[27] Consequently, slaveholders aligned with the Stone-Campbell Movement felt the rumblings of the mid-nineteenth century as they too had much at stake with their so-called "property."

That the anxiety of the 1850s penetrated the Stone-Campbell Movement can be seen in the immediate aftermath of the Fugitive Slave Law of 1850, which required any citizen in the free states to assist in the capture of runaway enslaved Africans or be punished. Campbell, citing Paul's epistle to Philemon, urged his readers to comply with the measure. John Kirk, a white Christian and abolitionist from Ohio, denounced Campbell's position: "I have come to the conclusion that I will neither patronize priest nor paper, that is not strictly anti-slavery." Campbell retorted that Kirk should keep his extreme "opinionism" to himself.[28] The Campbell-Kirk exchange illustrates that while tension and tempers flared among members of the Stone-Campbell Movement, it did not officially fracture it, perhaps because the movement lacked a central organization, but was composed of rather independent congregations.

In addition to the tumultuous episodes of the nineteenth century, the 1850s witnessed a number of people born in bondage who later emerged as potent leaders in the late nineteenth- and early twentieth-century black

Churches of Christ, such as Samuel W. Womack and Samuel R. Cassius, born in 1851 and in 1853, respectively. The following year, the Stone-Campbell lost a premier white leader when Thomas Campbell died. And in 1855, two preeminent white leaders, Tolbert Fanning and David Lipscomb, collaborated in Nashville, Tennessee, to publish the *Gospel Advocate*, destined to become the most influential journal in shaping and molding the theological perspectives of African American Churches of Christ.[29]

Enslaved Blacks in the Civil War

Defense of the enslavement of four million black people in 1860 precipitated the secession of eleven southern states and ignited the American Civil War. Both sides initially barred black men from armed service. Abraham Lincoln's Emancipation Proclamation not only expanded the war's goal of preserving the union to include the intent of freeing enslaved Africans—but it also led to the recruitment of black soldiers. By the war's end, 186,000 black men had fought in the Union army, and some 10,000 more served in the Union navy.[30] Some black men who later committed to the Stone-Campbell Movement had participated in the Civil War. Limited records indicate that Samuel R. Cassius, after relocating from Prince William County, Virginia, found work as contraband for Union troops while Preston Taylor, an enslaved African from Louisiana and Kentucky, served as a drummer boy for the 116th U. S. Colored Infantry, defenders of Camp Nelson in 1864. Researcher Annie C. Tuggle has identified Henry Clay as a Civil War veteran, insinuating that he most likely saw action as a Union soldier in a black regiment from Tennessee.[31]

Armed with moral rectitude and spiritual courage, such men as Cassius, Taylor, and Clay emerged from the old world of bondage into the new world of hope and freedom, but not without physical and emotional scars. After converting to the Stone-Campbell Movement, this trio, among others, toiled as torchbearers of racial justice and religious unity in the complex and chaotic world spawned by the Civil War. They forged the way for other formerly enslaved people who joined their noble cause to advance what they believed was the "pure gospel."

Alexander Campbell, who had declared that he possessed more love and sympathy for American whites than he did for black people,[32] clearly did not highly value African Americans. Nevertheless, pioneering black preachers in Churches of Christ still held the white evangelist in high regard. Samuel Robert Cassius lauded him as "that great man of God" who was "sent of

God" to correct religious error in America.³³ G. P. Bowser, another postwar black leader, held that African Americans in Churches of Christ owed "the Campbells much honor."³⁴ Such a theological affinity and even affection overshadowed for them any racial animosity Campbell may have espoused toward black people. Black leaders in Churches of Christ committed themselves to Campbell's principles, carefully studied his sermons and writings, and so imbibed his debating tradition that they helped to birth a new religious fellowship that still thrives. The following chapter explores the origins of these African American Churches of Christ.

— 2 —

Mother Churches

The Emergence of African American Churches of Christ

> "As a race, we know nothing of God but what white people have taught us."
> —S. R. Cassius, "Among Our Colored Disciples"

The origins of African American Churches of Christ remain nebulous. With no central organization for the movement, there was no nexus for gathering or preserving records, and the general illiteracy of the enslaved population only increased the difficulty. The resultant paucity of useful sources makes it virtually impossible to obtain a thorough understanding of this fellowship's history. Black Churches of Christ seem to have sprung up sporadically and disparately. While located initially in the South, there was no specific geographical area where the group clustered. The handful of congregations that emerged after the Civil War apparently came into being because formerly enslaved people had embraced the religious traditions of their owners and chose to remain loyal to that faith. Historian William E. Montgomery has persuasively argued that black people "tended to remain in the churches they had joined before the war."[1] In other words, the earliest black Churches of Christ seem to have originated on the same plantations where their members had toiled before the Civil War and often remained as paid laborers after that conflict ended. While the eminent black preacher Marshall Keeble once dubbed the Jackson Street Church of Christ in Nashville, Tennessee, the "mother church" for African American Churches of Christ,[2] several black congregations actually emerged long before Keeble's home religious community in Nashville.

Free Hills Church of Christ in Celina, Tennessee

The oldest known African American Church of Christ is the Free Hills Church of Christ in Celina, Tennessee. Situated in Clay County, Tennessee, the Free Hills Church of Christ dates to 1816,[3] two decades after the founding of the Volunteer State and just forty years after the signing of the Declaration of Independence. 1816 also marked the year that Alexander Campbell preached his famous "Sermon on the Law" before the Redstone Baptist Association in (West) Virginia, establishing a new hermeneutics of distinguishing between the Old and New Testaments.[4] Barton W. Stone and Thomas Campbell, co-religionist and father of Alexander, actively preached and taught across the American frontier, establishing the congregations called Churches of Christ or Disciples of Christ. Such churches constituted what is commonly referred to as the Restoration Movement or the Stone-Campbell Movement. The *Christian Chronicle* recently listed nineteen Churches of Christ established by 1819; of that number, ten originated in Tennessee.[5] Yet the origins of the Free Hills Church of Christ remain opaque.

Contemporary historical sketches reveal that Virginia Hill, a wealthy white woman from North Carolina, relocated to Overton County, Tennessee (Clay County was formed in 1870 from parts of Overton and Jackson counties), bringing with her several enslaved Africans. Betsy Manny, a free black woman, also accompanied Mrs. Hill to Celina. Mrs. Hill reportedly manumitted her other enslaved Africans and divided among them several hundred acres of land. The new landowners subsequently named their community "the free Hills." The freed people soon organized the first known and continuous black Church of Christ—the Free Hills Church of Christ.[6] It remains unclear exactly when Virginia Hill relocated to Tennessee, whether or not she was part of the Stone-Campbell Movement, precisely how many enslaved Africans accompanied her from the Tar Heel State, and what inspired her to free them.

Notwithstanding this uncertainty, it is likely that the all-black Free Hills Church of Christ, established in 1816, evolved from the predominantly white congregation, the Rock Springs Church of Christ in Celina, Tennessee, formed eleven years earlier. Still it remains unclear whether the separation was voluntary or mandatory in the antebellum South.

Even though the inception of the Free Hills Church of Christ remains obscure, what is clear is that the congregation gradually gained strength in both spirit and number even into the twentieth century as different black ministers visited and preached the "pure gospel," baptizing believers for the remission of sins, evangelizing through the local church, and worshiping without instruments of music. In 1907, G. P. Bowser, an emerging black preacher and educator, reported preaching in Celina, Tennessee; his return the following year produced eleven baptisms.[7] In 1911, John T. Ramsey, an African American evangelist from middle Tennessee, reported that he ended his "first annual meeting with the Free Hills Church of Christ" in Celina, Tennessee, "with fine attendance day and night." One of Ramsey's converts was Zelma Estella Shoffner, a teacher in the Celina community. "This is a hard field," confessed Ramsey. "I promised to hold a meeting for them next year, if the Lord wills."[8] A decade later, Gilbert A. Johnson, a black preacher from nearby Cookeville, Tennessee, experienced considerable success after preaching in Celina for two weeks, happily announcing that "fifty-four souls [were] added to the one body."[9]

George Ricks and the Christian Home Church of Christ in Alabama

Approximately fifty white advocates of New Testament Christianity arrived in antebellum Alabama between 1825 and 1850.[10] After the Civil War, these white proponents of the Stone-Campbell Movement reached out to their black neighbors. Among the earliest black converts to Restoration principles was George Ricks. Born into chattel enslavement in the mid 1830s, Ricks belonged to Abraham and Charlotte Ricks, white immigrants from North Carolina. Owner of approximately ten thousand acres of land worked by his three hundred enslaved Africans, Abraham Ricks Sr. adhered closely to the Stone-Campbell Movement and sent his son, Abraham Jr., to study at Alexander Campbell's fledgling school, Bethany College, in Virginia. The Ricks family reportedly treated their enslaved Africans cordially and gave them biblical instruction. George Ricks acquired both literacy and a love for the Bible under the tutelage of Charlotte Ricks, a courageous white Christian who violated the slaveowner's code of prohibiting the enslaved from reading and writing.[11]

George Ricks put this learning to good use, as he so toiled and saved his earnings, even managing to purchase fifty acres of land, becoming the first black property owner in Alabama.[12] Shortly after the Civil War, Ricks came under the influence of James Srygley and entered the preaching ministry. In 1867, Ricks appealed to *Gospel Advocate* readers to assist him and his small congregation of fifty to help them pay off their debt. The paper's editor, David Lipscomb, supported Ricks's appeal and assured his audience that the black evangelist was "most worthy" and accomplished a "good and faithful work for the Lord and his people."[13] Seventeen years later Ricks, while visiting and preaching in Nashville, Tennessee, reported that he had baptized about three hundred people in Alabama. He also noted that his home congregation, the Christian Home Church of Christ near Muscle Shoals, Alabama, numbered ninety-six members; and he worked to develop a flock of fifty in Fayetteville, Alabama, as well.[14] The former congregation, which surfaced in the post-Reconstruction era in the Yellowhammer State, became the "mother church" for African American Churches of Christ in that state; the latter congregation represented one of several offspring, including the High Street Church of Christ in Tuscumbia; the Cherokee Church of Christ in Cherokee; the Sterling Boulevard Church of Christ in Sheffield; the Westside Church of Christ in Leighton; the Reedtown Church of Christ in Russellville; and the Fayetteville Church of Christ in Talladega.[15]

Mount Zion Church of Christ in Tate County, Mississippi

In neighboring Mississippi, the oldest African American Church of Christ grew from a white congregation: the Thyatira Church of Christ in Tate County in north Mississippi. White members who comprised the Thyatira congregation had migrated from middle Tennessee where they had been members of the Cathey's Creek Church of Christ in Maury County. These Anglo believers not only brought with them their "property," but they also carried with them their religious convictions. In 1844, ten enslaved Africans aligned themselves with the Stone-Campbell Movement in north Mississippi. Two years later, the Thyatira Church of Christ had sixty-nine members, fourteen of whom were of African descent, and six of these belonged to the Cathey family of T. G. and Alexander Cathey.[16] After the Civil War, black and white Christians in Tate County agreed to form separate congregations. In 1882, Alexander Cathey donated one acre of land for black Christians to erect the Mount Zion Church of Christ in Thyatira. Charter members of the congregation included Isaac and Susie Cathey, Edmond Cathey and his wife, and Ben Cathey and his wife, Rene Locke, and Manuel Carter, all of whom were formerly held in bondage.[17]

The Cathey family holds significance in the history of African American Churches of Christ in that Nathan Cathey, a formerly enslaved African, emerged as a church leader in Maury County, Tennessee. Documentation attests that Cathey ordained Levi Kennedy Sr. to the preaching ministry in 1879. Perhaps more importantly, Nathan Cathey and his wife Geneva reared R. N. Hogan, who became as one of the most influential preachers in twentieth-century Churches of Christ.[18] The Locke family, who also held membership in the Mount Zion Church of Christ in north Mississippi, left a noteworthy legacy in black Churches of Christ as well. C. C. Locke, born in Tate County, Mississippi, in 1909, came under the mesmerizing influence of Marshall Keeble. After preaching and developing congregations across the state of Mississippi, Locke in 1944 answered a call from black members of the Ninth Street Church of Christ in Dallas, Texas. Within the next two decades, Locke's indefatigable efforts increased the church's membership from sixty to 615 members. In 1963, the Ninth Street Church of Christ became the Cedar Crest Church of Christ, the "mother church" of African American Churches of Christ in Dallas, Texas.[19]

The Antioch Church of Christ in Midway, Texas

Even though President Abraham Lincoln had issued the Emancipation Proclamation on January 1, 1863, and the Civil War had ended on April 9, 1865, enslaved Africans in Texas did not learn of their freedom until June 19, 1865. On that day, Union soldier Gordon Granger landed at Galveston on the Texas coast and read the proclamation declaring all enslaved Africans in Texas "free." This announcement sent shock waves all across the Lone Star State, especially 145 miles northward to Madison County, where the Hayes plantation was located.

The story of African American Churches of Christ in Texas began on this plantation owned by Hugh L. Hayes. A son of Irish immigrants who had come to Texas in the 1830s, Hayes was one of four children. After the Civil War, Hugh enrolled at Washington and Lee University, then under Robert E. Lee's leadership. Even though scant information exists about the Hayes family and their plantation, it is known that the white family adhered to the Stone-Campbell Movement. The black preacher F. F. Carson, who was born on the Hayes farm in the early twentieth century, recalled that Hugh Hayes was a "deeply religious man" and that in 1865 he had established the Antioch Church of Christ in Midway, Texas. Carson's great grandfather, Anthony Carson, came to America on a slave ship. After learning to read, Anthony Carson's Bible led him to the Churches of Christ. When asked why he never considered aligning with Baptists, Methodists, or other religious groups, the great grandfather quipped: "I just never believed in any of the stuff they taught."[20] It can be safely conjectured that the religious devotion of the Hayes family rubbed off on Anthony Carson, influencing him to adopt the Stone-Campbell Restoration principles.

F. F. Carson's parents, Perry and Sarah, also became members of the Stone-Campbell Movement. Upon graduating from high school in 1925, Francis enrolled the following year at Jarvis Christian College, a school established for black Disciples in Hawkins, Texas. At the all-black East Texas college, Francis excelled in football, basketball, and baseball. Upon graduating from Jarvis Christian College, he coached basketball in Midway before relocating to Dallas, where he came under the influence of K. C. Thomas, a pioneering black preacher who organized the oldest black Church of Christ in Dallas. Thomas drew a distinct line between Disciples of Christ and Churches of Christ, as the Restoration Movement had by now split into two divisions. He swayed young Francis to enter the preaching ministry. Francis would go on to serve and stabilize a number of fledgling black Churches of Christ in Oklahoma, Texas, Kansas, and California.[21]

F. F. Carson was not the only gift from the Antioch Church of Christ in Texas. Several other men who later became noteworthy black preachers in Churches of Christ traced their origins to the Hayes plantation in Madison County. Mack Allen Bailey, William M. Childress, Jessie Warrick, and the Nixon brothers, Kermit and Walter, all Antioch products, served African American congregations in Texas. Bailey gathered a black flock in Riverside, Texas, while Childress ministered to struggling churches in Dallas, Houston, Jacksonville, Lyons, and Palestine. Kermit preached for many years at the Sinclair Street Church of Christ in Gladewater, and his brother, Walter, helped congregations in Madisonville and Lovelady.[22] At the same time some preachers who sprang from the Antioch Church of Christ found evangelistic success outside the Lone Star State. Jessie Warrick worked to plant congregations in Brownwood, Coleman, and Fort Stockton, Texas, before settling in California in the 1940s where he established Churches of Christ in Richmond and Stockton.[23] Carl Baccus, whose mother, Edna Nixon Baccus, was born in Midway, has enjoyed an even more impressive preaching career beyond Texas. Launched from the Figueroa Church of Christ in Los Angeles, California, in 1956, Baccus's dramatic preaching and administrative skills propelled the Southside Church of Christ in the same city to a membership of eighteen hundred over four-decades.[24]

Unfortunately, the exact dates and circumstances surrounding the origins of all these black churches cannot be determined. Yet two facts remain indisputable: first, like white Churches of Christ, African American Churches of Christ originated in southern states, taking up the theological tenets and assuming the religious characteristics of their Anglo brothers and sisters. Their view of scripture, their commitment to restoring the "ancient order," and their aversion to instrumental music and missionary societies mirrored the theological perspectives of their white cohorts, confirming the veracity of S. R. Cassius's observation: "As a race, we know nothing of God but what white people have taught us."[25] Second, after the Civil War, white and black Churches of Christ went their separate ways, forming two distinct fellowships. Racism evidently overpowered and overshadowed the bonds of full Christian unity even as doctrinal unity remained firm. Although some black Christians in Mississippi chose to stay with white believers after the demise of chattel enslavement,[26] African Americans in Texas and Alabama voluntarily and cordially severed ties with their former owners and charted their own paths—even though often relying on white monetary support for a variety of projects.[27]

Most whites in Churches of Christ forced African Americans out of their congregations as the Jim Crow era dawned. A black man once presented himself for membership at a white congregation in McKinney, Texas, but the members rejected him. The editor of the *Gospel Advocate* David Lipscomb intervened, denouncing the church's action. "A church that will tolerate the persistent exhibition of such a spirit certainly forfeits its claims to be a church of God." The distraught editor added: "Our treatment of the negro at best, is that of criminal indifference and neglect. To discourage and repel him, when, despite that cruel neglect on our part he seeks membership in the church of God, is an outrage that ought not for a moment to be tolerated."[28] For Lipscomb, racism in God's house was unacceptable. His voice was strong, but he was unable to stem the rising tide of racism which infiltrated white Churches of Christ in the era of Jim Crow. Such racially turbulent waters kept black preachers out of most white pulpits, barred black students from white Christian schools, and helped to create two separate and disparate fellowships within Churches of Christ.

— 3 —

Founding Fathers

Pathfinders in African American Churches of Christ

"Remove not the ancient landmark, which thy fathers have set."
—Proverbs 22:28

"Thus saith the Lord, Stand ye in the ways, and see, and ask for the old paths, where is the good way, and walk therein, and ye shall find rest for your souls. But they said, We will not walk therein."
—Jeremiah 6:16

A brutal four-year Civil War left more than 600,000 casualties in its aftermath, more than all other American wars combined. The savage conflict ended when generals Ulysses S. Grant and Robert E. Lee shook hands near Virginia's Appomattox Courthouse on April 9, 1865. Five days later, John Wilkes Booth fatally shot President Abraham Lincoln, spiraling a fragile nation into widespread chaos. The death of the sixteenth president meant the end of presidential Reconstruction, as radical Republicans, led by Charles Sumner and Thaddaeus Stevens, gained control of Congress in 1866.

Even though the Radical Republicans' record may be faulted in a host of ways, they did push through Congress the Thirteenth, Fourteenth, and Fifteenth amendments. The first of these, passed in 1865, abolished chattel enslavement; the next (1868) bestowed citizenship rights on black Americans; finally, the Fifteenth Amendment (1870) granted black males the right to vote. The Civil War and these Reconstruction amendments eradicated black chattel enslavement but failed to eliminate white racism. Racism, the passage of new "Black Codes," and the proliferation of terrorist groups such as the Ku Klux Klan worked to keep African Americans in a state of subservience, all of which profoundly affected the course of religious life in black—as well as white—America.[1] In this conflicting and tumultuous context emerged white and black leaders who helped set African American Churches of Christ on a separate and distinct religious and theological course.

In his definitive work on Richard Allen, a black Methodist clergyman in antebellum America, historian Richard S. Newman's *Freedom's Prophet: Bishop Richard Allen, the AME Church, and the Black Founding Fathers* juxtaposes George Washington, Thomas Jefferson, and Ben Franklin with such black counterparts as Allen, Paul Cuffee, James Forten, and Absalom Jones. Newman defines black founders as men and women who "fought against racial oppression in some public way, shape, or form during the early republic and thereby set models of public protest for later activists."[2] Just as Richard Allen toiled as a premier leader for enslaved Africans in pre-Civil War America, four black men emerged as "founding fathers" for black Churches of Christ in the postbellum period: Levi Kennedy Sr., S. W. Womack, Alexander Campbell, and S. R. Cassius.

The Life and Labor of Levi Kennedy Sr.

Details are sketchy about black leaders who helped launch African American Churches of Christ after the Civil War. One of these pioneers, whose story was virtually unknown until the recent uncovering of salient documents, was Levi Kennedy Sr. Born into chattel enslavement in Maury County, Tennessee, in 1846, Levi Kennedy grew up in the Stone-Campbell Movement because his owners belonged to that religious community. At age thirty-three, Kennedy was ordained into the preaching ministry at the Pleasant Union Church of Christ in middle Tennessee. Two elders, Nathan Cathey and Jefferson Bennentt, "set apart" Kennedy to the "work of teaching and preaching the gospel." Soon afterward, Kennedy began his career as an itinerant preacher, traveling by horseback and serving congregations across middle Tennessee. In 1891, he found time to marry Sarah Alice Anderson who supported him in his ministry until his death 1911.[3]

Keeping House for the Lord: The Life and Legacy of S. W. Womack

Another pivotal black minister was Samuel W. Womack who, together with Alexander Campbell and the influential white editor David Lipscomb, formed a biracial theological coalition which helped spread the development of African American Churches of Christ. Born in 1851 in Lynchburg, Tennessee, young Samuel felt the tremors generated by sectional tension and, ultimately, war. Shortly after the Civil War, Womack heard the Gospel proclaimed by white preachers and transitioned from Methodism into the Stone-Campbell Movement. White evangelists, especially Thomas J. Shaw, "the man with the old Book in his head," fundamentally shaped Womack's life and theological perspectives. More specifically, white leaders in Churches of Christ bequeathed to Womack a high view of scripture and high ecclesiology.[4]

During the postbellum era, Womack married a woman named Sallie and had two daughters, Minnie and Hattie. In 1879, Womack began subscribing to the *Christian Standard*, a journal established by Isaac Errett and white Disciples in the North.[5] More than a mere subscriber, Womack frequently contributed to the journal, highlighting his preaching excursions across the state of Tennessee as well as his collaboration with black Disciples there. But in this period the Stone-Campbell movement was developing a fissure which would result in two groups, the Churches of Christ and the Disciples of Christ (often referred to as the Christian Church). Around 1900 Womack, swayed by black evangelist Alexander Campbell, severed ties with Preston Taylor and the Gay and Lea Christian Churches in Nashville. Womack decried "innovations" which he felt distracted from the work of black Disciple churches.

Like many of his white comrades who comprised Churches of Christ, Womack viewed the Disciples' evangelism through missionary societies as a direct violation of God's will because they found no precedents for them in the New Testament. When gathering funds for the Jackson Street Church of Christ in Nashville in 1902, he explained: "We have no entertainments, no clubs, no ladies' aid societies; but we believe in meeting these obligations through the church, the God-given institution provided for all his work."[6] Womack adhered rigidly to his interpretations of scriptural teachings, asserting: "I know of no other way taught in the Book to succeed in the work, but to work, talk, and trust God by doing what he says, just as he says it."[7] Seventeen years earlier, David Lipscomb had echoed this view, stressing: "It is wrong for members to refuse to work in harmony with the church and to form individual associations for doing the work committed by God to the church."[8] In the view of men such as Womack and Lipscomb, the Church of Christ was superior to missionary societies or any other auxiliary organization. This theological premise became a pivotal issue in dividing the Stone-Campbell Movement into Churches of Christ and Disciples of Christ.[9]

Alexander Campbell and the Quest for "Pure Worship"

Like his colaborer Samuel W. Womack, the black Alexander Campbell grew up in the tumultuous environment of chattel enslavement, the Civil War, and Reconstruction. Committed to sustaining his wife, Mattie, and "large family," Campbell had two jobs. A theological turning point occurred for him in 1900, when he abandoned black Disciple Churches in Nashville "because of the introduction of innovations into the churches, and began the pure worship in my own hired house...." Shortly thereafter, Womack joined him and "took his stand with us on apostolic grounds."[10] For Campbell, "pure worship" and "apostolic grounds" meant evangelizing without the aid of missionary societies and worshiping without the accompaniment of instrumental music.

Similar to his co-worker Womack, Campbell devoted himself to the practice of "pure worship" and to a rigid stance on "apostolic grounds." Yet two things differentiated Campbell from Womack. First, Campbell never hesitated to solicit financial assistance from white Christians. He boldly stated in 1909: "Dear white brethren, some of the loyal colored brethren have the zeal, the whole truth, and the courage to do the right thing, and you white brethren who are loyal have the zeal, the whole truth, the courage, and the money."[11] Such constant prodding swayed white Christians in the mid-South to purchase Campbell a tent for his evangelistic efforts. During the Christmas season six years later, Campbell appealed to his white audience to send him a monetary gift "to make my wife and children feel a little better once a year."[12]

Second, Campbell bore an ire and fire that animated his preaching. Annie C. Tuggle, a black educator in Churches of Christ, recalled hearing Campbell's sermons. "If God says in the Bible for me to jump through that wall," exclaimed Campbell, "I'm going to jump, and I believe God will open that wall for me to go through." Sometimes Campbell passionately threw his Bible to the floor, after which he would stand on the book, proudly declaring that he was "standing on the Word of God."[13] Campbell manifested his theological rigidity in 1920 when for three nights, he debated J. B. Booth, presiding Elder of the African Methodist Episcopal Church in Marshall County, Tennessee. Campbell affirmed: "The church of Christ, with which I [Alexander Campbell] stand identified, is apostolic in origin, doctrine, and practice." Booth denied the proposition. On the first night, Campbell argued that the Church of Christ originated "in Jerusalem in the days of the apostles, on the first Pentecost after the ascension of Christ." T. G. M'Lean, a white member of the Church of Christ, witnessed the debate, observing that Campbell "quoted passage after passage in proof, giving book, chapter, and verse." Conversely, Booth insisted that the church began in the lifetime of Abraham. Campbell retorted that "if there was a church then, it was not the church of Christ, for Christ's blood had not been shed; therefore, it was a bloodless church, a church without a head, and as the Spirit had not come, and as 'the body without the spirit is dead,' so it was a dead church." Campbell rejected such a bloodless, headless, spiritless, and lifeless church. His argument reflects the belligerent and exclusivist disposition that developed in African American Churches of Christ in the first quarter of the twentieth century.[14]

On the second night of the Campbell-Booth debate, the two men discussed the doctrine of the church. Booth, according to M'Lean, failed to make a sensible case because he read from the Methodist Discipline that "we are saved by faith only." Campbell, however, called on him for book, chapter, and verse, and he [Booth] consumed most of the time hunting for the passage in the Bible, but finally gave it up and said he was mistaken." On the last night, the preachers debated the practice of the church. On the one hand, Campbell "gave quotation after quotation showing the practice of the church of Christ to be apostolic." On the other hand, Booth, unable to refute Campbell's contention, told "the story of his childhood and early struggles and ridiculed Campbell and his argument." M'Lean noted that throughout the debate: "Booth would not stay on the proposition." When the debate ended, Campbell challenged Booth to another public discussion on the subject of water baptism, but the latter refused, "saying he never expected to debate again." M'Lean, after having observed the three-night debate, concluded: "Brother Campbell is an able preacher of the word, and the truth in no wise suffered, but was victorious in his hands."[15]

The Campbell-Booth debate is instructive for two reasons. First, it shows that after Campbell and other black evangelists broke from the Disciples of Christ, they, like many of their white counterparts, espoused an exclusivist posture, contending that Churches of Christ constituted "the one true church." This exclusivism, which developed in the first half of the nineteenth century among white leaders in the Stone-Campbell Movement, became a cardinal tenet of African American Churches of Christ during the next century. Second, a combative mentality accompanied their rigid position. Instead of viewing black Baptists and Methodists as fellow Christians, African American preachers in Churches of Christ ordinarily viewed them as religious enemies, who needed to be castigated, corrected, and converted. Campbell, then, embodied and presaged what historian Richard T. Hughes has called the "hard style" of black preachers, who denounced religious groups that deviated from what Churches of Christ perceived to be the "pure gospel."[16]

S. R. Cassius and the "Race Problem" in Churches of Christ

While S. W. Womack and Alexander Campbell stood firmly on "apostolic grounds" in middle Tennessee, S. R. Cassius similarly withstood what he viewed as religious error in the state of Oklahoma. Born to an enslaved mother and a white plantation owner in 1853 in Prince William County, Virginia, Cassius converted to the Stone-Campbell Movement three decades later after hearing a white preacher's sermon on "Faith." Around 1883, two white leaders, W. R. Jewell and Hiram Woods, ordained Cassius into the preaching ministry. Eight years later, Cassius and his family took up residence in the Oklahoma Territory, which many contemporary African Americans envisioned as the black man's "paradise."[17]

Like Womack and Campbell, Cassius exhibited a rigid theological posture toward other religious groups as well as a high view of scripture, especially the New Testament. A combative mindset accompanied his biblical perspective. In 1903, Cassius challenged a Primitive Baptist leader on the following premise: "Resolved, that the Church of Christ, of which I am member, is apostolic in faith, doctrine and practice. I affirm." When the Baptist preacher failed to show up, Cassius fumed: "I carried two large solid rocks—one in each hand. In my right hand I had the four Gospels, in my left the Acts of the Apostles, and belted about my waist I had all of the pistols of Paul, James and Peter, and between my teeth I carried the sword of the Spirit." Here with his creative paraphrase of Ephesians 6:10–18, Cassius clearly perceived scripture as an instrument to assail what he deemed to be aberrant religion.[18]

Yet for Cassius, the Bible functioned also as a weapon against racial and social wrongs. He melded the teachings in Matthew 7:5, Acts 17:26, and Colossians 3:25 to chide white Christians for excluding him from pulpits in the North, asserting: "Men may preach about the goodness of God, and pray about loving one another, and being one in Christ, but as long as they scorn me on account of my race or color, and tell me that their people will not tolerate me as an equal, I am compelled to say to all such, 'Thou hypocrite!' Do you believe the Bible, when it says that God is no respecter of persons, or that God made of one blood all men, for to dwell upon the face of the earth?"[19]

Most African Americans in the Stone-Campbell Movement did not so appropriate scripture to address racism in their chosen fellowship. Moreover, very few constantly leveled racial complaints against the white establishment in Churches of Christ.

In so doing Cassius stood out from Womack, Campbell, and other leaders in African American Churches of Christ for several reasons. First, Cassius, unlike Womack, Campbell, and other formerly enslaved Africans who transitioned to the Stone-Campbell Movement, met and "shook hands" with Abraham Lincoln, the black man's "Moses." This unforgettable experience inspired him to name his oldest son, Amos Lincoln Cassius. While residing in the nation's capital, Cassius had also met presidents Andrew Johnson, Ulysses S. Grant, Rutherford B. Hayes, and James A. Garfield.[20] These encounters not only distinguished Cassius from other black preachers who assumed leadership roles in the Restoration Movement, but they also stirred his interest in politics.

Second, while living in Washington, DC, Cassius was on "intimate terms" with such black statesmen as Frederick Douglass, Hiram Revels, Blanche K. Bruce, and John M. Langston.[21] All of these men were formerly enslaved and emerged as political leaders in the African American community, agitating for civil rights for their people. These black leaders indelibly stamped their views on Cassius and set for him a blueprint for his own quest for racial and social justice.

Additionally, Cassius most likely met Booker T. Washington when the Tuskegee educator traveled to all-black Boley, Oklahoma, in 1907. Washington so inspired Cassius that he sent his son, Amos, to study at the Tuskegee Institute in Alabama. Indeed, after Cassius launched his Tohee Industrial School in Tohee, Oklahoma Territory, in 1899, his good friend and white editor Frederick Rowe christened him "the Booker T. Washington of Oklahoma."[22] Womack and Campbell without question admired Washington; and they might well have exhibited the Washington-like traits of industry, fidelity, and humility. Yet none of them received such accolades from white Christians as did Cassius.

Third, although Womack, Campbell, and other preachers in Churches of Christ were former bondspeople, no known extant writings reveal their experiences in chattel enslavement, nor did they make any effort to denounce the institution. On the other hand, Cassius openly and often excoriated the past enslavement of black people as the "cancer of human slavery" and the "curse of slavery."[23] Cassius further traced lingering moral deficiencies among African

Americans to their experiences in chattel enslavement, since they were held in the "most degrading circumstances" and since they were "taught no morals, no sense of virtue, and no regard for the marriage ties." In fact, black men who witnessed the sexual violation of their mothers, wives, and sisters by white men during chattel enslavement acquired a "brutal desire to do the same." Cassius's own mother had been raped by her owner, James W. F. Macrae, in antebellum Virginia.[24]

Fourth, and perhaps most importantly, S. R. Cassius, unlike contemporary black preachers in the Stone-Campbell Movement, unabashedly injected political, racial, and social issues into the columns of religious journals. In a 1904 edition of the *Christian Leader*, for example, Cassius denounced the inauguration speech of Mississippi governor James K. Vardaman, calling it an "insult to every great mind on earth, and blasphemy against God." Vardaman, a virulent racist, declared that the abolition of chattel enslavement had made African Americans "more criminal as freemen than as slaves." Immorality among black people, replied Cassius, derived from the moral decadence of white men. J. S. De Jarnette, a *Christian Leader* subscriber and a white Christian from Oklahoma, angrily protested Cassius's criticisms of the governor's address, arguing that most northern whites were clueless about the state of race relations in the South. De Jarnette especially opposed Cassius's discussing social matters in a religious journal. "I seriously object to discussion of political questions in religious journals," fumed De Jarnette, "and, I believe, in this nine-tenths of your subscribers will agree with me."[25]

Most whites in the Stone-Campbell Movement failed to grasp that the dire social and political circumstances of black Americans compelled their preachers to reach beyond the pulpit to help their people. Henry McNeal Turner, an African Methodist Episcopal (AME) leader, adroitly and unabashedly linked religion and politics in the postbellum era.[26] As historian Leon F. Litwack has noted: "For black churchmen to have drawn a line between political and religious concerns in the years immediately following emancipation would have been ideologically and tactically impossible."[27] Most white and black leaders in the Stone-Campbell Movement, however, obviously did draw such a line of demarcation between politics and religion; S. R. Cassius uniquely and distinctly did not.

In addition, even though both Bishop Henry McNeal Turner and S. R. Cassius shared a deep abhorrence for white racism, the duo differed markedly on two main issues. First, Cassius would have vehemently disagreed with Turner's 1895 declaration that "God is a Negro," which repudiated the "idolatry of whiteness that he saw all around him."[28] While Cassius scoffed at the idea that "Christ was a fair-haired, blue-eyed, Anglo-Saxon, and that God is a white man and the devil is black," he refused to argue that God was black. He instead contended that "God is King, a Ruler, a Creator, a Maker and a Giver of Life" to all nations.[29] So while Cassius joined the chorus of black critics who assailed the "whiteness of Christ,"[30] he spurned the notion that Jesus had dark-skin and that God was black. Cassius furthermore emphatically rejected Turner's proposal that African Americans should return to Africa, largely because uncivilized native Africans would demoralize the "civilized life" of black Americans. "Instead of winning respect and educating the [black] heathen, we would simply gain their pity, or receive their contempt, and in a few years, instead of transforming them to our ways, we would ourselves be compelled to conform to their ways."[31]

Moreover, while Cassius relied on financial support from white Christians, he consistently contested their racial views and racist practices. Cassius admitted to this moral ambivalence. On the one hand, he highlighted his need for white monetary assistance to evangelize black people. On the other hand, he knew some white believers treated him as a pariah. In 1915, he rebuked Christian whites who sought to make the black man simultaneously "a spiritual equal and a social outcast."[32] Seven years later, he more frankly expressed his motive for interacting with white Christians: "I have not gone to the white churches because I liked to preach to white folks," he wrote poignantly. "I went to them to get aid that I might go to my own race. There was nowhere else to go to my own race. They had my bait in their pockets...." Cassius preferred to "never face a white audience," since some embraced him as a "man of God," while others spurned him as a "case of small pox."[33]

While there were certainly other men who helped to provide the foundation upon which African American Churches of Christ grew, regrettably very little information, if any, survives to illustrate their contributions to this unique fellowship. A perusal of the work of Levi Kennedy, S. W. Womack, Alexander Campbell, and S. R. Cassius nevertheless attests that these four men were spiritual trailblazers who forged a separate and distinct identity for black Churches of Christ. Furthermore, an examination of these "founding fathers" reveals a certain diversity and complexity that stamped African American Churches of Christ in the late nineteenth century. Kennedy worked mostly in obscurity in middle Tennessee, while Womack and Campbell—laboring primarily in the same region—gained greater visibility because of their access to the pages of Lipscomb's *Gospel Advocate*.

Womack bequeathed to his spiritual progeny not only a high view of scripture, but he also transmitted a rational view of "the Book." Campbell combined a feisty demeanor with his exclusivist posture.

Cassius, however, converted to the Stone-Campbell Movement in the 1880s, took up residence in the Oklahoma Territory in the 1890s, and became a thorn in the side of many of his white fellow Christians. Cassius, who began writing for the *Christian Leader* as early as 1895, acquired a greater visibility and voice than all the others. His preoccupation with race and his fusion of religion and politics stirred the ire of many white Christians.

Such variety and diversity of perspectives are both noteworthy and crucial to our understanding of black Churches of Christ in their fledgling state. On the one hand, most black Churches of Christ espoused a high ecclesiology and a rigid exclusivism; on the other hand, Cassius showed little tolerance for racial discrimination from his white brothers and sisters. This divergent theological and racial posture, surfacing in the late nineteenth century, continued into the twentieth century; and as the following chapters will reveal, it continues to mark twenty-first-century African American Churches of Christ.

PART TWO

African American Churches of Christ and the "Race Problem" in America, 1900–1930

—4—

"Making Love to Our Daughters"

The Racial Thought of White Churches of Christ

"The world did not start the 'Jim Crow' law; it was started by the church because the white members of the church did not think that negroes were good enough to worship God in the same house that they did."
—S. R. Cassius

"Behind white America's fear of the black male there
lurked an abhorrence of miscegenation."
—Colin Kidd

In 1913, Thomas Pearce Bailey, a white South Carolina educator, delineated the "racial creed of the Southern people" with these fifteen tenets:

1. "Blood will tell."
2. The white race must dominate.
3. The Teutonic peoples stand for race purity.
4. The Negro is inferior and will remain so.
5. "This is a white man's country."
6. No social equality.
7. No political equality.
8. In matters of civil rights and legal adjustments give the white man, the benefit of the doubt; and under no circumstances interfere with the prestige of the white race.
9. In educational policy let the Negro have the crumbs that fall from the white man's table.
10. Let there be such industrial education of the Negro as will best fit him to serve the white man.

11. Only Southerners understand the Negro question.
12. Let the South settle the Negro question.
13. The status of peasantry is all the Negro can hope for, if the races are to live together in peace.
14. Let the lowest white man count for more than the highest Negro.
15. The above statements indicate the leadings of Providence.¹

In his socio-religious study, scholar David Edwin Harrell has shown that American nationalism and racism such as Bailey's infiltrated the mindset of nineteenth century whites in the Stone-Campbell Movement. "Disciples shared with their fellow Americans not only a nationalistic view of providence but also a racist view," asserted Harrell. "A belief in Anglo-Saxon superiority was never far beneath the surface in Disciples thought."²

In the late nineteenth century, two significant events helped to shape the American mind in the first three decades of the twentieth century. First, Herbert Spencer, a disciple of Charles Darwin, coined the phrase "survival of the fittest" and applied his mentor's theories of natural selection to the whole of society. Since the strongest must rise to the top, in economics the rich must dominate the poor because the former were fit and the latter perceived unfit. Known as Social Darwinism, this concept advanced the notion that whites were a superior race.³

Second, the Spanish-American War helped to solidify the United States as a national empire in 1898, when the country acquired Puerto Rico, Guam, and the Philippine Islands. Lasting 113 days, the war against Spain bore racist overtones, as American imperialists appropriated Social Darwinism to defend their conquest of supposedly weaker brown peoples. Historian Richard Hofstader has succinctly noted: "During the fight for the annexation of the Philippines, when the larger question of imperial policy was thrown open for debate, expansionists were quick to invoke the law of progress, the inevitable tendency to expand, the Manifest Destiny of Anglo Saxons, and the survival of the fittest."⁴

White Churches of Christ and the "White Man's Burden"

Racist sentiment, engendered by the Spanish-American War, spilled over into the Stone-Campbell Movement, as whites in that fellowship believed they shouldered the "White Man's Burden." Just as American imperialists felt socially obligated to spread supposedly superior white culture to supposedly inferior brown and black peoples at home and abroad, Anglo adherents of the Churches of Christ believed they were divinely responsible for providing religious guidance to their black neighbors. Poet and author Rudyard Kipling, writing on the heels of the Spanish-American War, captured the essence of the "White Man's Burden" in verse:

> Take up the White Man's burden—
> Send forth the best ye breed—
> Go bind your sons to exile
> To serve your captives' need
> To wait in heavy harness
> On fluttered folk and wild—
> Your new-caught, sullen peoples,
> Half devil and half child.[5]

Kipling's poem succinctly expresses the racial attitudes of many, if not most, white leaders and members in Churches of Christ.

Apart from any consideration of evangelism in the nation's new colonies, most white Churches of Christ seemed overwhelmed by the perceived responsibility of "Christianizing" American blacks. In 1902, the *Christian Leader* published an article, stressing that African Americans needed to be taught the virtues of New England Puritans, virtues of temperance, selflessness, and morality. "It is the old spirit of Puritanism," the editor declared, "that needs to be infused into the negro race."[6] Three years later, the *Gospel Advocate* produced a piece on white Christians' moral obligation to black Americans, asserting: "The negro is here, and the responsibility is upon us. How to elevate him is a great problem, but we cannot dodge the responsibility." For white leaders in Churches of Christ, the Gospel message was crucial to black uplift. "The best way, evidently, to elevate the negro is to fill him with the gospel of Christ," the editorial maintained. "Ignorance, darkness, and superstition cannot dwell in the soul that is thoroughly saturated in the gospel of Christ." The editor concluded that domestic missions should be as important as foreign missionary work, pleading: "While we are giving attention to the heathen [abroad], we should not neglect the heathen at home."[7]

Writing in a similar vein, John M. McCaleb, a white preacher in Churches of Christ and missionary to Japan, expressed confidently that converting African Americans to Christianity would be an easy task, if white believers put forth a more earnest effort. Yet McCaleb admitted that racial hostility stood as a massive obstacle. "Race prejudice," he noted, "stands as a great barrier to such work. If the white man makes it a custom to preach to them and mingle with them, he is severely criticized by his own people, and imposes upon himself a burden few are willing to bear."[8] Ensnared in a tug-of-war of the "White Man's Burden" and God's mandate of disseminating the Gospel among black people, white leaders in Churches of Christ believed themselves caught between human excoriation and divine wrath. When white evangelists preached to their black neighbors, their white friends criticized and ostracized them; if they failed to reach out to African Americans, they felt condemned by God.

Beyond this, the "White Man's Burden" incorporated the corollary of black inferiority and white superiority. Price Billingsley, a renowned white evangelist in Churches of Christ, expressed the duties and difficulties in shouldering the burden of black elevation. Billingsley argued that white Christians had a moral and spiritual "obligation" to the black man. "That the black race is weaker than, and somewhat dependent upon, the white race, is no matter for dispute here. But this position of the white race over the black is a trust, and it, therefore, involves the superior race, toward the inferior people, in certain unescapable [*sic*] duties." Billingsley insisted that so-called "superior" whites owed their supposedly subhuman black neighbors "certain debts which the white race must pay or answer for; if not here on earth, then in eternity."[9]

A native Mississippian, Billingsley espoused racist perspectives of African Americans, viewing them as "degraded, weak, unstable," and "festering and incurable moral sores." The Anglo evangelist, however, excoriated some fellow whites who proved "themselves capable of even worse depravity." The black man, added Billingsley, "has a vague and very imperfect idea of the binding nature of the marital ties, of the sacredness of the home, and of the grave necessity for honor and purity in these relations." But Billingsley partly blamed white Christians for the black man's supposed moral deficiencies, lamenting: "What pity that the race in the midst of which he lives and to whom he has a right to look for models, inspiration, and guidance in these fundamental life matters, should be indifferent to his soul's welfare, should often illegally take his property, and should add unspeakable insult to injury by wickedly exploiting the black's home by dragging down his women folk in coming in illicit relations with them!" Billingsley then chided whites in Churches of Christ for ignoring the millions of "poor, weak, dying blacks" at home, while praying for the conversion of the "heathen over the seas."[10]

Billingsley's testimony plainly demonstrates that some white leaders in Churches of Christ took seriously their obligation of uplifting African

Americans morally and spiritually. He and others felt the heavy weight of rescuing "weaker" and "inferior" black Americans from sin and barbarism, attesting that white racism often accompanied white beneficence. Notwithstanding this vitiation, some white Christians viewed the spiritual and eternal welfare of black people as inextricably bound with their own.

Leaders other than Price Billingsley expressed the dichotomy of white superiority and black inferiority of the "White Man's Burden." In 1923, G. F. Gibbs, a white evangelist in Greenville, North Carolina, commented that the "Church of Christ is burdened with the preaching of the Gospel to every creature," including the almost one million black residents in the Tar Heel State.[11] H. C. Denson, a white Christian who perused the *Christian Leader*, responded to Gibbs's plaint, acknowledging that American blacks are "inferior to white people in many respects, yet I believe they are human, and as such are entitled to the privileges accorded them by the Constitution of the United States. I feel quite sure they are entitled to all Gospel privileges."[12] Many whites in Churches of Christ shared Denson's assessment that black people were simultaneously "human"—deserving of constitutional and spiritual "privileges"—and "inferior."

Some Anglos in Churches of Christ, however, contested the corollary of black inferiority and white superiority in the "White Man's Burden." In 1920, when a reader asked the *Christian Leader* the following questions: "Is the negro a beast? Has he an immortal soul?" G. A. Klingman, editor of the "Query Department," replied emphatically: "The negro is not a beast, but a human being with a soul." Citing Colossians 1:23, Klingman added that he believed the "apostles preached to negroes."[13] Two years later, E. W. Moon, a white preacher from Holland, Georgia, argued for the equality of black and white Americans. Alluding to Acts 17:26, Moon maintained that since the "Lord made of one blood all nations," this fact placed the "negro on a blood equality with all men." Indeed, Moon further contended that in some respects, African Americans were superior to their white counterparts, observing: "Given equal advantages many of them are equal to the white man intellectually, many superior. You cannot rub this out." Moon, a firm believer in the equality of black and white people, concluded: "God made man in his own image, the negro is a man. Therefore, God made the negro in his image. Did God 'equalize' himself with the negro by this likeness? We must honor God's handiwork, 'Honor all men,' says the Book." From Moon's view, "the Book" not only provided guidance in spiritual and religious matters, but it also regulated race relations in Churches of Christ. Moon championed white and black equality in that he practiced what he preached. W. U. Benton, a black convert to Churches of Christ in Holland, Georgia, praised Moon, who "assisted me at night in my studies, being kind and patient and always seeming glad to instruct me." In the Jim Crow South, where de jure as well as de facto segregation prevailed, Moon, a white minister, gave biblical instruction to Benton, a black seeker. Over the span of a decade, according to Benton, Moon showed consistency and courtesy by "handing me something good to read and always manifesting an unusual interest in me." Moon's genuine concern for Benton convinced him to "give up the church of my dear old mother" (probably Baptist or Methodist). The black believer credited Moon and another white evangelist with helping him extricate himself from the "bondage of sectarianism."[14]

Benton also thanked both the *Gospel Advocate* and the *Christian Leader* for their contribution to his spiritual development, praising the former paper for leading him into God's kingdom,[15] while the latter enabled him to glean "many valuable lessons... from its pages, and I thank and praise God for the gift of his Son, who washed me in his own blood, making me a son of God."[16] Benton's grateful statement suggests that E. W. Moon placed Benton on the *Christian Leader*'s subscription list, confirming that journals published by white Christians could profoundly shape the lives of black believers.[17] It further attests that Benton yearned for other black Georgians to enter the fold of Churches of Christ. "My heart's desire and prayer to God," Benton wrote, "is that my people, the unfortunate and neglected colored race, may begin to hear the glad story of the Cross of my Redeemer." Benton then challenged *Christian Leader* readers to introspection: "Ask yourself the personal question: 'Have I not discriminated against the colored race in America?' I think you have." He further asked: "Will the Lord hold you guiltless? I think not."[18]

While Benton lauded the *Christian Leader* and its benefits to his life, some white Christians accused the paper of promoting racial and social equality. G. W. Davis, a white Christian from Columbus, Georgia, charged *Christian Leader* writers, T. Q. Martin and A. A. Bunner, with "trying to mix the [white] with the negro." Davis angrily terminated his subscription, protesting: "I don't want such stuff taught to my children." An appalled Frederick L. Rowe, the paper's publisher, retorted that Davis "must believe in the theory of some shallow thinkers that the negro has no soul." Rowe, taking his inspiration from James A. Harding, David Lipscomb, and his own father, John F. Rowe, insisted that the Gospel "is for the whole world, whosoever will, and excludes none and favors none." Rowe then recalled an experience he had in west Texas in 1920, when a black evangelist gave "a talk" before a group of twenty-five preachers. A white preacher at the small gathering impressed Rowe when he introduced the black minister as "your brother and my brother." "I was glad I was there," Rowe remembered proudly, "to hear it and to know the attitude of the consecrated, God-fearing preacher, North or South, toward those whose skins may be black, brown, red, or yellow."[19]

These testimonies of E. W. Moon, W. U. Benton, G. W. Davis, and Frederick L. Rowe clearly reveal competing and conflicting racial views and practices. On the one hand, some whites in Churches of Christ genuinely viewed African Americans as spiritual and social equals. On the other hand, others plainly deemed their sable neighbors as biologically and morally inferior. The history of nineteenth- and twentieth-century African American Churches of Christ, however, confirms that the latter racial mentality dominated as white Christians largely excluded black people from their schools and churches. Like their white neighbors in American society, whites in the Stone-Campbell Movement imbibed the racial views and racist practices that defined black people as generally unethical and untrustworthy. David Edwin Harrell has again rightly concluded that white "Disciples were not unique; they behaved like their neighbors. They behaved like nineteenth-century [white] Americans, which, after all, is what they were."[20]

The Ku Klux Klan and White Churches of Christ

The racial ambivalence that pervaded white Churches of Christ can be seen in the revival of the Ku Klux Klan. Inspired by the incendiary film *The Birth of a Nation* and the Leo Frank trial, William J. Simmons, a Methodist cleric, revived the Klan on November 24, 1915, in Stone Mountain, Georgia. The second Klan, unlike the first Klan, which was mostly anti-black and mainly confined to the South, not only directed its racist venom against African Americans, but also aimed it toward Jews and Catholics. The revitalized organization, composed of a wide range of middle-class whites such as entrepreneurs, lawyers, ministers, physicians, and politicians, spread rapidly into southern and northern states alike. Women also joined the Klan and comprised a membership of half million.[21]

In 1923, the *Christian Leader* allowed its readers to debate the question, "Can a Christian Join the Klan?" Certainly, some whites in Churches of Christ endorsed the violently racist organization. D. H. Bates, a native of Whigville, Ohio, stated: "If the K. K. K. teaches and practices only New

Testament principles, why, so do all Christians." Ben J. Elston concurred: "I have no doubt God is using, and will use it, as a world force." A person writing under the pseudonym "One Whose Heart Is in the Work" viewed the organization as a reform movement, concluding: "I am glad the Ku Klux Klan exists today, for I believe they are going to help rid the land of the greatest evils of the age."[22]

Many other *Christian Leader* readers vehemently denounced the Klan. Mrs. W. F. H. stingingly wrote: "I really believe the Ku Klux Klan is the most deceptive organization that has ever been organized; that is, in relations to the Christian faith. There is so much good in it that it is quite hard for the Christian to see the harm unless he is a close Bible student." She further asked: "Does not the Bible teach the brotherhood of man in Christ Jesus? Are we not to take the Gospel to all nations and all who are in Christ are brethren regardless of color or race?" In agreement, and after delineating seven reasons why he opposed the Klan, C. G. Vincent, a white Christian in Corsicana, Texas, concluded: "Finally, who can believe for a moment that any of the New Testament Christians would have joined such an organization had there been one in their day? Who would dare assert that Thomas and Alexander Campbell, B. W. Stone, Benjamin Franklin, J. W. McGarvey, David Lipscomb and J. A. Harding, and a host of other Restoration preachers would look with favor upon such an organization?" Fred M. Little, a Christian in Montgomery, Alabama, affirmed: "I say it is not according to the Word of God for a Christian to belong to the K. K. K. or any other secret order, therefore I have never joined any of them."[23]

The foregoing exchange in the *Christian Leader* clearly attests to the racial ambivalence in white Churches of Christ. One group of Christians saw the Ku Klux Klan as an agency with restraining influence; the other group of believers' commitment to biblical principles as set forth by such white restorationists as Barton W. Stone, Thomas Campbell, David Lipscomb, and James A. Harding held distinctly negative views of the organization.

The following year, Frederick Rowe, editor of the *Christian Leader*, had planned to publish two more series on the subject of the Klan, but chose to abandon the topic, largely because Klan headquarters refused to furnish a "concise printed statement of their principles or platform." A white preacher for Churches of Christ in the South, "who is lecturing for the Klan," sent the *Leader* office a "printed card which he said is 'official.'" Rowe said that the card claimed to be "strictly American in its declaration and demands."[24]

Notwithstanding the *Christian Leader*'s withdrawal from the subject, questions about the Klan surfaced in the pages of the *Gospel Advocate*. When church member James F. Killebrew asked in 1927, "Can a man be a member of the 'Invisible Empire' (the Ku-Klux Klan) and at the same time be a follower of Christ?," H. Leo Boles, president of David Lipscomb College (now Lipscomb University), vigorously rejected the organization. "No one can follow Christ and go into this," railed Boles, "because Christ did not got [*sic*] into it, neither did he give any instruction for any of his people to go into it. Therefore, no one can claim Scriptural authority for being a member of it."[25] Boles's understanding of scripture, especially the silence of the Bible, inspired his opposition to the Ku Klux Klan. For Boles, then, accepting the Klan's platform of "100% Americanism" meant a rejection of Christ's teachings. The divergent ways in which white members and ministers in Churches of Christ viewed the Ku Klux Klan simultaneously reflected how they saw and treated African Americans. White Christians who approved of the Klan evidently viewed American blacks as subhuman; those who opposed the racist organization tended to be more accepting of blacks as human, even if they barred them from their churches and schools. Therein lies the paradox: Boles openly blasted the Klan, yet he and other white administrators of the all-white David Lipscomb College denied black students admission into the school. The same Bible used to pummel the Klan served to exclude people of African descent.

White Churches of Christ and the "Ghost of Social Equality"

At the heart of the exclusion of black people from their homes, schools, and churches seemed to be the fear of interracial sex. Even though white owners of enslaved Africans freely and frequently raped their so-called "property" in the Old South,[26] whites feared a reversal which would lead to black men's sexual interaction with white women in the New South. North Carolina journalist and author Wilbur J. Cash pointedly called this racial mindset the "Southern rape complex." "What Southerners felt," Cash argued, "was that any assertion of any kind on the part of the Negro constituted in a perfectly real manner an attack on the Southern woman." Any perceived assertion and aggression by black men "justified" their lynching by white men in order to defend white women. The demise of chattel enslavement threatened order in the Old South and engendered political, educational, and social advancement for African Americans during the Reconstruction era. Such progress, most white southerners feared, qualified black males for the "ever crucial right of marriage." Intermarriage between black men and white women imperiled white supremacy, "the great heritage of white men."²⁷

The "Southern rape complex" saliently manifested itself in 1901 when President Theodore Roosevelt invited notable black educator Booker T. Washington to dine in the White House. White southerners construed the Washington-Roosevelt meeting as black aggression against southern white womanhood, the "perpetuator" of white supremacy. "The President," the *Richmond Times* decried, "is willing that negroes shall mingle freely with whites in the social circle—that white women may receive attentions from negro men; it means that there is no racial reason in his opinion why whites and blacks may not marry and intermarry, why the Anglo-Saxon may not mix negro blood with his blood."²⁸

The *Greenwood Commonwealth*, a paper from the Mississippi Delta, published a poem entitled: "Niggers in the White House." A stanza of the poem succinctly noted:

> I see a way to settle it,
> Just as clear as water—
> Let Mr. Booker Washington
> Marry Teddy's daughter.²⁹

Whites in Churches of Christ certainly read such newspapers or at least ingested the racial rhetoric and racist sentiment of such editorials. And even if most southern whites vehemently opposed Republican President Theodore Roosevelt, they generally admired Booker T. Washington for his overt stance against "social equality" as well as his burgeoning educational enterprise in Tuskegee, Alabama.³⁰

Regardless of their admiration for the "Tuskegee Wizard," whites in the Stone-Campbell Movement vigorously denounced any hint of black men interacting with white women. In the first decade of the twentieth century, white minster John M. McCaleb voiced his ire and displeasure when he observed a young black southerner address a white woman as "'Bessie' in the familiar style of her own brother." "I voice the sentiment of the brotherhood generally," fussed McCaleb, "when I say that boy was out of his place. That upstartish disposition, especially among younger negroes in which they vainly try to be white people, has done much harm."³¹ A native Tennessean, McCaleb obviously imbibed the racism of his era and strongly contested any kind of imagined misdeed of black men against white women. McCaleb proposed that white leaders in Churches of Christ link with such black schools as Fisk University and the Tuskegee Institute, yet this cooperation and collaboration must be done "'professionally,' not socially." He then cautioned white Christians against black "intrusions" in white colleges. "Give him the privilege of attending our schools," lamented McCaleb, " . . . and next he will be making love to our daughters and will seek a place in the social circle."[32]

This neurotic fear of black men "making love" to white women was in large measure the basis for racial segregation throughout the twentieth-century Jim Crow South. *Brown v. Board of Education*, which declared segregated public schools unconstitutional, stirred "sex fear" across southern states. "The real fear," according to a noted historian, "was the white female staying out of reach of the Negro man."[33] This phobia shaped whites' attitudes in Churches of Christ and provided the impetus for racially divided congregations in twentieth-century America.

Indeed, when black evangelist Marshall Keeble planted a black Church of Christ in a southern community, he would return the following year astonished that white Christians had so quickly erected a separate facility to accommodate African Americans.[34] White believers in Huntsville, Texas, similarly puzzled R. N. Hogan when they built a new church building for "only one member (Colored) of the Church of Christ in the entire town." The new facility eliminated the objection that black people "did not have a place to worship."[35] Generous white donors in Churches of Christ funded African American evangelists to establish and develop separate black churches to keep black converts out their own congregations and to keep black men in particular away from their white women.

Such perspectives, policies, and practices would not go uncontested, however. A formerly enslaved man from Virginia would stir the race pot in Churches of Christ and urge his white comrades to dethrone the "ghost of social equality" from their hearts and houses of worship. He railed constantly against his white brothers and sisters who espoused the racist binary of white superiority and black inferiority, who bore the so-called "White Man's Burden," who subscribed the "racial creed of the Southern people," and who feared the "ghost of equality." His eventful, laborious, and tumultuous tale is told in the subsequent chapter.

— 5 —

"In a Class by Himself"

S. R. Cassius and the "Race Problem" in Churches of Christ

> "Of all the forms of negro hate in this world, save me from the one which clothes itself with the name of loving Jesus."
> —Frederick Douglass

The lynching of Sam Hose, a black man accused of crushing white man Alfred Cranford's skull with an ax, drew more than four thousand white Georgians in the spring of 1899. Hose, it was claimed, killed Cranford, snatched up his baby, dashing the infant to the floor, and then committed "outrage" against his wife, Mattie. The *Atlanta Constitution* lynched Hose in print long before a mob could carry out the brutal execution. The *Constitution*'s incendiary headline blared: "Determined Mob After Hose; He Will Be Lynched if Caught." The paper's subhead added: "Assailant of Mrs. Cranford May Be Brought to Palmetto and Burned at the Stake." This brand of race-baiting journalism, all too common in the era, sealed Sam Hose's fate, denying him due process under the law.[1]

Approximately ten days after the alleged assaults, white Georgians apprehended Hose, burned him, cut out his heart and liver, sliced off his genitals, and scattered remaining body parts throughout the Atlanta area, even sending pieces of the corpse to Governor Allen D. Candler. Contemporary sources branded Hose as a "monster in human form," a "black devil," who had been justly "barbecued," even as esteemed educator W. E. B. Du Bois lamented: "Sam Hose was crucified."[2]

S. R. Cassius, an African American who converted to the Stone-Campbell Movement in the 1880s and planted congregations in Oklahoma and California, devoured newspapers, particularly black journals, and read with dismay of the crucifixion in Georgia. A month after the heinous act, a white brother in the Stone-Campbell Movement sent Cassius ten cents to assist his educational enterprise, the Tohee Industrial School, in the Oklahoma Territory, delightfully asking him: " . . . what do you think of the 'fiend,' Sam Hose, whom the good people of Georgia burned?" The black educator thundered in return: "My brother, you had better ask what I think of the 'fiends' who did the 'burning.'" Cassius, acknowledging that Hose likely killed in self-defense, rejected the charge of rape, exclaiming: "Just think of burning a man and cutting up his body in small pieces to send to their friends! Ouh!" He repudiated a contribution from a white brother who "believes in mob violence."[3] In the view of this white donor, Sam Hose was a monstrous "fiend"; in the mind of Cassius, the black victim was still "a man," a human being who deserved due process under the law. In short, Cassius was stirred by what theologian Reinhold Niebuhr has called "madness in his soul."[4]

In his deeply felt and publicly expressed horror, Samuel Robert Cassius stands unique in the history of African American Churches of Christ. No other black leader in the Stone-Campbell Movement left behind such a racially charged paper trail; no other African American preacher in Churches of Christ consistently incorporated and injected racial and social issues into the articles he wrote for church journals. In a religious fellowship that looked askance at the imagined mixing of theology and politics, Cassius merged the two issues without trepidation. Historian David Edwin Harrell Jr. has observed that a certain theological ambivalence gripped white leaders in the Stone-Campbell Movement. On the one hand, conservative preachers such as David Lipscomb argued that Christians should stand "aloof" from social and political issues; on the other hand, liberal leaders such as James H. Garrison insisted that the church must champion causes of justice and equality for all men.[5] This intense theological dichotomy ensnared Cassius, making him an outsider in Churches of Christ.[6]

In his perceptive study, historian Edward J. Blum has pointed out that such African American leaders as Frederick Douglass and W. E. B. Du Bois constantly railed against lynching and racial discrimination to show that the "American nation was anything but Christian." "African Americans served," Blum observed, "as the most astute and brilliant critics of the spiritual state of the nation and repeatedly highlighted connections between northern Protestantism, sectional reconciliation, and the formation of an American nationalism premised upon whiteness."[7] What Blum has noted about Douglass, Du Bois, and others clearly holds true for Cassius as well.

Born into slavery to a black mother and a white man in Prince William County, Virginia, S. R. Cassius joined the ranks of the 406,000 biracial or "new people"[8] living in the United States in the mid-nineteenth century. Of course, in the Old South biracial persons automatically fell into the category of "black." He spent most of his adolescent life on Meadow Farm, where he learned to read from his mother, Jane, who had received instruction from her white "young mistresses." The outbreak of the Civil War led Cassius and his mother to relocate to Washington, DC, where Cassius enrolled at a public school and met a white educator, Frances W. Perkins, who "fixed it in my mind that the Bible was God's revealed will to man, and made it impossible for me to ever be anything [but] 'a Christian only.'" Cassius's residence in the nation's capital spanned the administrations of five American presidents.[9]

By the early 1880s, Cassius had married his first wife and moved to Brazil, Indiana, where he labored as a coal miner. At some point he heard a white preacher's sermon on "Faith," and converted to the Stone-Campbell Movement. Within a two-year period, Cassius had assumed the preaching mantle and apparently briefly held ministerial posts in Chicago, Cincinnati, and Sigourney, Iowa.[10] Around 1895, John F. Rowe, editor of the *Christian Leader*, introduced Cassius to his readership and the black evangelist emerged as one of the most visible—and vocal—African Americans in the Stone-Campbell Movement.

Cassius brought his antiracist sentiment to both pulpit and paper. Writing his first known letter to the *Christian Evangelist* in 1889, he argued against the appointment of a white "superintendent of colored missions," revealing his deep resentment of notions of black inferiority and white superiority. White leaders in the Stone-Campbell Movement had appointed J. W. Jenkins as "Superintendent of Missions and Schools for the Colored People"; black education, in the mind of the white board, should precede or at least coincide with evangelism among blacks.[11] From Cassius's perspective, however, the appointment of white preachers to supervise black missions revealed whites' distrust of African American ministers as well as their belief in blacks' supposed incompetence, irresponsibility, and inferiority. "Therefore the public is given to understand," Cassius contended, "that we are all a set of numbskulls, and must needs have a white man as overseer over us."[12]

The *Christian Evangelist*'s editor, James H. Garrison, disagreed with Cassius's assertion and defended the board's decision to place a white administrator over black missions. African Americans required wise and prudent supervision, he argued, since most of them were "ignorant" and "need education and religious training." Exclusion of white leaders from supervisory roles would, in Garrison's words, preclude black preachers from a "higher religious life" and "superior advantages."[13] A curious admixture of paternalism and racism often accompanied white benevolence, since white leaders in the Stone-Campbell Movement viewed themselves as wise fathers reaching downward to childlike African Americans.

Unlike many white and black leaders in Churches of Christ who opposed missionary societies largely on theological grounds,[14] a concern over racism prompted Cassius's opposition. He discerned both overt and covert racism manifesting itself in economic disparity and unequal treatment of black evangelists. In 1890, white leaders in the Stone-Campbell Movement formed the Board of Negro Education and Evangelization, an organization committed to disseminating the Gospel to African Americans. Two years later, C. C. Smith accepted appointment as the board's corresponding secretary; in 1893 Smith wrote that black Americans required an industrial education to equip them for domestic life, religion, and citizenship. "It was not the negro's fault, if he never discovered any relation between his religion and morals," believed Smith. Unlearned, untrained, and undisciplined, African American men and women possessed no "virtue," "chastity," or "regard for the marriage tie."[15] Cassius adamantly rejected Smith's racial smugness, marking him as unique in the Stone-Campbell Movement context in that he boldly contested his chosen fellowship's racial stance.

The imagined corollary of white superiority and black inferiority, in Cassius's view, fueled the economic disparity in the board's policies. In 1895, the black leader, after perusing the board's annual financial statement, rebuked the unjust remuneration practices. The organization paid $1,500 to Adoniram J. Thompson, a white instructor at the Louisville Bible School in Kentucky, yet it gave but $255 to Octavius Singleton, a black teacher at the same institution. Cassius protested: "notice the difference in the pay the white man gets—$1,245 more than the negro—and I honestly believe the negro is the smarter of the two." He labeled the missionary program "a pious fraud," adding: "There never was anything in it, either for the negro or the cause of Christ."[16] Cassius maintained such antipathy throughout his long preaching career.

Cassius further linked "progressivism" in the Stone-Campbell Movement with racism. In the fall of 1902, he read over the program for the Disciples of Christ convention in Omaha, Nebraska, and complained that African Americans had "entirely been left out." After attending the conference,

Cassius asked: "What right has such a body of people to call themselves Christians? Can a Christian use race discrimination and do the will of God and of Christ?"[17] Cassius particularly excoriated white "society men" who refused to compensate white and black evangelists equally. A competent black preacher, complained Cassius, "is not tolerated among the great leaders in the mission work of the Christian Church. They say that able colored preachers expect too much simply because they ask the same treatment given to white missionaries"[18]

Cassius understood something that most white Stone-Campbell leaders failed to comprehend: namely, that centuries of chattel enslavement had tainted their view of black people, causing them to underestimate "our intelligence" and overestimate "their ability to give us what we needed then and still—a pure gospel."[19] White decision makers, explained Cassius, "forgot that four hundred years of slavery had bred a prejudice that even zeal for the cause of Christ could not overcome, and that in the mind of every white man lurked the thought the Negro was, in some way, inferior and that the Negro himself had been taught to suspect and fear the white man."[20] Cassius held to a conviction that erroneous racial assumptions about black people in general not only caused the Negro Board of Education and Evangelization to fail, but also that racist views about black men in particular resulted in "division, which is doing us much harm."[21] Cassius, as a formerly enslaved African American, brought a singular perspective to bear on the policies and practices of white board leaders.

Beyond addressing racist presumptions in the Stone-Campbell Movement, S. R. Cassius vehemently denounced racism in America's broader society. Taking his instruction from scripture, the black evangelist studied white and black newspapers and often responded to antiblack sentiment. In 1904, when Mississippi governor James K. Vardaman labeled southern blacks as morally decadent and intellectually unfit for education, Cassius promptly scorned the Mississippian's inauguration remarks as an "insult to every great mind on earth, and blasphemy against God." The enslavement of black people kept them ignorant and "taught them no moral precepts, no sense of virtue, and no regard for the marriage ties," as they witnessed the rape of women until all moral decorum was stamped out of their hearts, inspiring black men to imitate their white oppressors."[22] A white Christian in the Oklahoma Territory objected to Cassius's criticism of Vardaman's speech and especially to his injecting political questions into religious journals.[23] Yet this very criticism pointed to the uniqueness of Cassius's role in the Stone-Campbell Movement:

a black man who consistently and courageously merged moral, political, social, and racial matters in church-controlled papers.

Cassius, cognizant that many whites in the Stone-Campbell Movement nursed a deep phobia concerning black males mingling with white women, insisted that the "fear of social equality" prevented Churches of Christ from becoming a more potent force in American society. Borrowing a reference from William Shakespeare's *Macbeth*, he compared whites' horror of biracial sex to Banquo's Ghost—the ghost of social equality frightened white Christians away from the black man in the United States. This phantom, declared Cassius, "howled that if the American negro is converted to Christ he will want to fill your churches and homes and drawing rooms and court your daughters, and in every way be your social equal." Long before Wilbur J. Cash coined the phrase "the Southern rape complex," Cassius understood the white man's phobia and branded it "false and absurd." Expressing a sense of black pride, he concluded that black men generally possessed no desire "to mix with any other people under heaven. We believe we are just as good morally, and socially as any other people on earth."[24]

S. R. Cassius's Fight against *The Birth of a Nation*

In the first three decades of the twentieth century, Cassius expended much time and energy fighting what he called "mind poisoning," that is, the proliferating racist literature devised to turn sympathetic whites against black people.[25] Thomas Dixon Jr., a white Baptist minister turned lawyer, orator, and novelist, composed a trilogy of inflammatory works: *The Leopard's Spots* (1902), *The Clansman* (1905), and *The Traitor* (1907). The second book proved to be his most racially explosive effort, becoming the basis for the blockbuster movie *The Birth of a Nation*. Dixon articulated his goal clearly: to "foment racism and convert viewers against the Negro," to "revolutionize Northern sentiment," and to "transform every man in my audience into a good Democrat."[26]

Within a decade, D. W. Griffith, a native Kentuckian who had imbibed racist perspectives about black people as an adolescent, adapted Dixon's novel for the big screen. The first movie to have an accompanied orchestral score, the first film to debut in the White House, and the costliest of its time, *The Birth of a Nation* portrayed African Americans as despicable creatures, venal politicians, and savage rapists. In contrast, the movie glorified the Ku Klux Klan as the savior of white civilization and white womanhood. Griffith exclaimed, in a veiled reference to President Woodrow Wilson's endorsement, "I was gratified when a man we all revere, or ought to, said it teaches history by lightning."²⁷ In Wilson's view, the racist caricatures of black men and the heroic work of the Klan were historically accurate.

If the white public generally applauded *The Birth of a Nation*, African Americans across the nation joined Cassius in assailing it. W. E. B. Du Bois, the Harvard-educated activist, helped to organize the National Association for the Advancement of Colored People, which brought together white liberals and concerned blacks to protest the controversial movie.²⁸ William Monroe Trotter, also a Harvard graduate and editor of a black newspaper, *The Guardian*, stood as a principal opponent of Griffith's film. Trotter summed up the movie's rationale: to "disparage the Colored race." The portrayal of black men "preying upon and raping white girl children" was, in Trotter's view, designed to "convert the North to believe in the South's repression and disfranchisement" of African Americans. Trotter's laborious efforts scored a victory in the spring of 1915, when the Massachusetts State Senate voted to censor the inflammatory film.²⁹

Consequently, in the broader political and religious context, Cassius was not altogether unique; as scholar Dennis C. Dickerson has shown, African Methodist Episcopal leader Archibald J. Carey used his position on the Chicago Board of Moving Picture Censors to condemn openly *The Birth of a Nation*.³⁰ In the Stone-Campbell Movement, however, S. R. Cassius stands as the only known opponent—black or white—to denounce publicly the racist theatrical production. Like William Monroe Trotter, Cassius captured the true motives behind both Thomas Dixon's *The Clansman* and Griffith's film, branding them as an effort "to poison the minds of Northern and Western white men against the negro by picturing the negro as a licentious brute that was roaming around seeking an opportunity to assault white women." The fundamental goal of the racist propagandists, added Cassius, was "to influence the minds" of white people against black people.³¹

Notwithstanding the vigorous stance of Cassius and others against *The Birth of a Nation*, the antiblack movie indelibly marked America: the Ku Klux Klan revived, lynchings increased, and—significantly in Cassius's case—race relations in the Stone-Campbell Movement suffered irreparable damage. In Cassius's view, white Churches of Christ endeavored to make the black man "a spiritual equal and a social outcast." "Brethren," Cassius commented, "it cannot be done. You simply cannot stand on a prostrated man's body and lift him up...."³² Regrettably, the works of Thomas Dixon and D. W. Griffith helped to influence white Christians to view the black man more as a social pariah than a brother in Christ.

"In a Class by Himself": The Legacy of S. R. Cassius

S. R. Cassius was not, certainly, the only former slave to emerge as a black leader in the Stone-Campbell Movement. Other men, such as S. W. Womack, Levi Kennedy, Alexander Campbell, George Ricks, and Preston Taylor, had endured life in chattel enslavement and emerged as religious leaders in their newly free world. Still, these men never publicly addressed race and racism in American society in general and in the Stone-Campbell Movement in particular, as did Cassius. He made it his mission to "make the Church of Christ see its duty to the Negro of the United States."³³ White Christians who poured monetary resources into foreign nations but neglected the plight of black people at home deeply troubled Cassius. "Brethren, when you think of heathen," Cassius demanded, "don't look beyond the United States. 'You have Africa at your door.'"³⁴

Cassius's commitment to the spiritual uplift of black Americans revealed his complex and contradictory stance on more than one level. First, he faced two stiff obstacles: "religious prejudice" from African Americans he desired to evangelize and "race prejudice" from whites in Churches of Christ. His exclusivist posture of "I am right and they are wrong" alienated the very people he loved and sought to assist.³⁵ Second, Cassius greatly admired the Wizard of Tuskegee, Booker T. Washington. Indeed, whites in the Stone-Campbell Movement christened Cassius the "Booker T. Washington of Oklahoma," for he had patterned his short-lived Tohee Industrial School after the Tuskegee Institute in Alabama. Yet Cassius, while outwardly displaying a Booker T. Washington persona, espoused a racial antipathy more strikingly similar to that of Frederick Douglass, Ida B. Wells, W. E. B. Du Bois, and William Monroe Trotter.³⁶ Third, Cassius unabashedly contested the racial and racist views of whites in the Stone-Campbell Movement; nonetheless, he frequently appealed to them for financial support. He detested going to white congregations; he went only seeking otherwise unavailable funds to minister to "my own race." At the same time, Cassius understood that many white Christians viewed him as an outcast, repelling as a "case of small pox."³⁷ A fourth example of the complexity of his personality is that, notwithstanding his constant railing against white believers and white racism, Cassius espoused an unfeigned affection for many Anglos in Churches of Christ. He felt a certain affinity with Frederick August Wagner, a German immigrant who converted to the Stone-Campbell Movement and took up missionary work in Japan. Upon learning of Wagner's death in the fall of 1901, a grief-stricken Cassius felt "too sad even to work." Comparing Wagner's toil among Asians to his own labor among black Americans, Cassius wrote that "Yes, Bro. Wagner's work and mine were very much alike; but he has been promoted, while I am still left in the field of battle." Cassius believed that Wagner went to heaven "from the dark, sin-cursed land of Japan; I will go from the Black Belt of sin-cursed America."[38]

In 1904, Cassius lost another dear white friend, J. C. Myers. Explaining the reason for his affection for Myers, he confessed: "I loved him because he seemed to realize my task and pity me. And not only was he my friend, but every one that was in trouble of our family received a word of encouragement from this man of God." He then appealed to *Christian Leader* readers to support Myers's ailing wife, volunteering to establish a fund for the new widow. "When I was hungry he fed me," reflected Cassius. "Naked, he clothed me. Sick and imprisoned by debt, he visited me. Brethren, my heart fails me."[39]

If Cassius had a best white friend, however, it was Joseph E. Cain, a preacher from Kansas and editor of the *Christian Leader*. "He found me alone, naked, as it were," Cassius recalled, "and he gave me food, clothes and comfort, and it is to him, more than any other man I owe my success in spreading the Gospel." Genuine love often reached across racial barriers even in a segregated society and religious community. "The white brethren indeed had great reason to love him," explained Cassius, "but I had more reason than they could ever have[;] he came into my life . . . at a time that I indeed needed a friend, and from that time to the very end he remained a friend to me. . . ." Cassius confessed that when he "did well," Cain praised him; but when "I erred, he lovingly rebuked me." The black evangelist called Cain the "whitest, broadest and most Christlike man I ever knew, and, above all, he was my friend."[40] The foregoing testimony confirms that even though Cassius uncompromisingly contested white racism, he harbored no hatred for all white people. He grew to love those whom he admired, just as they learned to admire and appreciate him.[41]

Finally, Cassius, too, admired black men. While residing in Washington, DC, as an adolescent, he claimed to have been on "intimate terms" with such black statesmen as Frederick Douglass, Hiram Revels, Blanche K. Bruce, and

John M. Langston. Cassius deeply appreciated Booker T. Washington; he sent his oldest son, Amos Lincoln Cassius, to study at the Tuskegee Institute. Moreover, when Washington died in 1915, Cassius eulogized him in the pages of the *Christian Leader* and *Gospel Advocate*, celebrating the Alabama educator as being "in a class by himself. His race did not make him great, but he reflected greatness on the race." Taking inspiration from Washington's success, Cassius remarked that what the former had achieved in a "worldly way," he was attempting to do spiritually and for an eternal reward.[42]

Fifteen years after Booker T. Washington's demise, Cassius died in Colorado Springs, Colorado. In light of his unflagging zeal in contesting racism both in the broader American society as well as in the Churches of Christ, S. R. Cassius stood, like Washington, "in a class by himself." In an era when federal, state, and local officials virtually abandoned black Americans, after stripping them of their citizenship rights and dignity; in an age when racist literature and movies portrayed black men as essentially subhuman; and in a religious fellowship that essentially spurned black Christians as pariahs, no man—white or black—toiled more diligently than Cassius to lift up American blacks to a plane of spiritual equality and social dignity with their white fellows.

When S. R. Cassius died on Monday night, August 10, 1931, a fifty-five-year-old black evangelist from middle Tennessee was hammering away with the "pure gospel," leading 166 black souls into Churches of Christ. The demise of Cassius arguably coincided with the rise of the most effective African American preacher in the history of Churches of Christ, Marshall Keeble. Cassius unwittingly helped pave the way for Marshall Keeble's success by calling attention to the "needs of my race." Unlike Cassius, however, Keeble had no desire to "rock the boat" of race relations in white America or white Churches of Christ. Consequently, he received something never accorded Cassius, namely, the constant and abiding monetary support of concerned white Christians. Such contaminated generosity both fueled the rise of African American Churches of Christ and empowered the Age of Marshall Keeble.

PART THREE

The Age of Marshall Keeble,
1931–1968

— 6 —

Setting the House on Fire

Marshall Keeble and the "Hard" Theology of African American Churches of Christ

"Then I said, I will not make mention of him, nor speak any more
in his name. But his word was in mine heart as a burning fire
shut in my bones, and I could not stay."
—Jeremiah 20:9

"Brother David Lipscomb put a coal of fire among the brethren
before God took him, which will never die."
—Marshall Keeble, *Gospel Advocate*

As S. R. Cassius lay dying in Colorado Springs, Colorado, earlier in the summer of 1931, Marshall Keeble was half a continent away in Valdosta, Georgia, setting Jeremiah's "burning fire" ablaze among often-enraged religious opponents. In Valdosta, an African American Baptist family hosted Keeble and his song leader, Luke Miller. When the wife of the family obeyed the Gospel at Keeble's evangelistic gathering, her husband became a "hot man," but Keeble pretended not to "know he was mad." After her baptism into Churches of Christ, Keeble reported that the "house was on fire—that man was mad enough to fight when we got back from services that night."[1] Of course, Marshall Keeble never literally set a house blazing, yet his combative sermons and his exclusivist theological stance—"I am right and they are wrong"[2]—emotionally fired the hearts and souls of many black Baptists, Methodists, and other religionists.

A native of Nashville, Tennessee, Keeble grew up in the tumultuous post-Reconstruction Era. In 1892, he received baptism into the Stone-Campbell Movement at the hands of evangelist and entrepreneur Preston Taylor.

Around 1900, his father-in-law broke ranks with Taylor and the Lea and Gay Christian Churches and aligned with the Jackson Street Church of Christ in Nashville, and Keeble joined him. Keeble's fiery sermonizing and exclusivist theology sprang from three sources. First, in the early 1900s, he confessed that he acquired a "burning desire to preach the Word" full time, much as did the biblical Jeremiah. This spiritual yearning inspired Keeble to commit his life solely to the task of evangelism from 1914 to his death in 1968. "I have given up all," he reported in 1917, "that I might preach the gospel to my people."[3] In addition, Keeble ingested the fiery preaching of his two black mentors, S. W. Womack and Alexander Campbell. The former presented the "pure gospel" in a "cool and slow" manner; the latter, with his "fiery and passionate" demeanor, brought a degree of animation and theatrics into the pulpit. Keeble merged the two preaching styles with his theological exclusivism, acknowledging that the duo "fired me up and left here."[4]

In an era which denied American blacks the opportunity of learning at southern theological institutions, Keeble could gain no formal training in religion, so white leaders in Churches of Christ and papers affiliated with the churches fueled Keeble's passion for advancing the "pure gospel" by providing an informal theological education. If Womack and Campbell influenced Keeble's style of sermon delivery, Joe McPherson, a white postal worker and preacher, profoundly contributed to the content of his messages. During a protracted meeting conducted by McPherson in 1914, Keeble "copied every lesson" the minister delivered. Even after his mentor's death, Keeble acknowledged that he was "still preaching" McPherson's sermons and they "still bring men to Christ."[5] Additionally, Keeble relied on the *Gospel Advocate*, edited by David Lipscomb, a key figure in the Stone-Campbell Movement, for spiritual sustenance. Regardless of how far and how frequently his preaching excursions kept him from his home in Nashville, Tennessee, he never divorced himself from the pages of the *Gospel Advocate*, the fundamental source of his theology, confessing that the paper always gave him "great strength." He also credited Lipscomb for lighting a "coal of fire among the brethren," a spiritual blaze "which will never die."[6]

Armed with the torch of the "pure gospel" and backed by generous white Christians, Keeble roamed southern communities, theologically setting ablaze the houses of black Baptists, Methodists, Pentecostals, and others, leading them into the fold of Churches of Christ. Indeed, the "fire" of Marshall Keeble differed markedly from his religious counterparts in two principal ways. Keeble often decried emotional expressions in public worship,

David Lipscomb (1831–1917), as editor of the *Gospel Advocate*, profoundly and decidedly shaped the theological mindset of African American Churches of Christ. After establishing black congregations across the South, Marshall Keeble often added those new church plants to the *Gospel Advocate* subscription list. Courtesy of Abilene Christian University.

especially dancing, shouting, and running "up and down the aisle like he is having a spasm." When preaching before a large biracial audience in Valdosta, Georgia, in 1931, he lamented that the true worshiper did not have to engage in such disorderly conduct to "prove to you he can't help it, that the Holy Ghost makes him do it."[7] Many black denominational adherents, however, believed that God's Spirit set them "on fire," prompting them to whine, sing, dance, and shout. Scholar Albert J. Raboteau has persuasively shown that "when the [black] preacher states that he is 'filled with' or 'set on fire by the Spirit,' he is not only claiming that he is a channel of God's grace or that God is telling him what to say; he is also describing his own ecstatic experience of preaching. As he preaches, he feels that a force or power other than his ordinary self takes over."[8]

Furthermore, the ardor burning in the hearts of black Baptists and Methodists often inspired them to protest racial injustice and social inequality. Wrestling with the weighty burden of persecution and threats to his life and family, Martin Luther King Jr. testified that he heard an "inner voice" urging him to "stand up for righteousness. Stand up for justice. Stand up for truth."[9] Keeble's fire motivated him to save the souls of his religious neighbors from what he perceived to be theological error, but King's fervor stirred him to "save the soul of the nation." The soul of the American nation, in King's view, was inextricably bound to the struggle for racial and economic equality.[10]

In the summer of 1939, a few weeks before the outbreak of World War II, Marshall Keeble declared his own war, not on racism, but on sin and sectarianism. Joe Morris, a white host minister in Huntington, West Virginia, lavished praise on the black evangelist. "I have never heard nor seen greater power in the pulpit," testified Morris. "Sin was condemned, error exposed, and the church of Christ exalted to the heavens, and no man can do this with a greater degree of success than Marshall Keeble."[11] Keeble's preaching efforts at Huntington yielded eight baptisms, including a Baptist and a Methodist preacher. His potent sermons, added Morris, not only established black believers, but also "greatly strengthened" the white Churches of Christ in the area. Morris then chided white preachers in Churches of Christ for their timid and soft sermons, pleading: "May God speed the day when soft-soaping preachers and neutrals among the white preachers will have the courage to condemn sin and error and preach righteousness as does M. Keeble."[12]

Certainly, Marshall Keeble was no "soft soap" preacher; on the contrary, he espoused a "hard" theology which touted the Church of Christ as the one "true church." Inspired by Alexander Campbell and his iconoclastic nineteenth-century *Christian Baptist*, white advocates of the "hard style" such as John R. Howard, Arthur Crihfield, and Moses Lard insisted that all who refused to align with the Churches of Christ had "rejected Christ and that no sectarian—including Methodists, Baptists, Presbyterians, Quakers, and others—could possibly be saved."[13] Through the pages of such journals as the *Gospel Advocate*, *Firm Foundation*, and the *Christian Echo*, Keeble absorbed this radical theology and frequently infuriated his black listeners, who at times threatened to "tar and feather" him.[14]

In 1918, Keeble planted his first congregation in Henderson, Tennessee. When black Baptists there denied Keeble the use of their building, N. B. Hardeman, a white educator and evangelist in Churches of Christ, used his influence to arrange for Keeble to preach in the Oak Grove school. Keeble's "hard" sermons aroused the ire of many black residents who complained: "Keeble is a trouble-maker and he's tearing up the churches." Notwithstanding such complaints, the three-week meeting produced eighty-four baptisms, the nucleus for the Oak Grove Church of Christ. Reports that "Marshall Keeble was setting Chester County 'on fire'" quickly reached his hometown of Nashville, Tennessee.[15]

When Keeble returned to his first church plant in the mid-1920s, he recalled that when he had first come to town the "sects were real angry." Yet he delighted to see that after several years those who "so opposed the doctrine have been baptized and are harder fighters than I am."[16] Keeble's sharp theology often created converts more zealous and rigid than himself; consequently, these disciples often generated lingering "strife" among their African American neighbors.[17]

Shortly after World War I, Keeble set up a tent in Whitehaven, Tennessee, a "hotbed of sectarianism" just outside Memphis. His messages linked the "seed of the kingdom of Christ" with the one true church, and his uncompromising sermons "made some awfully angry."[18] Twenty-seven miles east in Collierville, Tennessee, African Americans virtually chased Keeble out of town. Displeased with Keeble's "pure gospel," angry blacks in the city reported to white authorities that the black preacher was inciting a "race war." After investigating the accusation, white officials deemed his preaching "good and just what they needed." Disregarding the approval of the white establishment, enraged blacks addressed intimidating letters to Keeble, threatening him with bodily harm and vowing to burn up his tent.[19]

In the 1930s, as the Great Depression blanketed the United States, Keeble continued to infuriate many black hearers. In Valdosta, Georgia, an irate sectarian preacher stood and rebuked his former members whom Keeble had baptized into the Church of Christ. After the angry preacher denounced his former parishioners who "never got religion in the first place," an adroit Keeble defended his new converts by replying: "He's right. You never 'got religion.'" Quoting James 1:27, Keeble asserted: "Religion is something you do—not something you get."[20] Approximately 230 miles north in Atlanta, a "hot" Bishop Swanson accosted Keeble on his speaker's platform with a "sword cane" and thundered: "There was a good feeling in this town before you came." Keeble, after calmly diffusing his antagonist's rage, was able to teach and baptize him.[21]

Keeble owed his ability to quell friction between himself and his black hearers not only to his "wit and wisdom,"[23] but also to his understanding of human nature. He once acknowledged that he studied both scripture and people.[23] Indeed, Keeble at one time baptized an "angry man who said Keeble's preaching my mama to hell." On another occasion when a furious black listener shouted to Keeble, "Where's my mama?" the black evangelist quipped: "I don't know your mama," cooling a heated situation.[24]

"The Bouncing Time Is Over": Marshall Keeble and the "Hard" Theology

In the summer of 1931, as Marshall Keeble delivered sermons in Valdosta, Georgia, B. C. Goodpasture, an influential white preacher and staunch supporter of Keeble, hired Connie Alderman, an expert court reporter, to transcribe the black preacher's messages. The *Gospel Advocate* then marketed the sermons in book form and distributed them to African Americans in Churches of Christ. These transcriptions provide invaluable insight into Keeble's religious thinking, as well as a key to understanding his effectiveness. In his sermon entitled "The Power of the Written Word," Keeble displayed his biblical literalism, stressing that the source of all divine information emanated from "the written word."[25] Like B. F. Hall, Tolbert Fanning, and other white spiritual forbears, Keeble preached that the "Holy Spirit exerts no influence on the hearts of sinners over and above the word."[26] Keeble hammered the phrase "the written word" some eleven times in the discourse, explaining his intent to call his black listeners "back to the Bible, to do away with the disciplines, manuals and creeds from the people and get back to the written word."[27]

A master storyteller and practical preacher, Keeble linked "the written word"—that is, the Bible—with a "written deed," referencing the purchase of land or the significance of keeping a written receipt when buying furniture. To amplify his message and bring it down to earth, Keeble recalled a neighbor of his in Nashville, Tennessee, who bought land with a mere verbal agreement and without a "written deed." The buyer later lost his possession because he had no written documentation. "Poor John, lost his property," lamented Keeble, because he had "nothing in writing." He poignantly added, "when you stand at the bar of judgment after you have been slaving for a number of years and yet have no deed—got no eternal home. What was the matter? No written contract—went around guessing and feeling your way to heaven. Got to get your written contract."[28]

Keeble, with his aptitude for shaping spiritual concepts in worldly terms, then told his Valdosta audience about his wife, Minnie. She once thought she

Marshall Keeble (1878–1968) established the North Tenneha Church of Christ in Tyler, Texas, in 1935. Keeble's "hard" theology led to the formation of many such congregations that continue to flourish in the twenty-first century. Courtesy of the North Tenneha Church of Christ.

had satisfied a debt for furniture. The white bookkeeper, however, informed her that she still owed one more payment. Frustrated and confused, Minnie returned home; and after searching frantically for the receipt, she found it. "Thank God," her husband exclaimed. The couple hastily returned to the store, presented the receipt to the clerk, and verified that the debt had been paid. "Above everything," urged Keeble, "keep your receipts. If you are going to heaven and you appear before Jesus Christ at the final consummation of all things and at the judgment seat of Christ where all nations must appear and you stand there and you haven't got a written receipt by Jesus Christ, signed with His blood, you will have to check off with your debt unpaid."[29]

Scholar Michael Casey, in his study of preaching in Churches of Christ, has noted that African American evangelists such as Keeble often delivered sermons with a "double code" before racially mixed audiences. On the one hand, Keeble might drive home a spiritual message that his listeners needed a receipt from God, namely, baptism for the remission of sins in order to enter heaven. Such a message would have appeased his white supporters in Churches of Christ. On the other hand, Keeble's emphasis on "keep your receipts" was a subtle reminder to his black audience members that lacking documentation often translated into lingering financial debt imposed by white oppressors.[30]

In Keeble's mind, however, the "written word," illustrated with stories about the "written deed," inarguably pointed to the one true church, the Church of Christ. After denouncing Mormons and Jehovah's Witnesses in the Valdosta meeting, he then elevated the Church of Christ above Baptists and other denominations because the latter were not "in writing." He concluded his sermon by pointing to the chart he ordinarily used and challenging the audience: *"Have you obeyed the written word?"* On the one hand, Keeble's sermon elicited "grumbling" from many of his black auditors; on the other hand, his parabolic, exclusivist preaching swayed other hearers into the fold of Churches of Christ by meeting's end.

In his sermon the next evening, "Been to Worship, but Wrong," Keeble essentially lambasted Pentecostals and other charismatic groups. Inspired by his perspective of Campbellian rationalism,[31] which read the Bible virtually as a scientific textbook and viewed emotionalism with grave distrust, Keeble addressed those who relied on "feelings as an evidence of pardon. You have been taught to believe that you have got to go through some great excitement and emotional in order to become a child of God." Lifting his text from Acts 8:26–39, Keeble insisted the more one absorbed God's word the "less emotionalism" and the "less excitement" one experienced. "You are compelled to acknowledge," said Keeble, "that this is the quietest and least emotional service that you ever attended in your life and this is an intelligent audience, and when you accept the gospel of Jesus Christ, it knocks all the monkey notion out."[32]

Keeble, of course, didn't object to all emotional expressions, such as listeners exclaiming "Amen," in his preaching campaigns. Yet he berated those who shouted and danced excessively. "The gospel is like lead," he explained, "it's heavy, when you preach it to a man, it holds him down. He can't bounce around, but when you preach a false doctrine, it is light, it's like shucks, like cotton, can't help but bounce, nothing to hold it down. But my friends, the bouncing time is over." Instead of "bouncing," Keeble urged his hearers to: "Sit study, drink down the truth."[33]

Keeble vigorously opposed the emotional outbursts of Pentecostals because God did not have "a wild Holy Ghost." "They are about to dance themselves to death," he complained. "Old-fashioned buck and wild dance in the service and calling it Church of God."[34] Here, Keeble most likely had in mind the Church of God in Christ, which Charles H. Mason had founded in 1897.

Marshall Keeble (1878–1968) was without question one of the
most influential preachers in African American Churches of Christ.
His "hard" theology and high ecclesiology remain a key part
of many African American Churches of Christ today.
Courtesy of Abilene Christian University.

Mason and his followers, after severing ties with black Baptists, espoused the doctrines of baptism with the Holy Spirit, speaking in tongues, and sanctification.[35] Keeble roundly rejected such practices since the apostles of Jesus never "danced," "rolled around," or "were baptized with the Holy Ghost."[36]

After refuting Pentecostalism, Keeble then repudiated the beliefs of black Methodists and Baptists who attended his Valdosta meeting. Like his white teachers who stressed "baptism for the remission of sins,"[37] Keeble insisted that baptism was essential for salvation. Drawing his argument from the story of the Ethiopian eunuch in Acts 8, he declaimed that "you can't preach Jesus, you can't preach a complete Christ without getting into some water." Keeble also gleaned from the same narrative that "Baptism in the Bible always follows confession." During the discourse, Keeble rehearsed an experience he had in

Fayetteville, Tennessee, where a robust police officer approached the diminutive minister, asking: What if a man had confessed Christ, but on his way to be baptized he was killed in a car accident? "Is he lost or is he saved?" An unflinching 5' 4" Keeble responded: "according to the Bible, he is lost."[38] In the mind of Keeble, one had no hope without baptism for the remission of sins.

Keeble then chided black Methodists who practiced "three modes of baptism, sprinkling, pouring and immersing." The evangelist Philip in Acts 8 could not have been a "Methodist preacher," since he immersed the Ethiopian eunuch. Keeble deemed "Brother Baptist" worse off than "Brother Methodist," for the former was buried in water, but not "for the remission of sins." "There is not a Baptist in town, from the preachers on down," declared Keeble, "can tell you what he was baptized for, scripturally. He will tell you lots of things, but I say scripturally." Based on his understanding of Acts 2:38, Keeble affirmed that Baptists had received immersion for the wrong reason, since they believed that salvation was assured before baptism. He further reasoned that Philip, who baptized the Ethiopian eunuch in Acts 8, could not have been a Baptist preacher, since he did not carry the Ethiopian seeker to church to "hear his testimony and let him be voted on."[39] For Keeble, Baptists and Methodists, like their Pentecostal neighbors, held no place in the one true church.

Keeble concluded his Valdosta "Been to Worship, but Wrong" sermon by thanking white Christians who had invited him to their city, "furnished the tent, furnished the chairs and had me come and preach to you the pure word of God." Before singing the invitational hymn, calling hearers to come forward for salvation, Keeble delineated the five "conditions" one must meet in order to be saved: hear, believe, repent, confess, and be baptized.[40] Keeble's five-step plan, based on Walter Scott's so-called "five-finger exercise," emphasized the human tasks regarding salvation. A former Presbyterian minister who converted to the Stone-Campbell Movement, Scott developed a creative teaching device by emphasizing six steps to salvation: faith in Christ, repentance of sins, and baptism were mankind's responsibility, while forgiveness of sins, the gift of the Holy Spirit, and eternal life were the work of God. He then combined the last two gifts and reduced these six steps to the "five finger exercise."[41] This "plan of salvation" became and still remains a cornerstone teaching of African American Churches of Christ.

Before preaching his sermon, "Five Steps to the Church and Seven to Heaven," Keeble related to his Valdosta audience a story about Grandma

Clarke, a devout black Methodist whom he met and converted to Churches of Christ in Summit, Georgia. Before her transition into Churches of Christ, Mrs. Clarke brought her two adolescent grandchildren to hear Keeble preach. The grandchildren meticulously wrote down the Bible passages Keeble referenced each night. The grandmother reported that her two grandchildren would stay up until the next morning "trying to find those passages" and refusing to "sleep until they read every passage to grandma." Mrs. Clarke explained to Keeble that she so commissioned her two grandchildren because she did not know him; and she did not "know whether I was lying or not." Keeble then thanked the grandmother and suggested that his listeners in Valdosta "do like those children, like Grandma Clarke did."[42]

After her conversion to Churches of Christ, Grandma Clarke's pastor severely criticized her, berating her judgment: "I thought you had some sense." Mrs. Clarke, who had been a member of the Methodist faith for fifty-five years, replied: "I thought I did too, but I found out you had misled me." Keeble appropriated Grandma Clarke's story to rebuke his hearers for not reading their Bibles. "That is the trouble with this town, your pastors, and your moderators, and your superintendents or presiding elders, and your deacons and stewards ought to read the Bible so they wouldn't lead the masses astray."[43]

While in Louisville, Kentucky, Keeble met a woman who, like Grandma Clarke, believed the doctrine he preached, but she refused to "change from her church." She refused to jump "from limb to limb." Keeble, resorting to his quick wit, said that he agreed as long as the limb was a "sound one." It would be unwise, he added, to perch on a "rotten limb." "When the limb is so rotten it is cracking, it is time to change." Religious groups, who relied on manmade creeds and doctrines, Keeble explained, sat on "dead and rotten limbs" that were "cracking right now under you. You better change. Wise bird don't roost on a rotten limb."[44] For Keeble, changing from Baptist, Methodist, or Pentecostal to Church of Christ was tantamount to converting to Christ, since he held that the aforementioned groups were not accepted by God.

In the body of the sermon called "Five Steps to the Church and Seven Steps to Heaven," Keeble elaborated on the "five-finger exercise," accentuating the third step: repentance. He explained that repentance was a "reformation of life," quitting one's "devilment." Keeble believed that prohibition laws and enlarged prisons could not "stop men from sinning." Fully persuaded by Paul's statement in Romans 1:16, Keeble emphasized that God's message was "powerful enough to stop" a man from bootlegging, beating his wife, and cheating on his spouse.[45] For Keeble, a change of conduct must accompany one's transition from a denominational church into the one true church. Keeble, then, was considerably more than a rigid exclusivist evangelist; he strongly advocated moral values, arguing that religious commitment must affect one's behavior. In this regard, Keeble mirrored the very Pentecostals he pummeled from his pulpits.[46] Still, for Keeble "reformation" of one's life emanated not from the Holy Spirit, as Pentecostals maintained, but from one's compliance to the "gospel of Christ."

Such a stiff theological stance angered many of his black listeners in his Valdosta preaching campaign. Keeble acknowledged that he resembled Noah, who swayed only seven people to enter the Ark. Some who heard Noah's warnings laughed, mocked, and doubted him; others "got mad like you are doing here in Valdosta." When Keeble canvassed the community during the day, some black residents refused to speak to him. "One poke[d] his mouth out," said Keeble, "because I told him howdy." In spite of this often-unpleasant reception, Keeble's fourth sermon, "Nothing Too Hard for the Lord," reiterated: "God gives pardon in baptism for the remission of sins."[47]

Keeble's fifth homily in Valdosta, "Who Will Be Able to Stand?," attacked the use of instrumental music in worship. He recalled baptizing a "sanctified" preacher, Brother Swanson in Jacksonville, Florida, who had agreed to purchase a guitar on an installment plan. He had almost secured his guitar until he heard Keeble's message. After first angrily challenging Keeble, Swanson went home, read his Bible, "cooled off," and later received baptism into the Church of Christ. Keeble then advised his listeners in Valdosta: " . . . if you will go home and read your Bible, you will cool off."

After his baptism into the Church of Christ, Swanson chose not to purchase the instrument, went back to pawnbroker, and retrieved his money for "something more profitable." Keeble then indicted his listeners who had "fine pianos and organs sitting in the church," while widows and orphans suffered. "Hundreds of dollars wasted," he added, "and the world hungry for bread."[48] A humanitarian concern accompanied Keeble's rigid theological stance.

Anticipating the argument of pro-instrumentalists who argued that "there is music in heaven," Keeble proffered: "I generally suggest that you had better wait until you get there and then use it." He added that Revelation 19:11 referenced a white horse in heaven, "but you don't ride him in church, so you can't prove instrumental music is right because there is music in heaven." Keeble praised God for the "simplicity" of his word and for "that simple New

Testament worship." Elevating his chosen fellowship above all others, he avowed: "Nothing works like the church of Christ."[49]

Keeble went on to denounce preachers who wore the title "Reverend," reflecting his connection to Barton W. Stone's 1804 document "The Last Will and Testament of the Springfield Presbytery." Stone and his cohorts, all former Presbyterians, sternly rejected such labels.[50] Keeble and his spiritual descendants typically ignored such "roots,"[51] or traditional documents, and went back to the Bible to reject what they deemed manmade practices. "You have never read those titles in the Bible and you never will," Keeble stressed.[52]

Keeble next condemned Baptists, Methodists, and other religionists who required that preachers have a "license" to preach. Imagine, lamented Keeble, a man who has been "made to believe that he is called and can't preach until a set of men give him a license." Here again Keeble strikingly yet perhaps unwittingly based his theological stance on a platform by Barton W. Stone. In the abovementioned "Last Will and Testament of the Springfield Presbytery," Stone and his collaborators affirmed: "*We will*, that candidates for the Gospel ministry henceforth study the Holy scriptures with fervent prayer, and obtain license from God to preach the simple Gospel, *with the Holy Ghost sent down from heaven*, without any mixture of philosophy, vain deceit, traditions of men, or the rudiments of the world."[53] For Keeble, religious communities who required such practices were "not right." Consequently, such groups were not approved by God.

Marshall Keeble's five sermons, preached and recorded in Valdosta in 1931, in the shadow of the Great Depression, set on fire the houses and hearts of his countless black listeners. Keeble, then, might be called a spiritual arsonist who traveled the United States, primarily in the Jim Crow South, metaphorically torching black people who dared to give him a hearing. His bold, exclusivist posture often baffled African Americans entrenched in Baptist, Methodist, or other faith traditions. Many burned with anger at his "one true church" message, even threatening physical violence; yet by meeting's end in Valdosta, 166 black residents had received baptism at the hands of Keeble and his cohort Luke Miller, further stirring the ire of black pastors and family members who spurned his "hard" theology.

Notwithstanding this mixed response, Keeble succeeded by strengthening what is now the Woodlawn Forrest Church of Christ in Valdosta, Georgia. Keeble repeatedly accomplished this feat through his peregrinations, leaving behind scores of black Churches of Christ across the South. He struggled, however, to chip away at black denominations in northern and western cities in the United States when he occasionally ventured there.⁵⁴ As a Keeble biographer has observed Keeble, while preaching in California in the mid 1920s, failed to "set the 'golden hills' of California on fire."⁵⁵ Keeble's preaching and teaching style, born and nurtured in the South, remained most effective in that region.

Even though Keeble's evangelistic efforts found less success outside the South, his book of sermons had become the bestselling item produced by the Gospel Advocate Company by the mid-twentieth century.⁵⁶ More importantly, the teachings found in these sermons left an indelible mark on the history and theology of African American Churches of Christ. Keeble's recorded homilies not only offer insight into the mind of this singular preacher, but they also provide a window into the origins and development of the "hard" theology of his chosen religious fellowship. Indeed, Keeble's spiritual sons and grandsons⁵⁷ frequently revisited and reworked these sermons, subsequently transmitting their tenets to their audiences, and fashioning the teachings of what now stands as the core beliefs of African American Churches of Christ.

An appraisal of African American Churches of Christ over the thirty-seven years from 1931 to 1968 reveals this era as the Age of Marshall Keeble. He was inarguably the most influential black preacher in Churches of Christ. Yet Marshall Keeble was more than a fervent church planter. He was a careful strategist. After planting a local congregation, he then commissioned one of his spiritual sons to provide spiritual guidance for his new and fledgling flock. Keeble then added the new church plant to the subscription list of the *Gospel Advocate*, which profoundly shaped the theological perspectives of African American Churches of Christ.⁵⁸ By the 1940s, Keeble settled into the role of president of the Nashville Christian Institute, traversing the country raising funds and recruiting black students. At the same time in subsequent decades, Keeble's evangelistic campaigning slowed as he worked primarily as a moral counselor to African American members of Churches of Christ. He condemned Christians who played cards, smoked cigarettes, frequented movie theaters, drank alcohol, and used snuff. He particularly railed against any black preacher who flirted with women, calling it the "most dangerous thing he could allow himself to do, because it will surely destroy him." Three decades after Keeble's comments on morality, Eugene Lawton, an eminent and passionate African American preacher in Churches of Christ, urged fellow black preachers to "stand up for moral purity" during a National Lectureship in Dallas, Texas. He further admonished his ministerial colleagues: "You can't chase sisters and be pure, and you can't misuse church funds and be pure."⁵⁹ The pronouncements of both Keeble and Lawton attest to a deep concern for moral purity in twentieth-century black Churches of Christ.

Scholar Michael Eric Dyson, examining the moral climate of black Baptist Churches, has pointed out that many African American clergymen misused their position of trust to exploit women sexually. "The gift of sacred speech," noted Dyson, "has been used to lift the sagging souls of parishioners damned by disbelief in themselves and to rally bewildered troops in the war for racial and social justice. But black religious oratory has too often been employed to line the pockets of materialistic ministers or cause vulnerable women to swoon and sexually submit under the hypnotic sway of eloquence." Dyson claimed that "bedding women is nearly a sport in some churches."⁶⁰ As African American Churches of Christ became more visible and more vibrant, Marshall Keeble sought to stem any such tide of moral indiscretion in his chosen faith tradition.

Keeble boldly denounced what he deemed sins of sectarianism espoused by black denominations. In his own faith tradition, he railed against alcoholism and sexual immorality. Keeble, however, astonishingly never publicly condemned the sin of racism. Indeed, during the 1931 Valdosta campaign, white supporter B. C. Goodpasture made it clear: "Racial difference and the question of social equality were not discussed during the meetings. There was no occasion for it." Keeble's perhaps-studied evasion of the "race question" and his refusal to "rock the boat" of race relations in Churches of Christ made him a superstar in the eyes of his white supporters. But not all African American preachers in Churches of Christ adhered to the meek and mild racial path of Marshall Keeble. The "warhorses" discussed in a coming chapter charted a divergent course and courageously roiled the muddy waters of race relations in Churches of Christ and beyond.

— 7 —

Warhorses

G. P. Bowser, the "Big Four," and the Structuring of African American Churches of Christ

> "Hast thou given the horse strength? Hast thou clothed his neck with thunder? Canst thou make him afraid as a grasshopper? The glory of his nostrils is terrible. He paweth in the valley, and rejoiceth in his strength: he goeth on to meet the armed men. He mocketh at fear, and is not affrighted; neither turneth he back from the sword."
> —Job 39:19–22

Even though Marshall Keeble reigned supreme as the premier church planter of African American Churches of Christ, G. P. Bowser played a pivotal role in stabilizing and structuring the fledgling black congregations Keeble left behind. In 1931, Keeble reportedly preached 396 sermons, baptized 420 people, and planted six new congregations.[1] Keeble's evangelistic success often generated questions as to who would nurture these new black converts and guide these newly organized congregations. Keeble's threefold strategy for handling recent church plants entailed adding the new congregations to the *Gospel Advocate* subscription list, sending one of his spiritual sons to work with the novices, and relying on concerned white Christians to provide spiritual guidance and financial support for the new black flocks.[2]

While Keeble's strategy proved most helpful in the South, it did little to encourage black Churches of Christ nationally. As African American Churches of Christ both struggled and flourished in the 1940s and 1950s, G. P. Bowser and his "sons" filled a great void not only by providing black congregations with spiritual guidance but also by giving them a distinct identity through their own papers and lectureships. Bowser's biographer has correctly noted that Bowser recognized the "lack of teaching materials," "little communication," and "little contact" between black members of Churches of Christ and their fellow converts in other cities. Such deficiencies prompted him to establish both a journal and a school for his people.[3]

In the postemancipation era, African Americans occupied to the "lowest and lowliest position" in the nation's societal structure. The passage of the disfranchisement measures, the caricaturization of black people as lazy and stupid, and the horrific proliferation of lynchings and race riots coalesced to push race relations to their nadir.[4] In this dark and violent period, most African Americans turned to their God and to themselves. In their churches, homes, and schools, black instructors told their students to "pull yourself up by your bootstraps" and to be of "service to the race." Historians John Hope Franklin and Evelyn Brooks Higginbotham have observed succinctly: "Integral to self-help ideology is the belief in racial self-determination—the idea that blacks should speak for themselves and should control their own institutions."[5] G. P. Bowser clearly personified this idea.

Born in middle Tennessee in 1874, Bowser grew up in this disorderly, segregated age, searching for hope and security. Like many of his black contemporaries, Bowser absorbed the "self-help" ideology. Bowser, while crossing railroad tracks, stumbled and was hit by a train as a teenager; and he was left with a mangled arm. Notwithstanding this handicap, he aligned himself with the African Methodist Episcopal Church in Nashville, where he rose through the clerical ranks to become a licensed exhorter and church elder. He also studied at Walden University in Nashville, Tennessee, revealing a deep thirst for knowledge and reportedly mastering five languages: Hebrew, Greek, Latin, German, and French.[6] Bowser, like other black southerners in the Reconstruction and post-Reconstruction eras, believed firmly in the "magic of education."[7]

Even though Bowser obtained impressive academic training and found a certain sense of security in Methodism, that denomination's theology never fully satisfied him. In 1897, Bowser left the Methodist Church, becoming part of the Stone-Campbell Movement by receiving instruction from Sam Davis and eventually baptism at the Gay Street Christian Church in Nashville. Even there, however, Bowser felt dissatisfied and distraught over "innovations"; as a consequence, he left and became a member of the Jackson Street Church of Christ in the same city.[8] Bowser brought his gift of knowledge from Methodism into black Churches of Christ and helped to solidify and structure his newly found fellowship.

G. P. Bowser and Marshall Keeble shared striking similarities, but stark differences marked them as well. Both men hailed from middle Tennessee; both, after marrying, lived in the same segregated neighborhood in Nashville. Both men experienced a similar spiritual journey into Churches of Christ. Keeble, a former Baptist, received baptism into the Christian Church before coming into Churches of Christ. Bowser, a former Methodist, also aligned with the Christian Church before attaching himself to Churches of Christ. Both men espoused a "hard" exclusivist theology toward other religious groups. "Bowser was very dogmatic in his denunciation of all religious practice not consistent with New Testament Christianity," according to biographer R. Vernon Boyd. "His name-calling of sectarians sometimes made it difficult for the church members who had to live with their neighbors after Bowser left town."[9]

Yet in spite of such similarities, Bowser and Keeble differed in four important areas: their dress, educational training, preaching style, and racial posture. Keeble, receiving generous and sustained financial support from white Christians, ordinarily dressed professionally, whereas Bowser, relying mainly on impoverished black people for support, tended to dress shabbily. In 1930, F. B. Shepherd, a white preacher in Texas, heard and saw Bowser preaching and lamented that he was poorly attired with "barely enough clothes to cover him."[10] With little money at his disposal, Bowser customarily "dressed like a tramp" and because of his frequent and extensive travels, "his clothes often were ragged, unkempt, and unclean."[11] While Keeble may have been better attired, Bowser had acquired a better education. Indeed, Keeble's formal tutelage stopped at the seventh grade, while Bowser's academic training continued into the university level. Such schooling equipped him to launch the *Christian Echo*, a paper published by blacks in Churches of Christ. It further inspired Bowser to organize the Silver Point Christian Institute in Tennessee in 1907 and the Bowser Christian Institute in Arkansas in 1938, before his "sons" established the Southern Bible Institute (now Southwestern Christian College) in Texas in 1948.[12] Additionally, Keeble was a parabolic preacher, a storyteller who confessed, "If I can't make a parable, I'm lost."[13] Bowser conversely possessed a keen memory and in his closely reasoned sermons often quoted "passage after passage to establish his points."[14] Finally, the contrasting racial postures of Bowser and Keeble proved to be the most important difference between the two men. Keeble purposely evaded the issue of race, while

The Higby Street Church of Christ in Jackson, Michigan, was planted in 1924, when African Americans in Churches of Christ took their religious convictions from the South to northern cities in the early twentieth century. Courtesy of the Higby Street Church of Christ in Jackson, Michigan.

Bowser confronted it directly. In 1920, A. M. Burton and white Christians in Nashville organized the Southern Practical Institute for African American students. C. E. W. Dorris, a white minister and superintendent of the new school, demanded that students, all of them black, enter the building through the back door. Bowser, principal of the fledgling institution, vehemently denounced the practice since the school was only for African Americans. Keeble exhorted Bowser to accept the back-door policy, as long as the students obtained the "Christian education they so much desired." Unrepentant, Bowser abruptly resigned his post as principal, left the school, and urged other black parents to withdraw their children, resulting in the school's hasty demise.[15] Keeble passively accepted racism as long as he achieved his evangelistic or educational goals; Bowser adamantly repudiated racism even when it eliminated opportunities for himself or other African Americans.

Bowser refused to consider white people as innately superior to black people, viewing African Americans as equal to their white counterparts. This explains why Bowser prayed for the success of Marcus Garvey and his movement.[16] A Jamaican immigrant who came to the United States in 1916, Garvey founded the Universal Negro Improvement Association (UNIA), touted the beauty and dignity of blackness and urged black people to return to Africa.[17] In an era when white Americans deemed black people unattractive and inferior, Bowser held on to a keen sense of black pride and black self-respect.

In the pages of the *Christian Echo*, which Bowser founded in 1902 to advance the "teaching of pure New Testament Christianity,"[18] glimpses of his black pride surfaced. When subscriber Henry Robinson asked whether Christians should support the National Association for the Advancement of Colored People (NAACP), Bowser called the civil rights movement "the greatest organization in the world in helping" to ensure that African Americans get "justice before the court."[19] Founded in 1909 on a bipartisan and biracial platform, the NAACP initially floundered until the inflammatory movie *The Birth of a Nation* transformed it into a vigorous civil rights organization. Bowser knew both the movie and the organization, and he particularly understood the oppression of his fellow blacks in the United States. He felt, consequently, no misgivings about urging support for the NAACP.

In spite of these differences in their theology, both men maintained similar views. Bowser's *Christian Echo* not only furnished black people in Churches of Christ with a greater voice and greater visibility, but it also helped to bring structure to his chosen fellowship. Serious Bible students often raised doubts over scriptural passages to the editor, who in turn offered clarification over puzzling theological questions. One seeker asked: "Is it right for a brother of the church of Christ to ask a sect to lead us in prayer?" Bowser replied: "No. It is equivalent to saying that sects are right, and members of the church of Christ. No denomination has the right doctrine." Citing 2 John 9–10, Bowser concluded that allowing a Baptist or Methodist to lead prayer in a Church of Christ service was tantamount to granting him God's approval.[20] Bowser's response plainly reveals his "hard" exclusivist theological stance toward other religious groups, as he remained convinced that those beyond the fellowship of the Church of Christ were unsaved. Keeble would have soundly endorsed this perception of the church.

In the 1940s, *Christian Echo* readers peppered Bowser with a series of questions pertaining to the relationship between black Churches of Christ and black Disciples of Christ. While I have argued elsewhere that this was "the question of the decade"[21] for African American Churches of Christ in Texas, this was not merely a concern for African American Christians in the Lone

Star State; it became a national issue as black congregations proliferated across the country. To the general question, "When one comes from the Christian Church to the church of Christ should he be baptized again?" Bowser consistently answered: "If they have been baptized under the Christian Church a digressive faction of the church of Christ, [they are] hence our brethren." Bowser based his contention on the premise that both groups taught the same basic "five-finger plan of salvation."[22]

Regrettably, we do not have the complete volumes of the *Christian Echo* to aid fully in our understanding of African American Churches of Christ. Yet what we have at our disposal allows us to see that a certain theological ambiguity pervaded these churches. While they condemned black Baptists, Methodists, and others as non-Christians, they embraced black Disciples of Christ as Christians, even though they practiced certain "innovations."

Bowser's enduring legacy came not only from his tenure as editor of the *Christian Echo*, but also from his work as an educator. Armed with knowledge gained at Walden University as a Methodist minister, Bowser transmitted his passion for education to African Americans in Churches of Christ. In 1907, he launched the Silver Point Christian Institute in Nashville, Tennessee. Two years later, he relocated the school to the town of Silver Point itself, seventy-five miles east of Nashville, and offered classes in Bible, English, History, Latin, and Math. By 1916, just before the United States entered World War I, Bowser's school had reached its apex with an enrollment of fifty-seven students. The lack of financial support, however, forced the school's closure in 1918. But three of the pupils from Silver Point's classrooms became significant contributors to the growth and development of African American Churches of Christ.

First, Alonzo Jones, a native of Columbus, Mississippi, moved to Silver Point with his wife and children to study under G. P. Bowser. After the school closed in 1918, Jones and his family returned to the Magnolia State to farm one year. The family came back with him to middle Tennessee hoping to enroll at the short-lived Southern Practical Institute; however, the school's abrupt closure prompted Jones to make other plans. In Nashville, unfortunately, Jones's health so deteriorated that he came close to death. A. M. Burton, a wealthy white businessman, cared for his family and helped Jones get the medical attention he needed. Jones revived and relocated to Chattanooga, Tennessee, where he faithfully toiled in the ministry until his death in 1942.[23]

Second, T. H. Busby arrived at the Silver Point campus with a broken heart, after losing his wife and children to a sudden illness. Determined to equip himself for Christian service, Busby enrolled at Bowser's Institute. After the school's demise, Busby, a gifted song leader, accompanied both Bowser and Marshall Keeble on their preaching excursions before getting involved in more settled congregational efforts in the South as well as the North.²⁴

During an era where women of color had but slim educational opportunities, Annie C. Tuggle managed to find her way to Silver Point. In 1908, Tuggle had heard the "pure gospel," whereupon she immediately forsook her family's Methodist tradition, and became a member of the Church of Christ. After studying briefly at Lane College in Jackson, Tennessee, and LeMoyne Normal Institute in Memphis, Tuggle followed her heart's desire and enrolled at the Silver Point Christian Institute. Assigned to the ninth grade, the school's highest rank, Tuggle gladly ingested the wisdom and knowledge G. P. Bowser dispensed. To defray her expenses, Tuggle worked in the kitchen. "I liked my job very much," she testified, "because I believed God was pleased with me for helping a person like Bro. Bowser." During the summer, the school's principal commissioned Tuggle as fundraiser to solicit money for the struggling institution. Despite her burning zeal and tireless efforts, the Silver Point Christian Institute closed in 1918, breaking Tuggle's heart and those of all affiliated with the school. Still, Tuggle found a sense of humor in her burdensome situation, confessing that the Silver Point Christian Institute had many "points," but not much "silver."²⁵

Notwithstanding the school's demise, G. P. Bowser never abandoned his educational goals. After spending several years in Louisville, Kentucky, he eventually founded another school in Fort Smith, Arkansas. Named the Bowser Christian Institute, the school opened its doors in 1938 with twenty-three students from the neighborhood. But like the Silver Point project, the new venture suffered a short life, closing after eight years.²⁶ During the school's existence, Americans had wholeheartedly poured their efforts and resources into World War II, especially when the nation entered the fray after Pearl Harbor.

Three million black men registered for potential military service; of that number, approximately one million actually served. Joining their male counterparts, some four thousand African American women enlisted in the Women's Army Corps (WAC). At the same time, economic opportunities lured millions of black southerners to lucrative employment in major northern and western cities.²⁷ Such uncontrollable forces and external currents doomed the Bowser Christian Institute from its inception, just as World War I had undermined the Silver Point effort.

Bowser's enduring legacy was more than his paper and these educational projects, however; his protégés—termed the "the Big Four" by his biographer—became towering figures in the ongoing mission.[28] An impoverished and aging Bowser poured his own life into a quartet of men—Levi Kennedy, G. E. Steward, J. S. Winston, and R. N. Hogan—all formative architects in structuring black Churches of Christ.

The Work of Levi Kennedy

Levi Kennedy, a native of Hickman County, Tennessee, grew up the son of a Church of Christ minister. Baptized by Alonzo Jones in 1921, Kennedy and his new wife moved to Wheeling, West Virginia, where they established a small congregation. The Kennedys soon caught the waves of migration which carried them to Chicago, Illinois, where the husband worked as a truck driver while he assisted R. N. Hogan in establishing a black Church of Christ on the city's South Side.[29] When visiting Fort Smith, Arkansas, Kennedy gave such an impressive talk that Bowser chided him: "Well, well, well. I didn't know you could do that well. If you go back to Chicago and get on that truck and don't get out and help us do this missionary work, you're going to die and go to hell!"[30] Bowser's straight talk so stirred Kennedy that he returned to Chicago and helped through his preaching to develop the Michigan Avenue Church of Christ (now the Sheldon Heights Church of Christ) as well as other black congregations in the Midwest. And while Marshall Keeble flourished primarily in the South, and never experienced much evangelistic success in the Windy City, the spiritual sons of G. P. Bowser proved to be more efficient in planting and developing black Churches of Christ in the North.[31]

The Work of G. E. Steward

In the spring of 1931, G. P. Bowser found himself in Fort Worth, Texas, where he met G. E. Steward, a blind young Baptist preacher whom he led into the Church of Christ. Bowser recommended Steward for a number of preaching appointments in west Texas. Then in 1936, in the throes of the Great Depression, Bowser arranged for Steward to assume leadership of the Iowa and Lauderdale Church of Christ (now Norris Road Church of Christ) in Memphis, Tennessee, where he served for almost six years. Annie C. Tuggle, a diligent member of the Memphis congregation, called Steward "a God-sent man to fit in" where his predecessor left off.[32]

From Memphis, Steward and his devoted wife, Ella, made their way to Oklahoma City, Oklahoma, where he ministered to the East 7th Street

In 1945, G. P. Bowser and the "Big Four" organized the first annual lectureship for African Americans in Churches of Christ in Oklahoma City, Oklahoma. The specific place and date of the lectureship photo above is unknown. Courtesy of Phyllis (Holt) Davis.

Church of Christ. Here, Steward, with assistance from G. P. Bowser, R. N. Hogan, Levi Kennedy, and J. S. Winston, organized and hosted the first annual lectureship for members of African American Churches of Christ in the spring of 1945, six months before the end of World War II. Bowser and the "Big Four" shaped this into a national lectureship and an avenue to address divisions that they believed were developing in African American Churches of Christ. G. P. Holt, Bowser's grandson, recalled that G. E. Steward and his congregation in Oklahoma "decided to sponsor the first of these meetings, with hope of unifying our speech and teachings, in the light of Paul's commandment to 'speak the same thing, and let there be no division among you.'"[33]

In addition to "unifying" the speech of African American Churches of Christ, Holt explained that national lectureships afforded black Christians a chance to "know those that labor among us." Networking among preachers and other church leaders enabled congregations to fill empty pulpits. Holt then noted that the annual gathering of black preachers allowed them "to enjoy each other in Christian fellowship." "It always does my heart good," he said, "to see Brethren from other parts of our great brotherhood. It is so good

The thirty-ninth annual national lectureship convened in Fort Lauderdale, Florida, in 1984. G. P. Holt, G. P. Bowser's grandson and a powerful preacher in African American Churches of Christ, is sitting on the front row, fifth from the right. Courtesy of Phyllis (Holt) Davis.

to talk with them, to listen to them, to swap a sermon or two with them, and to share our common problems as Ministers of the Word.[34]

Understanding that racial discrimination excluded black ministers from the lectureships and other programs of most white Churches of Christ, Holt underscored the value of black ministers and members sharing their own camaraderie and their own connections. G. E. Steward, despite his physical blindness, sharpened his spiritual insight, playing a major role in helping to unify disparate black congregations.

The Work of J. S. Winston

As with Levi Kennedy and G. E. Steward, G. P. Bowser met J. S. Winston in the 1930s. Born and reared in Arkansas, Winston spent several years in Oklahoma before returning to his home state, where he received baptism into the Church of Christ at age seventeen. A gifted song leader, passionate preacher, and skillful organizer, Winston left an indelible mark on the

Building on the legacy of G. P. Bowser and the "Big Four," W. F. Washington, an influential preacher for the New Golden Heights Church of Christ in Fort Lauderdale, Florida, launched the Ministers' Institute Conference (MIC) to strengthen leaders and members of African American Churches of Christ. This photo is from the thirty-eighth annual MIC in 2014. Seated on the front row are the following (left to right): Harvey Jackson (kneeling), the late Arnelious Crenshaw, Harold Redd, Freeman Wyche, Ralph Smith, W. F. Washington, Jack Evans Sr., James Maxwell, the late R. C. Wells, Ben Foster Sr., and Stephen Thompson. Photograph by the author.

history and development of African American Churches of Christ. In his biography of Bowser, R. Vernon Boyd commented: "Young Winston became one of Bowser's most devoted and active 'Timothys' and led efforts to carry on Bowser's educational thrust."[35] After Bowser's death in 1950, Winston picked up the torch of the "pure gospel" and helped plant black congregations in Texas and strengthen many others across the nation. One Winston admirer called him a "fighter from the heart," who "tore up" black Christian Churches and transformed them into African American Churches of Christ.[36]

Yet Winston, more than a strong church planter and a religious zealot, succeeded as an organizer and church builder. Indeed, Winston helped to launch the Southern Bible Institute in Fort Worth, Texas, in 1948, which evolved into what is now Southwestern Christian College. His primary passion was

J. S. Winston (1906–2002), a protégé of G. P. Bowser, emerged as a potent church builder and a strong champion of educational efforts among African Americans in Churches of Christ. Winston stressed the importance of prepared leadership in black congregations.
Courtesy of Abilene Christian University.

to fill black congregations with sound spiritual leaders. Winston, when urging support for the nascent Bible school, declared: "LET US NOT FORGET OUR GREATEST NEED IN THE PROGRAM OF THE CHURCH IS PREPARED LEADERSHIP."[37]

As African American Churches of Christ expanded numerically, Winston saw the growing need for efficient leaders. In his 1947 historical sketch of black Churches of Christ, Winston noted that, by 1931, black membership in Churches of Christ numbered some 35,000 adherents in more than 250 congregations, served by 175 preachers. Five years later, Winston counted forty thousand black members with 225 preachers, most of whom had been mentored in some fashion by G. P. Bowser and Marshall Keeble. By 1946, by Winston's estimate, African American Churches of Christ had increased to encompass approximately seventy thousand members and three hundred congregations guided by at least 350 evangelists. Winston acknowledged, however, that "Many of the congregations are not very strong. Some of them have quit meeting. Lack of capable leadership is largely responsible for their condition."[38]

Winston devoted his life to the development of strong leaders in African American Churches of Christ. Black preachers were not only tasked with training other ministers, but they were also responsible for choosing and organizing local churches with elders and deacons. He keenly understood how ill-equipped ministers could damage a local congregation, explaining: "one unqualified preacher can do more harm to the church and brotherhood at large, than two or three elders of the local congregation; for his influence and work are national."[39] Basing his argument on Ephesians 4:11–16, Winston contended: "Leadership is requisite to the maintenance and development of the church and its work." In Winston's view black congregations lacking strong, scriptural leaders would never advance or succeed spiritually. Drawing his argument from Acts 20:27–30, he maintained that "well trained" preachers and teachers were essential for the "unity and fellowship of the church." He commended those who inspired men to become preachers, but he added: "We must do more to inspire men to become elders, deacons and teachers, for when a church has a qualified group of elders, to teach and lead it, the evangelist is then able to give more time to preaching the gospel and helping [needy] congregations."[40] Winston perceived preachers, elders, and deacons not as competitors, but as colaborers for Jesus.

Nearly two decades later, Winston reiterated his views on church leadership, maintaining that "elders in every congregation" were an "absolute need." He called the eldership a "most sacred, and weighty responsibility." The evangelist, explained Winston, also bore a heavy duty. Preachers needed assistance from qualified elders and deacons, since the evangelists could not possibly carry out their God-assigned tasks alone. Winston cautioned preachers never to be content with "increasing the membership, keeping peace," and building impressive houses of worship. Good trustees, he added, could never "fill adequately or completely the place and needs of the Church. . . . God has ordained as well that the mature congregation requires both elders and deacons."[41] Convinced that a "qualified Eldership is one of the greatest needs of the Church among black brethren of the Church of Christ," Winston reprimanded African American ministers who refused to ordain such men because of their desire to "control the money" and to "stay forever." Such preachers, demanded Winston, must be "exposed and dealt with."[42]

Consequently, nothing more thrilled Winston than when he helped to structure a black congregation with a "qualified evangelist and well trained elders and deacons." He upheld as a noteworthy example the all-black Northside Church of Christ in Jacksonville, Florida. Charlie E. McClendon, a native of Soperton, Georgia, received baptism into the Church of Christ at age twenty-four. Eleven years later, he accepted a call to become the minister of the Northside Church of Christ. From 1973 to 1979, McClendon led the new congregation in baptizing more than nine hundred people. Such exponential growth convinced McClendon of the need for scriptural leaders. Therefore, he turned to J. S. Winston. Over a thirteen-year period, Winston conducted a series of leadership workshops at the Northside congregation and helped the church to become a "Fully Scriptural Congregation, with over one thousand members" overseen by five elders working with three deacons. Winston joyfully testified: "It has been quite some time since I have witnessed an ordination service in which such beauty, solemnity, and thoroughness went into planning."[43] Winston yearned to witness this in every black Church of Christ.

The Work of R. N. Hogan

As did Levi Kennedy, G. E. Steward, and J. S. Winston, Richard N. Hogan came under the influence of G. P. Bowser. Yet, Hogan's relationship with Bowser began much earlier than that of the aforementioned trio. A native of Arkansas, Richard grew up in the care of his grandparents, Nathan and Frances Cathey. At age fourteen, Hogan enrolled at Bowser's Silver Point Christian Institute and quickly earned a reputation as a promising young preacher.[44]

After the distraught Hogan took a brief hiatus from preaching because of discouragement engendered by the death of his infant daughter, Hogan's devout wife, Maggie, "awakened" his soul. With her encouragement, Hogan returned to the pulpit with a fiery passion, planting several black congregations in California, Oklahoma, and Texas. Hogan accomplished his most important and enduring congregational work in the Golden State, where he planted the Figueroa Church of Christ in Los Angeles, California. From this congregation sprang other influential black Churches of Christ across southern California.[45] Remarkably, with his impassioned preaching and administrative skills, Hogan not only enlarged black Churches of Christ in southern

California, but the evangelist also found time to plant and organize congregations in other regions as well, particularly in Texas and Oklahoma.[46]

Even though R. N. Hogan left an impressive legacy as both an itinerant evangelist and a church builder, he lent his energies to three other major areas in twentieth-century African American Churches of Christ. First, Hogan devoted significant time and important resources to the growth and development of Southwestern Christian College in Terrell, Texas. As G. P. Bowser's health deteriorated, Hogan assumed editorship of the *Christian Echo* primarily in order to champion the cause of Christian education among African American Churches of Christ. "One of the greatest investments on earth today," wrote Hogan, "is the money and time invested in Southwestern Christian College."[47] He then highlighted several young men who had received training at the fledgling college and moved on to fill pulpits for black congregations across the country. Alvertice Bowdre preached in Ada, Oklahoma; Cloys Cecil ministered in Terre Haute, Indiana; A. C. Christman labored in Seattle, Washington; Isaac Dedrick in Baton Rouge, Louisiana; Arthur Fulson in Benton, Arkansas; Andrew Hairston in Waco, Texas; Roosevelt Wells in Okmulgee, Oklahoma.[48] Of course, graduates from Southwestern Christian College did not necessarily remain with the congregation where they began their ministry. Roosevelt Wells, a Texas native, enrolled at Southwestern Christian College in the early 1950s. After graduation, he then acquired several advanced degrees before settling in New York City's Harlem, where he has ministered for many years.[49] What was true for Wells stood true for other young men whom the college's faculty groomed and mentored.

Through four decades, R. N. Hogan helped to raise millions of dollars for Southwestern Christian College. His connections with city leaders in Los Angeles proved beneficial to Hogan's California work and to his school in Texas. His principal supporters included George Pepperdine, founder of Western Auto Supply , who loaned Hogan five thousand dollars to help secure a house of worship for the Figueroa Church of Christ. The black evangelist and his flock paid off the ten-year loan within ten months.[50]

Hogan also became close friends with Kenneth Hahn, a leading white politician in the Los Angeles area. A native of southern California, Hahn, after graduating from high school, enlisted in the United States Navy, serving as a pilot during World War II. He then earned a degree at Pepperdine College before winning a seat as a councilman in Los Angeles City District 8, soon becoming a major power broker in the burgeoning city. In 1969, Hahn

R. N. Hogan (1902–1997), a protégé of G. P. Bowser, exerted tremendous influence of African American Churches of Christ through his preaching and editorial work with the *Christian Echo*. Courtesy of Abilene Christian University.

appointed Bethel M. Smith, an African American Christian who worked faithfully with Hogan at the Figueroa Church of Christ, to the Board of Governors of the Otis Art Institute of Southern California. Hogan highlighted in the pages of the *Christian Echo* the occasion as well as his friendship with Hahn.[51] Indeed, Hogan's affiliation with Hahn informs us of his political leanings. Like most African Americans who aligned with the Republican Party after the passage of the Fifteenth Amendment, Hogan had probably been a Republican. Again like most black Americans who bade "farewell" to the party of Lincoln in the 1930s and turned to Franklin D. Roosevelt and the Democratic Party, Hogan joined the exodus. Indeed, after the election of Democrat Jimmy Carter in 1976, Hogan met the president-elect and expressed delight that although he was a native southerner, he seemed to be

Carl Spain, a Bible Professor at Abilene Christian College (now Abilene Christian University) in Abilene, Texas, boldly contested the racial segregation practiced by white members of Churches of Christ. His courageous efforts helped to desegregate Abilene Christian University in the early 1960s.
Courtesy of Abilene Christian University.

a "conscientiously religious person" with "no signs of racial prejudice nor unfairness in him during the time I was with him."[52]

Hogan pushed for ongoing financial support for Southwestern Christian College since white Christian administrators barred black students from their schools in the still-segregated South. Black graduates of Southwestern Christian College who sought to further their education experienced rejection when applying to such colleges as Abilene Christian College and Lubbock Christian College, Oklahoma Christian College, and Harding College in Arkansas, David Lipscomb College in Tennessee, and the like. Such racial discrimination at "Christian" colleges deeply pained Hogan, who lamented: "My Race can attend the denominational colleges, but not certain so-called Christian Colleges. What a shame!"[53] This shameful plight persisted until such white leaders as Carl Spain, a Bible professor at Abilene Christian College, openly contested the racial status quo by challenging his west Texas school to admit black students.[54]

Perhaps more importantly, the federal government passed the Civil Rights Act of 1964, threatening to withhold federal funds from any colleges that maintained segregation. But despite this pressure from the president and Congress, race relations in Churches of Christ often remained sour, especially after the closure of the Nashville Christian Institute in 1968 and the transfer of its proceeds to the white-controlled David Lipscomb College (now Lipscomb University). Hogan called the transaction "the grab of the century."[55] A subsequent lawsuit by the school's alumni pitted Fred D. Gray, a former student at the Nashville Christian Institute, against his black mentor Marshall Keeble and the white establishment in Nashville. Blacks in Churches of Christ felt (and still feel) that the almost half a million dollars in proceeds should have been transferred to the struggling Southwestern Christian College.[56]

Hogan further channeled his efforts and energy in bringing order to African American Churches of Christ. He particularly expressed concern over the inability of younger and older preachers in black Churches of Christ to work together. Hogan also addressed the frequently strained relationship between evangelists and elders in African American Churches of Christ. Taking his inspiration from the writings of Paul in 1 Timothy and Titus, Hogan argued that the preacher and elders should work together, but that the latter is not "over" the former. He offered this illustration: "here is a man out in the world living a filthy and ungodly life and I, an evangelist, go out there and preach the gospel to Christ to him. He hears and obeys the gospel and I continue to teach him until he is thought to be qualified for the office of an elder. As an evangelist, I appoint him an elder and as soon as he is appointed, I have to crawl under him. Pshaw! The Bible teaches no such thing."[57]

The Heritage of G. P. Bowser

R. Vernon Boyd has remarked that many of G. P. Bowser's admirers called him a warhorse because of the power of his mesmerizing preaching.[58] The "Big Four," like their spiritual father, must just as surely be denominated as warhorses. They deserve the appellation not simply because of their dynamic sermons, but also because of their moral courage in addressing the sins of sectarianism without and racism within their chosen faith tradition.

Boyd contrasted Marshall Keeble and G. P. Bowser by their roles in the church: "In a sense, Marshall Keeble filled the pews, while G. P. Bowser filled the pulpits."[59] Certainly Keeble filled many pews with new converts, but he also sent his numerous spiritual sons and grandsons to preach in places where he planted black congregations. These men left a lasting imprint on African

American Churches of Christ.⁶⁰ It seems, however, that the pews and pulpits Keeble's progeny filled were located primarily in the South, where leaders rarely focused on racial and social issues. Just as certainly, Bowser filled fewer pews than did Keeble, and perhaps even his preaching protégés may not have been as numerous. Still, Bowser succeeded in filling pulpits in regions beyond the South with such evangelists as Levi Kennedy, J. S. Winston, and R. N. Hogan who built churches beyond the old Confederacy's borders. More importantly, Bowser's preaching sons were organizationally inclined, politically savvy, and racially sensitive. G. E. Steward spearheaded the organization of the first annual lectureship for blacks in Churches of Christ. J. S. Winston toiled to see well-trained preachers and qualified elders and deacons in all-black congregations. R. N. Hogan, while adamantly opposed to racial discrimination, exercised political tact and acumen in gaining support for building African American congregations as well as for Southwestern Christian College.

While Marshall Keeble and his spiritual progeny planted scores of black Churches of Christ in the United States, Bowser and his protégés sought to structure them, to build them to last. As early as 1916, Bowser expressed his belief in delayed gratification as well as his interest in producing "lasting" work. "We realize that success of the lasting sort, the kind that has good staying qualities, does not usually come in a day."⁶¹ As a consequence, he poured his heart and soul into educating and equipping young black men and women at the Silver Point Christian Institute and the Bowser Christian Institute. And while his schools eventually closed, G. P. Bowser's "undying" spirit carved out a striking and enduring heritage among black Churches of Christ.

—8—

"Nonviolent Gadflies"

African American Churches of Christ and the Quest for Civil Rights

> "But let judgment run down as waters, and
> righteousness as a mighty stream."
> —Amos 5:24

> "But God—and I felt this even then, so long ago, on that tremendous floor,
> unwillingly—is white. And if His love was so great, and if He loved
> all His children, why were we, the blacks, cast down so far?"
> —James Baldwin, *The Fire Next Time*

In 1952, Ralph Ellison's *Invisible Man* captured the essence of race relations in Jim Crow America. In the novel's opening passage, Ellison wrote: "I am an invisible man . . . I am a man of substance, of flesh and bone, fiber and liquids—and I might even be said to possess a mind. I am invisible, understand, simply because people refuse to see me." On one level, black Americans were invisible to whites in America. On another level, blacks and whites were invisible to each other. A black character expressed the thesis of Ellison's novel when he said to Mr. Norton, a wealthy white man: "Poor stumblers, neither of you can see the other. To you he is a mark on the scoreboard of your achievement, a thing and not a man; a child, or even less—a black amorphous thing. And you, for all your power, are not a man to him, but a God, a force."[1] The darkness of racism dimmed the vision of both blacks and whites alike, rendering both groups virtually blind.

To address the invisibility of black youth in Churches of Christ, Orum L. Trone, in the same year Ellison's book appeared, organized the National Youth Conference (NYC). Born in Birmingham, Alabama, in 1915, Trone was

In an attempt to address social and moral issues among their young people, African American leaders in Churches of Christ launched the first annual National Youth Conference in 1952. Left to right: Ernest D. Wyrick of Dallas, Texas, the late Alvin Adkisson of Nashville, Tennessee, the late Calvin Bowers of Los Angeles, California, the late O. L. Trone Jr. of Brandon, Florida, and the late Carl Swanigan of Detroit, Michigan, in a reunion photograph, date unknown.
Courtesy of Phillip Wade.

caught up in the waves of the first Great Migration, relocating with his family to Detroit, Michigan. At age twelve, Trone received baptism at the hands of D. M. English. After graduating from high school, Trone studied under G. P. Bowser at the Bowser Christian Institute in Fort Smith, Arkansas, and then enrolled in Detroit's Wayne State University. Trone then served many years as preaching minister for black Churches of Christ in the Motor City.[2]

Shortly after World War II, Herbert Locke, a rising young preacher in African American Churches of Christ, talked with Trone about the possibility of organizing "interstate fellowship" between black youth in their common faith tradition. The interest of building fellowship among young people soon spread to other black leaders and congregations across the country. In 1952, Carl E. Swanigan and Trone hosted the first annual National Youth

Conference in Detroit. Over the next fifty years, thousands of young people were either baptized or restored to the Lord through the efforts of those involved in this movement. A dozen years after its inception, the conference developed the NYC Chorus. Shortly afterward, Orum L. Trone Jr. assumed direction of this musical pageant which afforded African American youth the opportunity to showcase their God-given talent. Beyond this, marches and rallies have served as evangelistic tools in the various cities which have hosted the conference.[3]

Over five decades, the NYC has convened all across the nation; Detroit, Chicago, Los Angeles, St. Louis, New Orleans, and other cities have hosted the gatherings. Historically white Church of Christ colleges and universities eventually opened their doors to the NYC at the end of de jure segregation, including Pepperdine University, Abilene Christian University, Lipscomb University, and Oklahoma Christian University. Non-Church of Christ schools such as Yale University, Washington University in St. Louis, Michigan State University, and the University of Illinois in Champaign-Urbana have also hosted the event. Reflecting on the success of the NYC over fifty years, Swanigan referenced three important things: the grace of God, fervent prayers, and committed Christians.[4] In a time of intense racial strife and tension, Trone, Swanigan, and other black leaders in Churches of Christ sought to provide African American youth with moral direction and spiritual strength to withstand the temptation of Satan and the onslaughts of Jim Crow. At the same time, other black leaders sought reforms in a different way.

"Nonviolent Gadflies" in African American Churches of Christ

In 1957, a white insurance salesman in Nashville, Tennessee, knocked on the door of the home of Andrew and Jennie Jenkins. When their fourteen-year-old daughter, Patricia, answered the door, the salesman demanded: "Gal, go get your mammy to come to the door." Patricia slammed the door in his face because the salesman disrespected her mother by not addressing her as "Mrs. Jenkins." Upon hearing the loud slam, Patricia's mother hastened to the door and said: "I'm sorry." The furious vender replied: "You need to get that gal straight."[5] Patricia, however, would never get "straight," as the racial hubris of many white southerners fired in her a passion to resist racism and propelled her into the civil rights movement.

At age sixteen, Patricia Jenkins worked part time at a Nashville hospital. One day in 1959, as she boarded the bus to work, Jenkins noted the sign

"Colored to the Rear," and became deeply disturbed. Her anger boiled even more furiously when the white bus driver commanded: "You know niggers belong in the back." Such unpleasant encounters stirred the teenager to contest the racial status quo in America. As Rosa Parks had done four years earlier in Montgomery, Alabama, Patricia sat in the "whites only" section of the bus in segregated Nashville. Officials summoned a black police officer, John Smith, who took Patricia off the bus and escorted her home because she was a minor.[6]

A Nashville native, Jenkins in 1959 received baptism at the hands of Otis H. Boatright, minister of the Jackson Street Church of Christ, home congregation of Marshall Keeble, the premier black evangelist in African American Churches of Christ. At Jackson Street, in earlier times, Jenkins recalled Keeble saying, "you, colored folk, get up and let the white folk sit down," an order which then reflected the prevailing sentiment of most African Americans in Churches of Christ.[7]

Yet unlike Keeble, who carefully avoided racial conflict, Jenkins confronted it head on, immersing herself in the civil rights movement. In August 1960, she enrolled at traditionally black Tennessee State University where she met classmate Frederick Leonard, who told her: "They are integrating downtown" Nashville and asked her to come and participate in the sit-ins. Her involvement led to her dismissal from the university as well as her arrest by Nashville police. However, the Southern Christian Leadership Conference (SCLC), a nonviolent organization formed by Martin Luther King Jr. in 1957, paid her and other students' bail, securing their release.[8]

Jenkins then joined Texas native James Farmer's organization, the Congress of Racial Equality (CORE). CORE coordinated the "Freedom Rides" to test southern states' compliance with rulings concerning the desegregation of interstate travel. On May 4, 1961, the first group of eighteen "freedom riders" left Washington, DC, for New Orleans, Louisiana. This initial group of racially mixed travelers were attacked and then arrested in Alabama. Patricia Jenkins joined the second group of twenty-two freedom riders as they boarded a bus in Nashville, Tennessee, bound for Montgomery, Alabama. She remembered signing her will, singing "freedom songs," and traveling with future U. S. Senator John Lewis and other courageous young people. In spite of verbal insults, physical attacks, and arrests, Jenkins and more than four hundred other audacious young people "initiated a turbulent decade of insurgent citizen politics that transformed the nature of American democracy."[9]

"Nonviolent Gadflies"   97

Patricia Jenkins was one of the many "nonviolent gadflies" who agitated
for social justice and racial equality. A Tennessee State University student
in Nashville and a devout member of African American Churches of Christ,
Jenkins in 1961 joined the freedom riders, who contested racial barriers
in interstate travel. Courtesy of Patricia (Jenkins) Armstrong.

Patricia Jenkins, then, stands as one of the "nonviolent gadflies" Martin Luther King Jr. referenced in his celebrated treatise "Letter from Birmingham Jail." Responding to eight white clergymen who criticized King's demonstrations in Birmingham, the black preacher compared himself to Socrates, who endorsed a "constructive, non-violent tension." King affirmed: "Just as Socrates felt that it was necessary to create tension in the mind so that individuals could rise from the bondage of myths and half-truths to the unfettered realm of creative analysis and objective appraisal, so must we see the need for non-violent gadflies to create the kind of tension in society that will help men rise from the dark depths of prejudice and racism to the majestic heights of understanding and brotherhood."[10]

Even though their rigid exclusivist theology and scriptural interpretations shaped their fellowship's tendency to downplay political and social issues, many African Americans in Churches of Christ contributed importantly to the death of Jim Crow. They were not always as vocal or as visible as African Americans in Baptist and Methodist Churches, yet they had a potent presence in the civil rights movement. In his 2007 dissertation, Barclay Key observed that few African Americans in Churches of Christ, "due in part to their exclusivist attitudes toward other Christians, participated in civil rights activities."[11] The stories of Patricia Jenkins and others, however, show that more black members of Churches of Christ publicly resisted racial discrimination in America than Key and others previously thought.

Indeed, the same year Patricia Jenkins contested racial barriers as a freedom rider, six-year-old Ethel Carr desegregated the all-white Buena Vista Elementary School in Nashville, Tennessee. One of nine children born to Virgil and Mary Carr in middle Tennessee, Ethel grew up in a loving and affirming environment. Her diligent and determined parents relocated from Silver Point, Tennessee, to Nashville; there they worshipped at the Jackson Street Church of Christ, and Virgil served as an elder for forty-two years. Carr remembered her parents as "good Christian people," not affluent but very hospitable. In the fall of 1957, Mary Carr escorted her daughter to Buena Vista Elementary School at a time when people were "anxious" amid the turbulent racial climate. After a "bomb scare" disrupted the first day of school, the white principal, Mr. Gamble, took the new student safely home. A cadre of supporters sustained Carr during this tumultuous time. Her mother's courage and determination encouraged her; her "very nice" white teacher, Mrs. Davis, instructed her; and her black neighbors, especially a Mr. Weatherspoon, "made sure that she got home safely" each day. Three years before Ruby Bridges, a six-year-old, precocious black girl, garnered national recognition for desegregating the all-white William Frantz Elementary in New Orleans, Louisiana, Ethel Carr was already knocking down racial barriers 533 miles away.[12]

"The Sting of Jim Crow": Dalton Gooden, A Firefighter in Waco

In the summer of 1961, Dalton Gooden, a black resident of Waco, Texas, after hearing that the local fire department had job openings, rushed downtown to City Hall and applied. Gooden's heart sank, however, when the white secretary remarked: "We don't give applications for the fire department to colored people." The twenty-three-year-old military veteran lamented that he "heard, felt and tasted the sting of Jim Crow." Dismayed but still determined,

1957 Buena Vista School Desegregation

In the fall of 1957, Mary Carr escorted her daughter, Ethel Carr, to the all-white Buena Vista Elementary School in Nashville, Tennessee. Young Ethel paved the way for other black children to enroll in the segregated school. Courtesy of Ethel (Carr) Crowder.

Gooden reapplied over the next few years, only to be advised that he was "knocking on the wrong door at the wrong time." In 1966, he enrolled at traditionally black Paul Quinn College, earning a bachelor of arts degree in English four years later. While studying there, Gooden trained as a fireman on the old James Connally Air Force Base (now McLennan Community College). Upon completing his degree and practical training, Gooden became Waco's first black firefighter in a department of all white firefighters in 1968 and worked until his retirement thirty-two years later.[13]

Gooden understood that he lived and moved during a pivotal time, acknowledging that 1968 was "the height of the Black revolutionary period" as civil rights protests and demonstrations—led by the Southern Christian Leadership Conference (SCLC), the National Association for the Advancement of Colored People (NAACP), Student Nonviolent Coordinating Committee (SNCC), Black Muslims, and Black Panthers—pressured America's white power structure and helped abolish racial and social barriers in the United States. Reflecting on his experiences forty-six years later, Gooden confessed to mixed emotions. On the one hand, he deplored an unjust system that had remained intact for so long; at the same time, he commended "fair-minded whites" who shared a common interest in serving humanity.

Additionally, Gooden viewed himself as a product of the times, drawing a parallel between himself and others who broke the color barrier. "But time," he explained, "had chosen me to build the bridge in Waco, Texas, for city hires—much like time chose Jackie Robinson to build that bridge in Major League Baseball."[14] More significantly, Gooden, while fighting flames and saving lives as a firefighter in McLennan County, simultaneously began preaching in 1968. In all this he represents many black ministers who, while contesting systemic racism in Jim Crow America (sometimes holding other full-time jobs), were equally committed to combating religious error and saving lost souls, fusing social justice and evangelistic outreach.

"Stench in the Nostrils of God": Norman Adamson's Fight against Racism

African Americans in Churches of Christ of course did not live in a vacuum. They heard the news flashes on radios, saw the reports on television, and read their newspapers. They stayed abreast of social and political happenings, since their own destinies were inextricably bound up with those of their black neighbors and friends. Even though Gospel singer Mahalia Jackson ascended to national acclaim, she experienced firsthand the pangs of Jim Crow. A native of New Orleans, Louisiana, Jackson at age sixteen moved with her family to Chicago. Her hit record, "Move On Up a Little Higher," catapulted her to national and international fame. White racism, however, deeply troubled Jackson when she and her entourage toured the South. Barred from hotels, restaurants, and some gas stations, Jackson called the experience a "nightmare." Emotional anguish often accompanied physical exhaustion and excessive monetary expenditures, as finding places to eat and sleep in black neighborhoods meant losing time, money, and energy. Many white southerners resented seeing black people driving expensive automobiles. "The looks of anger at the sight of us colored folks sitting in a nice car were frightening to see," Jackson lamented. "It got so we were living on bags of fresh fruit during the day and driving half the night and I was so exhausted by the time I was supposed to sing I was almost dizzy."[15] African American preachers and leaders in Churches of Christ who traversed the segregated South to do God's work shouldered the same burden. Indeed, regardless of their talents, gender, and economic status, virtually all black people in America felt the sting and smelled the odor of racism in the United States.

Norman Adamson, a native of Arkansas and Southwestern Christian College graduate, ministered to congregations in Illinois while earning advanced degrees at Governors State University just outside Chicago. Adamson grew preoccupied with resolving America's race problem, often weighing in on the subject by writing in secular and religious newspapers. "The white Christians are our brothers, some of them are practicing segregation; *which is wrong*," wrote Adamson. "We believe it to be stench in the nostrils of God, and therefore subjects them to eternal damnation."[16]

A firm believer in and an active supporter of the civil rights movement, Adamson confessed to his own racial presuppositions. "I thought when I left Chicago that my heart was free of all prejudices. I had not traveled far before I suddenly realized that I was wrong for I had unconsciously stereotyped all white people into a selfish class with ulterior motives based on evil." But "Bloody Sunday," the event in Selma, Alabama, where 150 white policemen on foot and horseback mercilessly beat nonviolent protesters, changed Adamson when he "walked along Highway 80, hand in hand with my Caucasian brothers and sisters."

Notwithstanding the continued racist pronouncements of Alabama governor George Wallace and the murder in Alabama of civil rights worker Viola Liuzzo, a white woman from Detroit, Michigan, Adamson deemed the civil rights movement a success. "We believe the non-violent way is the expedient way[;] for this cause we went to Alabama to MARCH."[17] In the mind of Adamson, the nonviolent actions of civil rights protesters helped to abolish racial barriers in both colleges and congregations aligned with white Churches of Christ. "We believe," added Adamson, "the march and the whole Civil Rights Movement is a success for many former pseudo Christian Colleges are now truly Christian Colleges for all Christians can attend. Many of the former pseudo Churches of Christ are now truly Churches of Christ for all Christians can worship." So-called Christians committed the murders and ignited the bombs that killed innocent black people, alleged Adamson.

In consequence he urged African American Christians to "take up the blood stained banner of the cross and do something about the unchristian, ungodly, social problem that is not only in the world affairs of man but is also rampant in the holy confines of God's kingdom." Adamson concluded: "You may not choose to march and demonstrate but let every person who nameth the name of Christ stand up and be counted by doing something to alleviate man's inhumanity toward man."[18]

Fusion of Pulpit and Politics: The Work of Fred D. Gray

Adamson's earnest words did not go unheeded. Fred D. Gray, a native of Montgomery, Alabama, and an alumnus of the Nashville Christian Institute (NCI), emerged a leader in the civil rights movement from its inception. After graduating from NCI, Gray matriculated at Alabama State College (now Alabama State University) in Montgomery, where he completed his degree in 1951. Because segregation then precluded black students from attending major white universities in the South, Gray chose to study law at Western Reserve University (now Case Western Reserve University) in Cleveland, Ohio. After earning his law degree, Gray returned to the South, determined to "destroy everything segregated that I could find."[19]

One of Gray's first clients was Claudette Colvin, a fifteen-year-old high school student, who was arrested on March 5, 1955, for refusing to vacate her bus seat for a white person in Montgomery. Even though Gray and Colvin lost the case, the attorney learned many valuable lessons that aided him nine months later, on December 1, 1955, when Montgomery officials arrested Parks for the same violation. Gray represented Parks, along with the newly formed Montgomery Improvement Association. At the same time, Martin Luther King Jr. emerged as a leader and led the 381-day bus boycott. As blacks in Montgomery stopped riding buses, they walked or strategically carpooled. Indeed, Arlette Nixon and K. K. Mitchell, both of whom were devoted members of African American Churches of Christ, supported the yearlong boycott. The former was married to Edgar D. Nixon, known as "Mr. Civil Rights" by African Americans in Montgomery and central Alabama. Mitchell, Gray's classmate at NCI, preached at the Holt Street Church of Christ in Montgomery, while his attorney friend assisted him. Mitchell also transported passengers in his own car during the boycott.[20]

Kelly K. Mitchell (1928–1998) preached for African American Churches of Christ in Montgomery, Alabama, for several decades. While preaching in Alabama, Mitchell immersed himself in the civil rights struggle and used his own vehicle to transport passengers during the Montgomery Bus Boycott. Courtesy of Kelyne M. Provitt.

The Montgomery Bus Boycott ended on December 20, 1956, touching off joyful expressions throughout the African American community in Montgomery and across the nation. Gray later called the Supreme Court's ruling that segregated buses were unconstitutional a "personal milestone" in his goal to destroy segregation, adding: "A pebble cast in the segregated waters of Montgomery, Alabama, created a human rights tidal wave that changed America and eventually washed up on the shores of such far away places as the Bahamas, China, South Africa, and the Soviet Union. And it all started on a bus."[21] That wave returned to the Supreme Court four years later, when Gray argued in *Gomillion v. Lightfoot* (1960) that redistricting laws in Tuskegee,

Alabama, disenfranchised black citizens and voters there. In 1975, Gray further pursued his goals by filing suit on behalf of African Americans who survived the Tuskegee syphilis experience of the 1930s. In both cases, Gray felt that he was fulfilling his pledge to destroy segregation.[22]

Significantly, Fred Gray had studied under and traveled with the esteemed evangelist, Marshall Keeble, who deliberately kept apart from the race problem in America. But Gray, parting with his older mentor's philosophy, chose to fight and dismantle racism through legal channels. Indeed, Gray even sided against Keeble and the white establishment of the NCI in 1967, when the all-black K-12 school closed and its assets were transferred to Nashville's David Lipscomb College (now Lipscomb University).[23] Gray and other NCI alumni admired and even loved their mentor, Keeble, but they abhorred racism more, following a different course than that chosen much earlier by their spiritual grandfather. In so doing, Gray felt no misgivings about merging preaching and politics, expressing that the brotherhood of African American Churches of Christ "soon saw that even though I was a lawyer, I was still very loyal to the church and continued to perform my ministerial duties. Over the years, I have been called upon many times by our leading church leaders across the nation to preach. There is no conflict in my mind about the two professions."[24] In Gray's view, his commitment to Christ profoundly affected how he practiced law.

Marshall Keeble also had other spiritual grandsons, such as Franklin Florence, who rocked the boat of American race relations. A Florida native and Keeble protégé, Florence has ministered several years in Rochester, New York. While there, he worked alongside civil rights leader Malcolm X in challenging racism and in protesting racial discrimination allegedly practiced by the Eastman Kodak Company in Rochester.[25]

Frustrated Fellows: The Fight against Jim Crow

Carroll Pitts, born in Arkansas in 1924, grew up under the oppressive system of Jim Crow segregation near Shawnee, Oklahoma. Pitts and his brothers walked three miles one way each day to attend an all-black school, even though his parents paid taxes to support the nearby white-controlled and carefully segregated public schools. A befuddled young Pitts often wondered why he and his brothers could not learn at the public schools closer to his house; after all, he and his black classmates saluted the American flag, pledging allegiance "with liberty and justice for all." Inclement weather frequently prevented Pitts from attending his own dilapidated school; as a result, he lost two grades of education. Thirty years later, Pitts lamented that a "Christian" elementary school in California denied his own two children entrance because of their race. "One can see," Pitts wrote from personal experience, "that the Negro's search for equality in America has been long, slow, and frustrating."[26]

The witness of Carroll Pitts not only attests that the system of unbending segregation emotionally and excruciatingly oppressed black people, but it also reveals that African American Churches of Christ saw no means of relief unless they entered the fray to slay Jim Crow. Orum L. Trone—who had moved with his parents to Detroit, Michigan, at an early age—became a minister for a black Church of Christ in the Motor City. He believed that God provided a solution for every difficulty (the racial problem included) "through his divine Word." Appealing to Acts 17:24–26, the Apostle Paul's Mars Hill sermon, Trone argued that all human beings were "related" because they descended from "one blood." In Trone's view, understanding this fact was crucial to resolving the race problem in America, for "if this one principle was taught and believed by every responsible individual in the church of the Lord, needless to say, it would be a great force in helping to make this world a better world to inhabit just for a little while leaving no room in man's heart for racial prejudice."[27] Failing to realize their common origin as well as the ringing words of the Declaration of Independence that "all men are created equal" has caused human beings to perpetuate "this great evil, RACIAL PREJUDICE."[28]

Like Trone, R. N. Hogan, one of G. P. Bowser's aforementioned "Big Four," cited Paul's encounter with Elymas the sorcerer in Acts 13:10 to condemn white Christian school administrators. Since they barred black students from their colleges, Hogan placed white college officials on the same plane with Elymas, labeling them "enemies of righteousness." "I wonder if my so-called 'white' brethren think that they are upholding the right ways of the Lord by barring christian Negroes from being taught the word of God in their churches and so-called christian schools?" Anticipating that he would lose some of his white friends through such comments, Hogan quipped "but are they really my friends"?[29]

Hogan further lamented that many white Church of Christ schools cordially welcomed Asians, Mexicans, and Native Americans, but rejected African Americans. "Only the Negro! They hate only the Negro!" Citing 1 John 4:19–20, Hogan asked: "Do you mean to tell me that these men love God and hate the Negro?" His greatest concern for African American youth in Churches of Christ was that they be taught "the word of God" and prepared for "qualified leadership" beyond the classroom. Knowing white segregationists in Churches of Christ would advise African Americans to "take your time" and "don't push this matter too fast," Hogan asserted: "Well, the Negro has taken his time for a hundred years and I think it is a terrible thing to tell people to take their time in obeying God. Take their time in repenting of their sins."[30]

Hogan clearly anticipated Martin Luther King's 1963 "Letter from Birmingham Jail," which King wrote in response to white clerics who criticized his "untimely" nonviolent protests. When the eight white clergymen asked King why he failed to give city administrators "time to act," the black prisoner replied: "For years now I have heard the word 'Wait!' It rings in the ear of every Negro with piercing familiarity. This 'Wait' has almost always meant 'Never.' We must come to see, with one of our distinguished jurists, that 'justice too long delayed is justice denied.'"[31] Hogan, however, differed from Martin Luther King Jr. on pivotal theological points. On the one hand, both men abhorred racial discrimination; on the other hand, Hogan espoused a rigid theological exclusivism, which condemned Baptists, Methodists, and "other denominational churches" for taking their time "coming out of that human institution."[32] A rigid sectarianism, then, accompanied Hogan's aversion to white racism.

At the same time, Hogan opposed racist practices in his Church of Christ fellowship. Fusing Matthew 23 and Mark 7, Hogan pointed to Jesus's denunciation of the Pharisees who elevated the traditions of men above God's word and who appeared virtuous outwardly but were full of corruption inwardly. Hogan applied these references to white segregationists in Churches of Christ, affirming: "It must be agreed that we have the same kind of people in the Church of Christ today. They are the prejudiced segregationists in congregations all over the Brotherhood whose hearts are filled with hate because of the color of another man's skin."[33]

The same month Martin Luther King Jr. delivered his famous "I Have a Dream" speech, Hogan railed against racial barriers in Churches of Christ. On the front page of the *Christian Echo*, Hogan published a picture of an African American couple who had been appointed ministers at an all-white Methodist Church. The Church of Christ, argued Hogan, "has sunken to a low when she allows denominational churches to show to the world a higher regard for the word of God, respecting love for brethren of other races than she does."[34] Hogan understood that most whites in Churches of Christ feared integrating their churches and schools because of the threat of miscegenation.[35] For Hogan, however, obedience to scripture superseded any human misgivings about black/white interaction. "The very idea of a College calling itself a Christian College that will not allow a Negro Christian to study God's word in it or be taught by it that he may be prepared to carry out the great world-wide commission of the Son of God. These Colleges are headed by so-called gospel preachers and they are living in rebellion against God, for God said, "Teach ALL NATIONS."[36]

Hogan specifically highlighted the segregationist practices of David Lipscomb College, Freed-Hardeman College, Harding College, and Oklahoma Christian College, whose boards consisted of church leaders in white Churches of Christ. They claimed, Hogan noted, citing Thomas Campbell's famous dictum, "to speak where the Bible speaks and be silent where the Bible is silent." Hogan, however, gave Campbell's adage a twist: "But they speak where the Bible does not speak and they are silent where the Bible is not silent." Citing Romans 2:11, Ephesians 6:9, and James 2:9 to accentuate the impartiality of God, Hogan asked why white church and college leaders remained silent on those verses.[37]

But Hogan did not neglect to commend those white leaders in Churches of Christ who championed racial equality and social justice in their congregations and schools. He lauded Gordon Teel, minister of the all-white Vermont Avenue Church of Christ in Los Angeles, California, for displaying a sign, "All Races Are Welcome," in front of their house of worship. He also applauded Carl Spain, a Bible professor at Abilene Christian College, who in 1960 challenged his school to admit black students. The following year, the west Texas college admitted its first black graduate students, later admitting its first undergraduates, Larry Bonner and Billy Curl.[38] Yet as historian Barclay Key has argued, economics, "not ethics," was the impetus behind the desegregation of Church of Christ colleges.[39]

Other church leaders also stood with Hogan in his critique of racism in white Churches of Christ. Like Hogan, Andrew J. Hairston, a native Texan and graduate of Southwestern Christian College, insisted that racial segregation was "wrong and evil." He also stressed that the division of Churches of Christ into white and black sectors must be undone. But unlike Hogan, Hairston also chided African Americans for their role in segregation. Such blacks were "just as wrong in accommodating segregation in the Church of Christ as white people are for having ever instituted it. The Negro has as much responsibility to reject segregation as the Whites do to stamp it out." Hairston refused to compromise, adding: "If we are brethren, we are brethren in Christ and not 'Negro brethren' and 'white brethren.'"[40]

In 1961, Hairston assumed the post of minister for the Simpson Street Church of Christ in Atlanta, Georgia. This congregation launched an outreach effort thirty-seven miles south of Atlanta in Newman, baptizing fourteen souls. Because of the difficulty of transporting these new black believers to Atlanta, Hairston and one of his elders appealed to white leaders of the Church of Christ in Newman. After initially allowing black converts to be baptized in their building, the Newman church halted the practice "because neighbors in the community had questioned it." One white elder, Hairston astonishingly recalled, "even told us to see if we could not find a Negro Baptist Church that had a pool that it would let us use. We are a long ways from the truth when we can obey the same gospel, make the same confession, but cannot be baptized in the 'WHITE CHURCH OF CHRIST' pool."[41] Hairston's comments underscore the reality that, for many white Christians, complying with segregation was more important than saving the souls of black people, so Jim Crow reigned in the Church of Christ. Hairston, therefore, concluded: "In reality, all so called CHURCHES OF CHRIST ought to stop being Church of Christ and take on the name 'CHURCH OF THE WHITE MAN,' and any Church of Christ among Negroes condoning such practices ought to be called the 'CHRUCH OF THE NEGRO.'"[42]

Together with R. N. Hogan and Martin Luther King Jr., Hairston repudiated the notion that "God will fix it one day." He instead urged white and black leaders in Churches of Christ to address racism immediately, as an issue of vital importance. Hairston rebuked white Christians who insisted that "the issue of race relations" had "nothing to do with the church," asserting: "The race issue is no more social and to be divorced from the life and preaching of the true church today than it was when Christ died for the demolition of that wall separating man from man."[43] James Maxwell, a native of Tulsa, Oklahoma, and a rising preacher and educator in African American Churches of Christ, also agreed that his chosen fellowship should lead the way in tackling America's race problem. "If any should be concerned with the magnitude of this problem, it should be the Church of our Lord," since racial discrimination disproportionally affected African Americans in areas of employment, education, voting, and public housing.[44]

The Politics of African American Churches of Christ

President Lyndon B. Johnson's signing of the Civil Rights Act of 1964 foreshadowed brighter days for African Americans as the law prohibited discrimination and segregation in education, employment, voting, and the use of public facilities. "In many places South and North, doors of opportunity once closed to African Americans opened for the first time."[45] Buoyed by the promise of this legal measure, African Americans in Churches of Christ continued to weigh in on the issue of race. Alvin S. Simmons, a native of Oklahoma and former NCI student, delineated six principles to enhance race relations in the Church of Christ. Included in these were recognizing the dignity of each individual, practicing the fellowship of believers, and trusting in the principle of democracy to break down walls of racial strife and division.[46]

In view of the impending 1964 presidential election between Republican candidate Barry Goldwater and Democratic nominee Lyndon B. Johnson, Humphrey Foutz, a native Texan and a black Church of Christ minister in Maryland, marked that the matter of civil rights as "an explosive and emotional issue." Foutz, therefore, refused to tell *Christian Echo* readers whom to vote for, instead urging them to consider Christian values when casting their ballots. "I do not suggest that we make the church a political entity but I must suggest, and quite strongly, that Christian principles and ethics are not something you leave outside of the voter's booth."[47]

The death of Martin Luther King Jr. in 1968 stirred African Americans in Churches of Christ to a still higher level of vocal expression concerning race and racism in America, as Calvin Bowers, an assistant minister to R. N. Hogan, noted: "While many of us will not agree with the theological point of view of the denomination which he [King] represented, we cannot deny that in many ways he identified with the teachings of Christ. He taught love and non-violence, and he gave his life to show that his method could work." King's canon of scripture included the Old Testament and the four Gospels, while African American Churches of Christ focused almost exclusively on biblical texts drawn from Acts 2 through Revelation. But King's death caused some, such as Bowers to rethink his chosen fellowship's emphasis. Bowers observed, "he made clothing the naked, feeding the hungry, visiting the sick and those in prison major goals in life. Without minimizing the significance of doctrine, we cannot ignore the fact that these are things Jesus said were important when he gave a preview of the judgment scene in Matthew's 25:31–46."[48]

A month after King's death, G. P. Holt bemoaned that racial divisions in Churches of Christ were our "weakest link." He chided white leaders in Churches of Christ who would fire their preacher for addressing the evil of segregation. "White churches," Holt insisted, "will move from their neighborhood rather than be channels of God's healing righteousness where they are." Appealing to Amos 5:15, 23, texts cited by King in his "I Have a Dream" speech, Holt added: "We as a church are not letting justice and righteousness come through. The answer to Cool Summers is *hate evil, love good* establish justice in the gate."⁴⁹ "Cool Summers" was a reference to the volunteer campaign launched in the 1960s in Mississippi to register as many African American voters as possible. These young white and black workers often faced stiff opposition from white Mississippians.

The Myth of a Silent Church

Although African American preachers in Churches of Christ did not fully immerse themselves in the throes of the civil rights movement and did not join all of Martin Luther King's marches and protests, many of these black leaders in Churches of Christ admired King and supported him from a distance. A year before King's assassination in Memphis, Tennessee, W. F. Washington, a Marshall Keeble protégé at the Nashville Christian Institute and preacher for the West Side Church of Christ in Marshall, Texas, penned an encouraging and sympathetic letter to the civil rights leader, offering support. After acknowledging the "unfavorable and undue publicity" King received because of his stance against the war the Vietnam War, Washington declared: "I am compelled to write to you. I feel that you have been unduly criticized for your stand. As a minister you had to take a stand and as a fellow minister I was elated when you came forward." Not only did Washington commend King for his courageous opposition to the war in Vietnam, but he also lauded him as a man who sought "peace for all mankind," as his being awarded the 1964 Nobel Peace Prize well attested. Washington then exhorted King to persevere amid the storm, "keep the faith, and *this too shall pass*."⁵⁰

The essence of Washington's 1967 letter to Martin Luther King echoed the feelings of many other leaders in his fellowship. When it came to denouncing and defying the horrors of war, Washington found common ground with the Baptist minister in spite of their theological differences. His heartfelt note revealed a deep sense of appreciation and admiration for King, unquestionably shared by countless other blacks in Churches of Christ who by television and radio had also heard the civil rights leader's impassioned speeches and witnessed his bold actions.

A number of black leaders in Churches of Christ publicly insisted that their chosen fellowship had been too reticent to address the race issue. James Kennedy, an African American minister in Greenville, South Carolina, wrote two months after Martin Luther King's assassination that Churches of Christ had been far too silent on the race issue. Kennedy averred: "The church cannot afford to hold her peace; she must not keep silent." Jesus, Kennedy argued, was not a segregationist; thus, preachers in Churches of Christ, bound by racism, have "no Authority to preach the gospel of Christ."[51] A perusal of extant copies of the *Christian Echo* reveals that African Americans were indeed vocal, vibrant, and visible on the issue of race. From the inception of the civil rights movement in 1954 to in the tragic death of Martin Luther King Jr. in 1968, the collective voice of African American Churches of Christ, while it may have begun as a whisper, soon cresendoed into a mighty shout across its brotherhood.

After King's tragic demise, leaders such as Andrew J. Hairston remained potent critics of race relations in Churches of Christ. At a conference on "Improving Race Relations in the Churches of Christ," Hairston pointed out that the sin of racism had hindered his faith tradition from becoming the "one true church." Hairston maintained: "This sin has never permitted the true Church to exist in reality on the American frontier; it has only accommodated a denominational Church of Christ that is obviously divided and deeply split asunder by racial antagonisms."[52] Hairston's balanced presentation indicted white Christians who "abused, mistreated, hated, despised and misused [African Americans] for no reason at all," but he also incriminated African Americans in Churches of Christ for accommodating racially divided congregations. "The blacks' greatest single sin in this matter of segregation is accommodation. It is the whites who created the system and it is they [black Christians] who are primarily yet maintaining it."[53] Clearly, the quest for civil rights had a checkered history in both black and white Churches of Christ.

Indeed, most preachers in African American Churches of Christ used the pulpit to address America's race problem during this period. Eugene Lawton, a native of St. Petersburg, Florida, received baptism at the hands of minister S. J. Dudley in 1951. After graduating from high school, Lawton enrolled at Southwestern Christian College (SwCC) in Terrell, Texas, where he earned top academic honors. He then studied at Pepperdine University in southern California, where he took bachelor's and master's degrees. Lawton eventually made his way to Newark, New Jersey, where he preached from 1963 to 1969. After a two-year stint at his alma mater in Texas as academic dean, he returned to New Jersey, where he continues to lead the vibrant Newark Church of Christ.[54]

A fierce opponent of racial discrimination, Lawton preached a sermon entitled "The Church Faces Modern Isms," in which he declared, "one of the most shameful chapters of American history is in race relations." Lawton chided Christians who supported "everything lily-white" and "everything all black." At the same time, he sternly rebuked advocates of "Black Power," cautioning his listeners not to be "brainwashed . . . with the idea that all white people are blue-eyed devils." Speaking in the vein of black abolitionist Frederick Douglass, who distinguished true Christianity from false Christianity, Lawton confessed that "all religious groups in America including the churches of Christ have been guilty of racism; but we must also understand that true Christianity never supported slavery, but distorted Christianity [did]. True Christianity broke down the walls of slavery in the Roman Empire." Seeking to dissuade black youth who might be drawn into the "Black Power" movement, Lawton warned: "Any group that knocks non-violence is knocking Jesus who advocated non-violence. Stand up for non-violence even if you are called an Uncle Tom or an Aunt Tom."[55]

Many others joined Eugene Lawton in his denunciation of both white and black racism. R. C. Wells, a native of Waco, Texas, grew up in Churches of Christ and preached his first sermon at age ten. Wells attended the Nashville Christian Institute for a short time before completing high school in his hometown; from there, he enrolled at Southwestern Christian College before advancing to Midwestern Theological Seminary and Temple Theological Seminary. Wells preached for Churches of Christ in Okmulgee, Oklahoma, and Pontiac, Michigan, before settling for four decades with the Washington Heights Church of Christ in Harlem, New York.[56]

Growing up in the segregated South and knowing the lure of the Black Power Movement, Wells boldly addressed racism within and outside of his chosen fellowship. In his homily, "Equal Heirs, Equal Members, and Equal Partners," Wells forcefully declaimed: "Fellow saints, the number one problem in America today is racism and so long as it exists, making millions struggle for *freedom, integration, justice, and equality,* the war will continue. Racism in our society is erecting a new middle wall of partisanship, a wall non-existent in New Testament times and which foolishly exists now." Wells then parodied the Pledge of Allegiance to make his point: "I pledge allegiance to the idol of racism and to the ungodly, unbiblical, and inhuman principle for which it stands; one exclusive ethnic union cemented together with persecution, suppression, and exploitation of others." Wells called this the "consistent creed of the racist."[57]

Wells blamed the biased views and practices of white Christians for turning black Americans away from Christianity. "The racist Christians," railed Wells, "have so dimmed the light of Christianity and so distorted the principles and teachings of Christ under the bushel of bigotry that many Black people totally reject Christianity as the White man's club of slavery, segregation, and exploitation." Perturbed by the black rage he encountered when preaching in urban America, Wells urged his audience: "Walk with me through the streets of any Black ghetto and ask Black men about Christ, the Bible, and Christianity, and hear them say, 'Don't give me your White Jesus, your White Bible, your White churches, your White philosophy, and your White man's Uncle Tom. Christianity is what has held us back.'" Wells of course did not share this view, but he admitted that "he understands it." For Wells, white racism demeaned Christ and perverted the teachings of the New Testament.[58]

The sermons and testimonies of such men as W. F. Washington, Eugene Lawton, and R. C. Wells give clear witness that African Americans in Churches of Christ were anything but "silent" on the race issue. On the contrary, Lawton and Wells offer unique perspectives and experiences on how black preachers in their chosen fellowship went about addressing and attacking white racism in American society. Both Lawton and Wells, black southerners transplanted to the North, felt the sting of racism in their native states of Florida and Texas. After relocating to northern cities and ministering for many years in New Jersey and New York, they found various forms of racism there as well. More significantly, they encountered angry black men in their communities who preferred the "Black Power" movement over a racist brand of Christianity. Lawton and Wells, then, not only bore the emotional scars of segregation from their southern communities, but they also felt the deep hostility and boiling rage of many black people to whom they preached in northern ghettos. To worsen matters, many whites in Churches of Christ championed a racist system that demeaned and dehumanized African Americans, making it difficult for men, in the words of R. C. Wells, to "really see the compassionate, concerned Christ."[59]

PART 4

Finding Their Own Way, 1969–2008

— 9 —

Making Something Out of Nothing

*Annie C. Tuggle, Thelma M. Holt,
and the Women's Movement in African
American Churches of Christ*

"I am my mother's daughter, and the drums of Africa
beat in my heart. They will not let me rest while there is a single
Negro boy or girl without a chance to prove his worth."
—Mary McLeod Bethune

In 1992, J. S. Winston, a dynamic African American leader in Churches of Christ, bestowed verbal bouquets on his spiritual father, G. P. Bowser, in commemoration of the ninetieth anniversary of the founding the *Christian Echo*. Winston recounted Bowser's transition from Methodism into the Stone-Campbell Movement as well as his disappointment upon learning that black Churches of Christ had no college or paper of their own. A dissatisfied Bowser devoted his life to create both a "Christian paper" and a "Christian school." With an irreparably damaged arm and insufficient money, Bowser struggled and sacrificed first to launch and then to keep his paper afloat. Winston recalled how during the eras of the Great Depression and World War II, Bowser often went to the "wholesale paper house" in order to "gather the paper to use for printing the Echo."[1] Bowser gladly collected these "scraps" to produce a quality paper in middle Tennessee to enrich, inspire, and inform African Americans in Churches of Christ.

African Americans in other faith traditions and in other parts of the South had similar experiences. In 1904, aspiring educator Mary McLeod Bethune transformed a "garbage dump" into a college for black youth in Daytona Beach, Florida. Bereft of monetary resources, Bethune relied on "faith in a living God, faith in myself, and a desire to serve" to produce a first-rate college. She recalled turning charred splinters into pencils and berries into ink. "I haunted the city dump and the trash piles behind hotels," Bethune remembered, "retrieving discarded linen and kitchenware, cracked dishes, broken chairs, pieces of old lumber. Everything was scoured and mended. This was part of the training to salvage, to reconstruct, to make bricks without straw."[2]

Making "bricks without straw" became a theme for African American Churches of Christ. What Mary McLeod Bethune testified about herself stood equally and especially true, if not more so, for black women in Churches of Christ. One of these remarkable women, Annie C. Tuggle, a prominent educator from Tennessee, has confirmed Winston's testimony, noting that during the Silver Point Christian Institute experiment Bowser's wife, Fannie "could take leftovers from different meals and make some of the most tasty dishes you ever ate. She could make something out of nothing so to speak, and everybody at the table liked it." A prudent and frugal woman, Mrs. Bowser determined to "make everything count."[3] African American women in Churches of Christ, like their male companions, struggled and sacrificed beyond measure to help support and sustain their fledgling congregations and schools. Even though black women in Churches of Christ played less public roles, their presence and participation in their chosen fellowship qualified them as "hard-fighting soldiers," marching alongside their male compatriots.

That black women have played seminal roles in the nation's history remains indisputable. From Phillis Wheatley to Sojourner Truth, from Ida B. Wells to Rosa Parks, African American women have proven indispensable in helping their people secure full freedom. Historian Jacqueline Jones has pointed out that throughout American history, black women have supplied "elbow grease" to meet the needs of both whites and their own families. Despite toiling in oppressive environments after emancipation, black women, Jones has argued, found relief in their faith, "and the church provided strength for those overcome by the day-to-day business of living. For many weary, hard-working sharecroppers' women, worship services allowed for physical and spiritual release and offered a means of transcending earthly cares in the company of one's friends and family."[4]

Yet African American women not only gained strength from their faith in God, but they also gave to their chosen fellowship. Scholar Anthea D. Butler, when appraising the contributions of black women in the Church of God in Christ, found assertive women who served as counselors to pastors, leaders of youth, and "spiritual avatars to the congregation."⁵ In her perceptive and exhaustive book, *Jesus, Jobs, and Justice: African American Women and Religion*, historian Bettye Collier-Thomas rightly noted, "the African American church as an institution would not exist without the membership and financial support of black women."⁶ The evaluations of Butler and Collier-Thomas hold true for black women of all denominations.

In the early 1930s, when Marshall Keeble ascended to his role as the most prominent black evangelist in Churches of Christ, he readily acknowledged that his wife, Minnie, stood at the "bottom" of his preaching endeavors.⁷ As Keeble's preaching campaigns and ministerial roles expanded and developed even more fully in the 1940s and 1950s, he came to realize that other women proved invaluable as well. To chronicle the stories of all these courageous black women would be virtually impossible; however, two of these can serve as exemplars: Annie C. Tuggle and Thelma M. Holt.

"The Tenacity of a Bulldog": The Work of Annie C. Tuggle

Born in 1890 in Germantown, Tennessee, to formerly enslaved parents Haywood and Mollie Tuggle, Annie C. Tuggle lived always in the shadow of chattel enslavement. Although free, Annie grew up under the burden of de jure segregation and all its attendant horrors, as *Plessy v. Ferguson* (1896) legalized the doctrine of "separate but equal." The legal and social structure of the southern states maintained the former but never the latter. Reared a devout Methodist, Annie at age seventeen heard the "pure gospel" and converted to Churches of Christ. Tuggle then committed herself to learning scripture "to know the will of God so that I could do it and live with him forever."⁸

After brief academic stints at Lane College in Jackson, Tennessee, and LeMoyne Normal Institute in Memphis, Tennessee, Tuggle fulfilled a dream of studying the Bible under evangelist G. P. Bowser at the Silver Point Christian Institute in Silver Point, Tennessee. While there Tuggle accompanied W. C. Baldwin, a young ministerial student at the Silver Point school, who was slated to preach in a Methodist Church. When a listener asked Baldwin, "What is wrong with the Methodist Church?" the young preacher turned to Tuggle whom he said was "well versed in the scriptures." Although astonished that the preacher called on her in the worship service, Tuggle immediately replied: "First of all, I would say that the Methodist church and its doctrine cannot be found in the inspired writings of the Bible." She then paraphrased 2 John 9: "Any church is wrong if it is without God and without Christ."⁹

After her statement, Tuggle felt guilty and "under a heavy burden because she had spoken in the midst of the congregation," knowing that black women were called on to be submissive to their male counterparts, even if they were more prepared economically. Yet Bowser, when learning what Tuggle had said, assured her that she had no reason to worry since Baldwin had given her "permission to speak."¹⁰ Notwithstanding her misgivings about her actions, Tuggle paradoxically revealed her rigid exclusivist theology, which denied women the right to speak in the assembly; she also thereby played down her own leadership in the early stages of African American Churches of Christ.

Not merely a teacher among African American women, Tuggle worked as a leader among black men in Churches of Christ. In 1913, black evangelist John T. Ramsey preached three weeks in Memphis, and he depended on Tuggle "to read certain scriptures that he needed while preaching."¹¹ Incompetent and illiterate black men in Churches of Christ made the Tuggle's work priceless.

In 1927, Tuggle married John Waller, a pharmacist, and relocated to Cincinnati, Ohio. Financial strain and her health difficulties ended the marriage, and Tuggle returned to her family in Tennessee. Distraught and heartbroken over her failed marriage, Tuggle regained her emotional, physical, and spiritual composure and poured her life into congregational and educational projects. Her failed marriage, in this sense, proved to be a blessing in disguise in that it provided for her another venue to serve God and others without restrictions.¹²

In addition to assuming leadership roles among African Americans in Churches of Christ, Tuggle advised white leaders in her faith tradition. In 1932, Anglo and African American Christians in Memphis, Tennessee, convened to discuss future plans for the city's all-black Iowa and Lauderdale congregation. Many in the business meeting recommended that the minister, William H. Owens, be fired to retire the eight-hundred-dollar debt on the church building; others disagreed. After much discussion, Tuggle boldly stood and stated, "when you take the gospel out of the church you have a dead church. The gospel is the power of God to save." She then recommended that Owens be retained as minister and that renowned evangelist Marshall Keeble be invited to Memphis to "help build up the church."¹³

After deliberating the matter, white leaders of the Union Avenue Church of Christ acted on Tuggle's suggestion and sponsored a four-week tent meeting.

An elated Tuggle called the event "one of the greatest gospel meetings perhaps since the day of Pentecost," as Keeble and song leader William Lee together engendered seventy-five baptisms, and "shook Memphis from center to circumference." Twenty-five more people received baptism into African American Churches of Christ shortly after the meeting's closure.[14] Tuggle never took credit for the campaign's success; she deflected it to the men—Keeble, Lee, and Owens. Still, the trio doubtless understood that Tuggle's wise counsel to white elders made possible their presence and collaboration in west Tennessee.

Signaling his confidence in her abilities, Owens urged Tuggle to "work among the sisters" at the Iowa and Lauderdale Church of Christ and "to teach them to do their best in every way for the good of the cause of Christ." The local minister knew firsthand that an "uninformed sisterhood in the church" soon resulted in an "uninformed brotherhood." Here, Owens acknowledged the vital contribution that African American women made to black Churches of Christ, intimating that strong and enlightened sisters undergirded weak and struggling men. Owens, as a consequence, exhorted Tuggle: "I want you to do your best in this respect as Phoebe and Lydia did in Paul's day."[15]

After Owens died in 1937, Tuggle worked closely with his successor, G. E. Steward, a blind preacher from Texas. She also grew close to Steward's wife, Ella. In 1943, Tuggle relocated to Nashville, Tennessee, where she served as a teacher at the Nashville Christian Institute (NCI). This post empowered her to influence many young pupils. Robert Woods, a student from Gallatin, Tennessee, came under Tuggle's tutelage, and it prepared him to serve more than forty years at the Monroe Street Church of Christ in Chicago, Illinois. She also helped mold K. K. Mitchell, a student from Georgia, into a most effective preacher who served for many years as minister to the Southside Church of Christ in Montgomery, Alabama. Tuggle helped the future civil rights leader Fred D. Gray, then a pupil from Alabama, open his first savings account at a local Nashville bank. When reflecting on his NCI experiences, Gray observed: "Our facilities were meager, but we had dedicated faculty members who were genuinely interested in the growth and development of its students. They gave us a good college preparatory education, and many of the graduates of NCI are leaders across the country and preachers in the Church of Christ throughout the nation." One of these "dedicated faculty members" was, of course, Annie C. Tuggle, who helped lay for Gray a good academic foundation, propelling him on to Alabama State University and

Case Western Reserve University to study law. She also prodded Woodie W. Morrison to do missionary work in Jamaica.[16]

In addition to her educational work, Tuggle raised funds for NCI and the Bowser Christian Institute (BCI) in Fort Smith, Arkansas. During the summer of 1942, Tuggle had relocated to Fort Smith in order to solicit funds for Bowser's new enterprise there. She canvassed parts of Tennessee, Arkansas, and Mississippi, appealing for money from both black and white members of Churches of Christ. While in Arkansas, Tuggle met A. J. Colston, a black evangelist from Muskogee, Oklahoma, who was preaching in Fort Smith. His declaration of the "unadulterated word of God" yielded eighteen restorations at a Gospel meeting. Neighboring white and black Christians convened to eat, worship, and contribute financially to the BCI. Tuggle then reported that Colston later returned to debate a Baptist preacher who metaphorically tried to bomb the Church of Christ. "In the midst of a great audience of both white and colored, Brother Colston seized him by the word of God, snatched his weapon of man-made doctrine away from him and burned him at the stake with the gospel of Christ." Tuggle's colorful, militant language suggests that a great deal of verbal conflict and theological friction occurred during the debate, as the black Baptist preacher contested Colston's claim that Churches of Christ comprised "the one true" body of believers. In Tuggle's view, Colston prevailed in "a great victory over the devil and his works."[17]

Beyond her educational and fundraising efforts, Tuggle also wielded a certain degree of power and influence in African American Churches of Christ as a writer and historian. In her 1945 book, *Our Ministers and Song Leaders of the Church of Christ*, Tuggle composed biographical sketches of African American preachers and singers in her faith tradition, thereby giving them national visibility and connecting them to each other. When explaining the book's purpose, she noted: "With the photos and biographies of these great ambassadors who represent the cause of Christ here on earth we believe there will be such an awakening throughout the Christian realm, that every soul will be refreshed and encouraged to press forward to the mark of the high calling which is in Christ Jesus." She also hoped that the "noble examples of perseverance and tenacity" would prompt young people to pursue high Christian morals and contend for the faith.[18]

In *Another World Wonder*, Tuggle recorded the "story of my life," simultaneously providing a historical overview of the rise and development of African American Churches of Christ. Even though black Churches of Christ,

After converting to Churches of Christ in 1908, Annie C. Tuggle (1890–1976) became one of the most influential women in her chosen fellowship. Tuggle worked as a counselor, educator, missionary, and writer in African American Churches of Christ.
Courtesy of Abilene Christian University.

along with their white counterparts, have been notoriously poor record keepers, Tuggle herself kept meticulous notes, chronicling the various events and encounters in her life from childhood onward. And even though blacks in Churches of Christ have espoused ahistorical perspectives, Tuggle worked diligently to trace her religious fellowship from its origins in the South, to the North, and on to the Caribbean Islands.

Tuggle further recognized that she was not a self-made woman, acknowledging that many Christians, both white and black, helped to mold her character. Her associations with such important white leaders David Lipscomb, N. B. Hardeman, B. C. Goodpasture, and A. M. Burton indelibly stamped her life. Many black believers also impacted Tuggle, especially G. P. Bowser, and Marshall Keeble. "My close associations with such spiritual giants as Marshall Keeble and G. P. Bowser," testified Tuggle, "along with many others all had an influence in shaping me into the kind of person I became."[19]

"My Mother Can Do It":
The Work of Thelma M. Holt

Annie C. Tuggle died in 1976, the same year the United States commemorated its bicentennial. In her article, "Happy Birthday—America!! 1976," Thelma M. Holt joined the celebration and expressed America's need for a "spiritual revolution." Refusing to rehash yesterday's wrongs, Holt instead exhibited a sense of black pride, observing that African Americans "have played an important part in the building of our nation, as have other ethnic groups. We are still working for freedom, for liberty, and for justice." Holt specifically addressed her article to African American women in Churches of Christ, urging them to thank "almighty God for our many blessings, His generous bounty, for the comforts and conveniences we enjoy." A staunch Christian moralist, Holt challenged her readers that in spite of the many "creative comforts," which they enjoyed, they must not "forget what is really valuable and to overlook the important." Reflecting a mixture of patriotism and spiritual commitment, Holt concluded: "It is wonderful to live in a country where we are free to love and serve God, and love and serve our less fortunate brothers."[20] In Thelma M. Holt's mind, commitment to Christ and his church superseded all other loyalties.

Born in Nashville, Tennessee, in 1902, Holt grew up during a period of religious transition, a time when her parents, G. P. and Fannie Bowser, had just recently switched from the Gay Street Christian Church to the Jackson Street Church of Christ. Holt also matured in a busy and noisy family environment, as her father worked diligently to establish his new paper, the *Christian Echo*, and secretly plotted to launch a school for African Americans in Churches of Christ. Holt recalled standing by her father in the pulpit when she was three and traveling with him when she was four. In 1907, Bowser organized a school in the building of the Jackson Street congregation, where his daughter received her early education. Two years later Bowser relocated the school to Silver Point, Tennessee, and named it the Silver Point Christian Institute. His precocious daughter called the experience "some of the happiest days of my life."[21]

Seven-year-old Thelma received baptism at the hands of Harrison Ramsey, a ministerial student at the Silver Point Christian Institute. After studying briefly at what is now Tennessee State University, Thelma met Marion F. Holt in Louisville, Kentucky, to which her family had moved after the Silver Point Christian Institute ended its brief life. On January 11, 1920, Thelma and

Marion married in Louisville, Kentucky. E. L. Jorgenson, a white minister of the Highland Church of Christ, performed the wedding ceremony on a Sunday before white and black guests.[22]

The day after their wedding, the newlyweds went to Indianapolis, Indiana, where Marion worked. From Indianapolis, the couple moved to Belfast, Tennessee, then to Richmond, Tennessee, where Marion taught eight grades in a one-room school while farming corn. The young couple had six children. Notwithstanding the challenges of rearing such a large brood on a meager income, Mrs. Holt testified: "If I had my life to live over I would select the same father and the same babies."[23]

A comparison of Thelma M. Holt and Annie C. Tuggle reveals many striking similarities, as well as differences. Both women descended from enslaved parents, were born in Tennessee, and bore the heavy burdens of race and gender in the Jim Crow South. Both acquired academic training at the college level. Both read avidly, immersing themselves in literature and the Bible. Both women authored books that provide unique glimpses into the historical development of black Churches of Christ. And both women, of course, profoundly impacted the lives of black adherents in Churches of Christ.

One obvious difference stands out. On the one hand, Tuggle married, divorced, and had no biological children; she dreamed of having a large family, but her dream ended with her failed marriage. Consequently, she poured her life into young men and women at the NCI and BCI, nurturing numerous "offspring" along the way.[24] Holt, however, married and in time gave birth to six children, three girls and three boys. As a wife and mother, Holt experienced the life Tuggle had hoped for but never realized. Rearing six children gave Holt little time for extracurricular activities. "Not only the children's school activities demanded a lot of my time," recalled Holt, "but also their religious training in which I had been taught was so greatly needed. I am glad I went to church with them instead of sending them."[25] Holt's patience and involvement paid off remarkably well, as two of her sons, G. P. Holt and Marion Holt Jr. emerged as potent and influential preachers in twentieth-century African American Churches of Christ.

Paradoxically, while Holt nurtured and guided her offspring, her children at the same time provided her with a sense of confidence she had hitherto lacked. When her daughter, Charlotte, attended Lincoln High School in Fort Smith, Arkansas, she gladly volunteered her mother to give a response to the welcome address, proudly announcing: "My mother can do it." Alarmed and afraid, Holt nevertheless went to her daughter's school and delivered a reply on the program, repeatedly echoing her daughter's words to herself: "My mother can do it."[26] This public speech boosted the mother's confidence and set her on a path to becoming a highly reputable presenter to women's groups in African American Churches of Christ.

"It Has Rubbed Off on Me": The Legacy of Thelma M. Holt

G. P. Bowser was unquestionably the most influential person in his daughter's life. Standing at his knees as he preached, riding with him as he drove to various locations, and singing in public places as he distributed tracts left lasting impressions on young Thelma. She later commented that her father was always "looking ahead, planning and hoping for a better day for the church." Under this influence, Thelma Holt, too, became a visionary. She believed that church work reached "far ahead of what it was in my youth," but she understood there remained "room for improvement." Holt added: "I believe living in this type of atmosphere, a little bit of it has rubbed off on me."[27] G. P. Bowser and his wife transmitted profound moral values to their daughter who in turn passed them on to black women in Churches of Christ.

In 1957, when racial tension roiled the South, Holt focused her attention on the black Christian woman in the home. Taking her admonition from Titus 2, which treats domestic relations among Christ's followers, Holt urged her *Christian Echo* readers to find "joy" and "contentment" in maintaining clean homes, preparing nutritious meals for their families, and sending their children to school "clean and anxious to return to a home in the afternoon and evening that is inviting and comfortable, a place where the cares of the outside can be forgotten for a while."[28] In Holt's mind, a clean, comfortable, Christ-centered home provided African American women and their families with a solid buffer against a world teeming with racial strife and scarred by social turmoil.

Seven years later, leaders of the Dorr Street Church of Christ in Toledo, Ohio, appointed Holt to organize the women's session at the annual national lectureship for African American Churches of Christ. Holt's appointment was one of delegated authority in that men appointed her to present the Gospel to black female Christians.[29] After making several oral presentations over the years, Holt eventually recorded moral instruction for African American women in Churches of Christ in two books: *Reach Out and Touch: A Book of Remembrances, Favorite Poems, and Thoughts from the Book of Psalms* and *My*

Making Something Out of Nothing 127

African American women in Churches of Christ have always been sources of strength in their chosen fellowship. In 1967, many wives of preachers and church leaders attend annual national lectureship in Newark, New Jersey. Courtesy of Phyllis (Holt) Davis.

Task. These two volumes mark Holt as a Christian moralist who devoted her life to imparting moral guidance to African American females in Churches of Christ.

In *My Task*, Holt addressed a plethora of topics: marriages, prayer, reading scripture, divorce, singlehood, fatherhood, Christian education, and race relations. Holt's experiences as a Christian homemaker supplied the impetus and shaped her perspectives on these social and moral issues. "With six children I found myself attending three schools' P. T. A. meetings, and being a room mother at the Sr. High School."[30] She wrote specifically to "inspire, encourage, and sustain" African American women in Churches of Christ.

Holt, who had been married to Marion for several years, viewed marriage as a sacred destiny. "God, in creating the home," affirmed Holt, "also ordained that it be the center, the foundation of a well organized society. Marriage is a beautiful life if the plan of God is carried out by both parties." Holt never

Women in the African American Churches of Christ who attended the thirty-eighth annual national lectureship in Fort Lauderdale, Florida. Courtesy of the author.

berated divorced or single people; she only urged the married to "keep in mind your vows."[31] Unfortunately she and her husband later dissolved their own marriage.[32]

In Holt's view, prayer sustained black Christian women, who often found themselves subjected to domination at home and oppression in the broader society. "We can't make it without prayer," she attested. Desiring an intimate relationship with God through prayer was "first in order to relate to my family and the world." Closely aligned with prayer was reading scripture: "Sisters, encourage the reading of the scripture. This is 'our task.'"[33]

While residing in Detroit, Michigan, Holt witnessed firsthand the rise of crime in urban America. She particularly expressed concern over crimes committed by young people. Therefore, Holt urged Christian black women to recognize the reality of crime, to devise a plan of action to combat it, and to persevere, adding: "The devil's reasoning is the cause of crime. Let's fight him!!!!! THIS IS OUR TASK."[34]

Not only rising crime but also America's divorce problem disturbed Holt. On the one hand, she exhorted married couples to remember their sacred vows; on the other hand, she counseled her divorced readers to "don't fail your children now, they need you more than ever." Holt urged black women suffering from divorce or separation to move forward and to "rely upon the Word. It alone will help when other cease to love us."[35] Holt's foregoing counsel emanated from her own personal experience as she and her husband separated from several years before eventually divorcing. Therefore, like Tuggle, Holt embraced scripture as her "all in all."[36]

A lover of literature and a student of history, Holt related to her readers a story about leaders in colonial Pennsylvania, who in 1751 ordered a bell from Thomas Lester's Whitechapel Foundry in London. The following year, when the bell arrived, overzealous and inexperienced bell hangers mishandled and cracked it. When enthused Philadelphians gathered to hear the bell's first rings, they heard a surprisingly strange sound. Over four centuries, the Liberty Bell was purportedly the only Whitechapel bell to have been cracked. Holt used the analogy of the cracked Liberty Bell to point out "cracks" in American society. While acknowledging America's "greatness," she poignantly highlighted moral decline, juvenile delinquency, and racism as "cracks" in America's system. The absence of moral integrity and honesty not only threatened the U. S. government, but it also menaced American families.[37] Holt might have had in mind the recent Watergate scandal unraveling the presidency of Richard M. Nixon.

Holt uncompromisingly addressed the issue of racism in America, stating: "Everyone has a right to [be] proud of their heritage. To be denied this right affects my life and my children's lives. Racism is the greatest, most potent illness in America today. Is there a cure for this illness? It eats like a cancer. 'This is a crack in the bell!'"[38] For Holt, racism was the most potent and porous crack in America's bell because she felt its sting firsthand as she accompanied her father, G. P. Bowser, across the Jim Crow South and as she reared her own six children in a racially divisive and hostile nation. The bite of racism was most painful and excruciating when it affected her own children. The "cracks" in America deeply concerned Holt, for she knew that when: "Our country is in danger; we are all in danger."[39]

Other topics in Holt's *My Task* included singlehood, fatherhood, Christian education, educators' influence, the role of Christian women in the community, gerontology, and America's bicentennial. Biblical references permeated each chapter and topic, attesting to Holt's faith. Like countless other African American women who trusted the Bible as their guide, Holt also viewed scripture as "an instrument of freedom and survival and a tool for development of literacy."[40] As a Christian moralist, Holt challenged African American women in Churches of Christ to "deal with sin wherever it is. That means in the cities, and the suburbs, as well. They are both deteriorating. When one suffers, the other suffers, as well.[41]

Thelma M. Holt and Annie C. Tuggle knew, admired, and loved each other. Both women came under the influence of Tuggle's mentor and Holt's father, G. P. Bowser. The devoted duo filled diverse roles to lead and guide black women in Churches of Christ. Holt's commitment to her husband and six children made her an insider, a diligent domestic who channeled her energies in molding the lives of her biological offspring. This experience equipped her to counsel and provide moral guidance for African American women in Churches of Christ, a work she accomplished in later years, even though she also went through a divorce.

Tuggle's failed marriage aborted her dream of having six children but liberated her to toil outside the home. Her work as an educator and missionary would have been virtually impossible with marital and filial ties. Both women, then, had the same goal—advancing the cause of Christ among African American women in Churches of Christ—but their experiences differed. The stories of Tuggle and Holt attest that African American women never comprised a "monolithic group."[42]

"Standing by His Side": The Legacy of African American Women in Churches of Christ

Women in African American Churches of Christ must have understood that the theological rigidity of their faith tradition barred them from the pulpit and hegemony over men. This stance stamped African American Churches of Christ as decidedly different from some of their black religious brethren. Black women in African Methodist Episcopal congregations, such as Jarena Lee, assumed preaching roles long before the Civil War. In 1885, Bishop Henry McNeal Turner stirred controversy among A.M.E. pastors when he ordained Sarah Ann Hughes as a preacher.[43] African American Churches of Christ, then, stood with many black Baptists in restricting women from leadership posts. Yet unlike black Baptists and Methodists who often championed racial uplift and social reform, African American women in Churches of Christ, like many of their male counterparts, espoused an exclusivist theology that virtually prevented them from openly raising their voices against racial discrimination in the broader American context.

Therefore, Thelma M. Holt and Annie C. Tuggle bequeathed an inspiring legacy to African American Churches of Christ. They were not perfect, nor were they the only black women in Churches of Christ whose lives shined brightly in their dark worlds. Countless other women toiled to sustain and strengthen the fellowship of black Churches of Christ. A full treatment of such women extends beyond the scope of this book. Thankfully, educator James Maxwell has recently told the stories of a number of black women in Churches of Christ who made substantive contributions to their chosen faith tradition. Such women included: Frances R. Bowser, Minnie Keeble, Maggie Hogan, Laura Keeble, Mizetta Winston, Ella Steward, Alberta Kennedy, Mary Carpenter, Bethel Smith, Imogene Cole, Izetta Sams, Patricia Evans, and Frances Harrison.[44]

Even though a full-length study of black women in Churches of Christ remains warranted, a cursory survey of pertinent sources clearly reveal that African American females in Churches of Christ filled varying and important roles in their congregations. They composed and submitted evangelism reports to the *Christian Echo*, cooked meals for church gatherings, offered prayers, read scripture in service, prodded prodigals to return home, taught and mentored black youth, reared talented children, and often outnumbered black male worshipers. In 1943, Ezekiel Z. Webster, after reporting that J. S. Winston had baptized ten women in Sweeney, Texas, noted: "We have no brother in the congregation, but the sisters are faithful."[45] What held true for the small congregation in Sweeney stood true for many African American Churches of Christ at that time.

R. N. Hogan reported that, when he abandoned the preaching ministry because of the untimely death of his child, his wife, Maggie, "remained faithful" and "awakened my soul and brought me to repentance."[46] Ella Steward led by hand her blind preaching husband, G. E. Steward, dressing him, grooming him, and editing his manuscripts. Patricia Evans, a native of Tennessee, has stood by her husband, Jack Evans Sr., during his almost fifty-year tenure at Southwestern Christian College. An able French instructor and gifted musician, Mrs. Evans and her melodious voice have helped to raise millions of dollars for the cause of Christian education.[47]

Indeed, Thelma M. Holt, when commending her father, captured the essence of the work of African American women in Churches of Christ: "I am proud of my father," averred Holt, "who was humble enough to go along the unbeaten paths, under brush harbors, with the message of salvation, and my dear mother going with him when she could, standing by his side."[48] Holt then added a humorous touch to her commendation of her mother, stating that her father was "the head" and her mother was "the neck." What Holt intended as humor was in many ways reality. As Fannie Bowser stood by her husband's "side," scores of other black women in Churches of Christ similarly soldiered alongside their spouses or other men of God who battled for the Lord. African American women in Churches of Christ, then, were also "hard fighting soldiers."

— 10 —

"I'm Coming Up Lord"

The Hymnody of African American Churches of Christ

"We are almost a nation of dancers, poets."
—Olaudah Equiano

"The African race is a music-loving one...."
—Solomon Northup, *Twelve Years a Slave*

Music has been an integral part of the African American experience from the beginning. Indeed, their music sustained and strengthened African Americans through chattel enslavement to emancipation; and it fortified and galvanized them from de jure segregation through the civil rights era. "The spiritual, then," affirms scholar James H. Cone, "is the spirit of the people struggling to be free; it is their religion, their source of strength in a time of trouble."[1] Author Andrew Ward has similarly noted, "nothing influenced the form and content of the spiritual more than the sheer experience of bondage."[2] In a special way, the spirituals flowing from the souls of enslaved people in antebellum America "first developed the signature of serious black involvement in American Christianity."[3]

The music of American blacks not only sustained them during the ordeal of chattel enslavement, but it also delighted their white audiences. Solomon Northup, a free black man from New York, spent twelve arduous years in bondage in the Deep South. Northup recalled being invited to play his violin for white audiences across the Louisiana bayou. "My master often received letters," Northup wrote, "sometimes from a distance of ten miles, requesting him to send me to play at a ball or festival of the whites."[4] Alexander Campbell, the white religious reformer, and his wife, Selina, owned a man named Ben, who possessed a "wonderful musical talent." Ben, according to Mrs. Campbell, "sang for visitors and charmed them with sweetness and pathos of his voice."[5] Even though it is unknown what specific songs Ben performed, it is obvious that the songs of the enslaved affected not only the performers but also their white listeners. Elizabeth Botome, a white teacher from the North, observed: "One who has not heard these spirituals under such circumstances cannot understand their power and pathos. I can never hear them, even at this date, without emotion."[6]

The spirituals indelibly marked the hearts and minds of African Americans who endured the pangs of chattel enslavement. While Frederick Douglass had initially viewed spirituals as "rude" and "incoherent songs," he came to see them as a "complaint of souls boiling over with the bitterest anguish. Every tone was a testimony against slavery, and a prayer to God for deliverance from chains." White apologists for the peculiar institution comfortably misunderstood these songs, claiming that they provided evidence of black people's "contentment and happiness." Douglass countered such simplistic and self-serving nonsense, declaring eloquently that enslaved people "sing most when they are most unhappy. The songs of the slave represent the sorrows of his heart; he is relieved by them, only as an aching heart is relieved by its tears."[7]

Prior to the Civil War, enslaved African Americans often encrypted their songs. As an example, white southerners assumed that "freedom," when appearing in a spiritual's lyrics, referred to the next life. But after the Union victory, Booker T. Washington noted that free blacks boldly "threw off the masks" and made it known that the "'freedom' in their songs meant freedom of the body in this world."[8] S. R. Cassius, like countless African American children, came to feel the joy of freedom but who had heard the rhythmic chants of emancipation songs in their early days. Cassius never forgot those spirituals of his childhood he had heard and doubtless sung around the campfires in the nation's capital district. One particular spiritual, "Lord, I Done Done," captured Cassius's heart for life, as he referred to it at age seventy-six to encourage himself to fulfill his God-given mission.[9]

Douglass, Washington, and Cassius clung to the songs which had been so vital a part of their youth spent in chattel enslavement, but it was the Fisk Jubilee Singers who first disseminated these "sorrow songs" to the nation and the broader world. Assembled by George White, a former Union soldier who named the new group after the Jewish festival "Jubilee" described in Leviticus 25, the Fisk Jubilee Singers began touring the United States in

1871. Seven of the original nine singers were newly freed. Overcoming the visceral racism that pervaded the South, the choral group gradually melted away racial opposition on their tours and moved audiences with their "burst of wonderful melody" in raising funds to save their struggling Nashville school from extinction. W. E. B. Du Bois, a Fisk alumnus himself and the first African American to earn a doctorate from Harvard University, offered the first scholarly analysis of the spirituals, referring to them as the "articulate message of the slave to the world." He further acknowledged the courage of the nine Fisk singers who fought their way through sneers, jeers, privation, and racism to share the music of African Americans with the world. "So their songs," declared Du Bois, "conquered till they sang across the land and across the sea, before Queen and Kaiser, in Scotland and Ireland, Holland and Switzerland."[10]

The music of the Fisk Jubilee Singers also touched the hearts and souls of African Americans in Churches of Christ. Minnie Womack, future wife of Marshall Keeble, completed the high school department at Fisk University.[11] Marshall and Minnie Keeble then collaborated in church: Marshall preached while Minnie sang. In 1916, Annie C. Tuggle stopped in Bell Buckle, Tennessee, where the Keebles conducted a preaching campaign. "They both sang like angels," remembered Tuggle. "Sister Minnie had the sweetest alto voice that one could imagine and Bro. Keeble with his heavy melodious bass voice had stirred the community from center to circumference with the work of the Lord."[12]

Indeed, singing with his wife and other black songsters proved to be a key element in Keeble's evangelistic strategy, as harmonizing voices often attracted a crowd of people, giving the evangelist an opportunity to preach. This strategy clearly succeeded in Fayetteville, Tennessee, where white Christians invited Keeble to preach. When Keeble, his wife, and a few others began singing before the Fayetteville courthouse, five hundred people, mostly whites, gathered around. "After we had sung a song and had prayer, I began to preach, touching on water baptism, showing the essentiality of it and showing by the Bible that one cannot be saved without it."[13] This blend of passionate preaching and heartfelt singing helped fuel the rise of African American Churches of Christ, and Keeble well understood this. In 1921, while preaching in Birmingham, Alabama, Keeble "led the singing under the 'big tent.'" When Anglo Christian supporters saw Keeble being "severely overtaxed with his double duties," they assigned the singing task to white hymnists.[14] From this time forward, in his travels Keeble ordinarily teamed with a black song leader. Luke Miller, a former furniture truck driver from Alabama, converted to Churches of Christ in 1920 after hearing Keeble. Miller soon flourished as Keeble's chief song leader, adhering to the evangelistic strategy of using Miller's voice to attract a crowd, bringing them under the tent to hear the "pure gospel."[15] Apart from his singing, Miller also developed into an effective evangelist and church planter.[16]

T. H. Busby, a student at G. P. Bowser's Silver Point Christian Institute and a "great and unusual singer," helped Keeble's effort in Sparta, Tennessee, before becoming a highly skilled preacher himself. In Lakeland, Florida, however, a white Christian led the assembly in singing until Keeble baptized a "good songleader" and turned the responsibility over to him.[17] William Lee, a black song leader, accompanied Keeble on preaching excursions in both West Virginia and Texas.[18] Keeble preferred a songster of his own race to lead the predominantly black audience in song. He likely wished to steer clear of leaving any impression that he sought social equality in the Jim Crow South.

Keeble's strategy with regard to music strikingly resembled that of the renowned Dwight L. Moody, a white New England shoe salesman who emerged as a premier evangelist in nineteenth-century America. Moody partnered with an effective song leader, Ira Sankey, and swayed scores of people into evangelical Christianity. Scholar Edith L. Blumhofer, in her study of hymn writer Fanny J. Crosby, has pointed out that "in Sankey's able hands and tied to Moody's energetic efforts, the gospel song assumed a larger life than before. Sankey made music indispensable to Moody's accomplishments."[19] Even though Moody and Sankey accomplished their greatest teamwork in Europe and in the northern parts of the United States, Blumhofer's observation applies as well to the emergence of African American Churches of Christ. Melodious singing and harmonic a cappella music proved "indispensable" to Marshall Keeble and other African American evangelists in Churches of Christ.

Thelma Bowser, blessed with a "good singing voice," often sang on the sidewalks as her father, G. P. Bowser, distributed tracts. In 1934, evangelist R. N. Hogan collaborated with song leader J. S. Winston and planted a black Church of Christ in Okmulgee, Oklahoma, by baptizing 189 Oklahomans.[20] In the fall of 1941, John R. Vaughner, a Keeble convert, preached two weeks under a tent in Shelbyville, Tennessee, baptizing eleven people and restoring one. L. C. Bradley directed the singing for Vaughner's efforts.[21] Two weeks after Pearl Harbor, R. N. Hogan preached in Denton, Texas, with J. Milton Butler, a native Oklahoman, rendering "good song service."[22] John Henry

Clay, another Keeble disciple who served black congregations in Texas, New Mexico, and California, relied on two musicians when conducting his preaching campaigns: Alms Arms, a Montgomery, Alabama, native, and Wonderful Small Richardson, a resident of Valdosta, Georgia.[23]

Educator Annie C. Tuggle valued song leaders so highly as she studied African American Churches of Christ that she entitled her 1945 publication *Our Ministers and Song Leaders of the Church of Christ*. In Tuggle's view, the story of the growth of black Churches of Christ in the United States would have been incomplete without highlighting of the role of songsters, who have "played an important part in the spread of the gospel."[24] Black ministers of music, in Tuggle's experienced view, deserved ranking alongside black preachers.

An examination of this pivotal role of music reveals three streams flowing into African American Churches of Christ which shape their hymnological tradition. First, a theological stream informed the hymnody of black Churches of Christ. In 1816, Alexander Campbell's "Sermon on the Law" drew a line of demarcation between the Old and New Testaments and argued that the latter covenant governed the personal and religious practices of modern Christians. Since they found no sanction in the New Testament for instrumental music in worship, Campbell and his *Christian Baptist* followers concluded that it was "criminal and wrong."[25] Based on their congruent understanding of scripture, African American Churches of Christ believed that God did not endorse using nonvocal instruments in worship. G. E. Steward, an African American preacher, summarized the position of black Churches of Christ when he stated: "We are not commanded to sing and play in the Church, on instruments of music in the worship of the Church today, that is purely a human invention and cannot be sustained by the New Testament."[26]

Second, European and Anglo influences pervaded the hymnody of African American Churches of Christ. Just as white hymnists such as Isaac Watts, Charles Wesley, and John Newton profoundly shaped black Methodists, Baptists, Pentecostals, Episcopalians, and Catholics,[27] the same occurred in African American Churches of Christ. R. N. Hogan's favorite song was "Blessed Assurance," a composition of white hymnist Fanny J. Crosby.[28] In 1828, Alexander Campbell issued his first hymnal, followed by Barton W. Stone the next year. When the "Disciples" and "Christian" churches merged in 1832, the two groups realized the need for one songbook as an aid in maintaining this new unity. Therefore, in 1834, Walter Scott and John T. Johnson collaborated in producing a single hymnal designed for Stone-Campbell congregations.[29]

When African American Churches of Christ emerged as a distinct religious group, they mostly sang hymns composed by Anglo believers both outside and inside the Stone-Campbell Movement. E. L. Jorgenson, a white hymnist, perhaps exerted the most compelling effect upon the hymnody of black Churches of Christ. A descendant of Danish immigrants and a native of Nebraska, Jorgenson displayed musical talent at an early age. After leading a music department at Western Literary and Bible College in Odessa, Missouri, for a few years, he and his wife relocated in 1910 to Louisville, Kentucky, where he ministered to the Highland Church of Christ. Eleven years later, Jorgenson produced the songbook entitled *Great Songs of the Church*; the spreading of this volume exercised the "greatest influence on the hymnody of the Churches of Christ in the twentieth century."[30]

When Jorgenson released *Great Songs of the Church* in 1921—the same year the horrific Tulsa race riot sent shockwaves across the entire nation[31]—G. P. Bowser had relocated to Louisville and worked to organize a black Church of Christ on Burnett Avenue. Bowser and Jorgenson enjoyed a cordial and collaborative relationship at a time when de jure segregation reigned in southern communities. More importantly, Bowser most likely perused Jorgenson's new hymnal, which inspired him to compose his own songbook, *Choice Selections*.[32] Additionally, Bowser, a former Methodist preacher, hailed from a religious tradition heavily steeped in collecting and composing hymns. Marshall Taylor, a black Methodist cleric, compiled the first new hymnal for black congregations after Emancipation. Taylor's 1882 *Collection of Revival and Plantation Melodies* contained more than 150 hymns and songs composed by white and black writers.[33] Bowser perhaps had Taylor's work at his disposal when he devised his own book of songs.

Even though it is unclear which songs comprised Bowser's hymnal, since no known example survives, what remains obvious is that the hymns composed by white Christians dominated the hymnody of nascent African American Churches of Christ. One of Marshall Keeble's favorite hymns was F. L. Eiland's "Hold to God's Unchanging Hand."[34] This song inspired Keeble and other blacks in Churches of Christ to stay "true" to the unchanging God in a turbulent and transient world. Many other compositions of whites in Churches of Christ which black believers frequently sang included T. S. Teddlie's "Heaven Holds All to Me," Robert S. Arnold's "No Tears in Heaven," Roy Harris's "Hilltops of Glory," and Albert E. Brumley's "I'll Fly Away" and "I'll Meet You in the Morning." These stirring songs, mostly composed in the Depression Era, reflected the yearnings of both white and black

Christians to look beyond this world of "sorrow" to "heav'n where all will be made new."[35]

All hymns composed by whites in Churches of Christ did not, however, express otherworldly themes. Black Christians often favored J. W. Dennis's "I'll Be a Friend to Jesus" which exhorted Christians to spend "each flying moment to prove" themselves worthy of Jesus's friendship. J. W. Ferrill's "A Soul Winner for Jesus" fueled Christians' passion to evangelize their lost neighbors. Songs such as W. L. Thompson's "Softly and Tenderly" have been regularly sung in black congregations to encourage the weary to "come home." At annual Gospel meetings and national crusades, A. W. Dicus's "Our God, He is Alive" remains a favorite for African Americans in Churches of Christ.[36]

The third stream of influence to shape music in African American Churches of Christ is that of black hymnists from other religious traditions. S. R. Cassius's favorite hymn was "We'll Understand It Better By and By." Composed in 1905 by Charles A. Tindley, a black Methodist songwriter and clergyman, this rhythmic selection inspired Cassius, an impoverished preacher and "race man" to soldier his way through "thirsty hills and barren lands."[37] Another Tindley song, "Leave It There," exhorted black believers, who struggled to cope with "meager fare," to look to God for sustenance. Baptist composer Thomas A. Dorsey's "Take My Hand, Precious Lord" comforted countless grief-stricken black parishioners, including those in Churches of Christ. Doris Akers's "Sweet, Sweet Spirit" taught blacks in Churches of Christ a sense of reverence for the Third Person of the holy Trinity, whom they had often ignored and relegated to a subordinate position.[38] Mahalia Jackson perhaps spoke for most African Americans in Churches of Christ when she asserted that European songs were "beautiful songs, but they're not Negro music."[39] Even as African Americans desired to control their own churches, they also wished to determine which hymns they sang in those churches.

"I'm Coming Up, Lord": Hugh Graham and the "Southwestern Sound"

Southwestern Christian College came to play a pivotal role in enabling African Americans in Churches of Christ to both develop and control their own hymnody. As noted earlier, G. P. Bowser and four of his protégés, Levi Kennedy, G. E. Steward, R. N. Hogan (who in 1938 organized the first known choral group in black Churches of Christ), and J. S. Winston established the school in Fort Worth in 1948; Southwestern moved to Terrell the following year. The school's first music instructor was Kenneth Davis Jr., a native of Dallas, who served briefly before transitioning to Harding College in Arkansas, enjoying there a lengthy and distinguished career.[40]

In 1951, A. Hugh Graham, a white native of Wolfe City, Texas, with an undergraduate degree in music from Abilene Christian College (now Abilene Christian University) and graduate degrees from the University of North Texas, began teaching night classes in Terrell. Choosing to cast his lot with people who were "short-changed," Graham taught music at Southwestern Christian College (SwCC) for twenty-six years in order to provide African American students with a "high quality music education." He fused "Negro spirituals" and classical motifs to fashion what became known as the "Southwestern sound." In 1967–1968, Graham led the college chorus on its first and only European tour. Willie Eva Burnett, a SwCC student, considered the overseas trip one of the highlights of her life, as she and fellow students performed in Belfast, London, and Paris. "We had an awesome time there," recalled Burnett.[41] After the death of the esteemed black evangelist Marshall Keeble in the spring of 1968, Graham launched the first Marshall Keeble Tour. Graham's most popular composition, "I'm Coming up, Lord," not only became a signature hymn for the college chorus, but it also gained wider national popularity in African American Churches of Christ.[42]

Graham taught numerous SwCC pupils who subsequently blessed African American Churches of Christ. One such student was Sylvia Rose, a native of Valdosta, Georgia, who studied in Terrell. Rose served as choral director at her alma mater for a year and a half, from 1978 to 1979. During her brief stint, Rose composed such popular hymns as "I Can't Come Down" and "Call Him Up," and assembled a chorus featuring such musical talents as Wayburn Dean, a native of Hobbs, New Mexico, and George Pendergrass, a New Yorker, who toured nationally with the vocal group Acappella.[43] After her brief time at SwCC, Rose compiled a hymnal, published in 1985, consisting of several songs which many African Americans in Churches of Christ sing weekly, including "All My Trials," "Holy Spirit," "Mansion, Robe, and Crown," and "Restore My Soul."[44]

A year after Sylvia Rose issued her hymnal, Veronica Williams became chorus director at SwCC. A Fort Worth native, Williams studied at SwCC under Barry Graham, a son of A. Hugh Graham and a gifted musician in his own right. Williams also received instruction under Kenneth Davis Jr. at Harding University. Hailing from a musical family, Williams worked at

A. Hugh Graham (1922–1980) committed his life to teaching and training black youth at Southwestern Christian College how to sing. He is credited with creating the "Southwestern sound."
Courtesy of Barry Graham.

SwCC for a decade. While there, she wrote such songs as "I'll Be Wearing a Crown," "He Worked His Power on Me," "City Beyond the Blue," and "Let the Words of My Mouth."[45] Her choral groups carried these songs across the country, enriching the hymnody of African American Churches of Christ. The choral groups of SwCC deeply influenced congregations across the nation, prompting musical groups in these churches to imitate the "Southwestern sound." Students of Veronica Williams followed in her footsteps by composing songs which remain popular in African American Churches of Christ. Ronald Walker's "Heaven's on the Other Side," John Green's "We Will

Serve the Lord," John Edmerson's "I'm Glad I Know You," David Wilson's "Keeping the Dream Alive," and Andy McNeal's "Send Us a Revival" remain staple songs known and sung in virtually all black Churches of Christ.[46]

Additionally, individual song leaders beyond the circle of SwCC have left their own enduring mark on the hymnody of African American Churches of Christ. Chris Turner, a native of Alabama, grew up in black Churches of Christ. An admirer of Sam Cooke, the Gospel-turned-rhythm and blues sensation, Turner combined the Cooke sound with his own melodious voice and musical talents in composing approximately eighty hymns. These include, among many others, "Somewhere in Paradise," "You Don't Know How Blessed You Are," "One More Day," and "If You Want to Go to Heaven."[47] Joining these singers are many arrangers: Willie Norwood, Harold Robinson, Thomas Fitzgerald, Johnnie Wilder Jr., and Jeff Murrah and Straight Company. Researcher Leroy Butler Jr. has noted that black Churches of Christ have several men who have served as both outstanding preachers and singers, including Warren Blakeney Sr., Elijah Bush, W. C. Edwards, the late N. L. Evans, Robert Ivory, Terry D. Wallace, and David Wilson.[48]

Joi Carr, a native of southern California, professional actress, and professor at Pepperdine University, stands out as a gifted female musician in African American Churches of Christ, having composed more than fifty songs, including "You Are Amazing," "Send Me a Friend," and "Let Go and Let God." Carr has acknowledged that blues and jazz artists outside of Churches of Christ have influenced her music, among whom are Ella Fitzgerald, Phoebe Snow, Carole King, Amel Larrieux, and Lionel Richie. While pointing out that many secular artists have molded her musical renditions, Carr also expresses her admiration for song leaders in black Churches of Christ, calling Chris Turner "one of the most influential voices" in the history of her faith tradition. Willie Norwood, Carr noted, was the first full-time music minister in African American Churches of Christ in Los Angeles. Jessie Murrah, a founder of the musical group Straight Company, and Johnnie Wilder Sr., a former member of the rhythm and blues group Heat Wave, have contributed substantially to the hymnody of African American Churches of Christ through their "melodic" and harmonic arrangements.[49]

Carr's musical talent and insightful comments attest that several noteworthy singers have emerged in black Churches of Christ beyond the confines of SwCC. Researcher Calvin H. Bowers has chronicled the power of music in strengthening and sustaining African American Churches of Christ in Los Angeles. William Lee, a native of Helena, Arkansas, and colaborer with renowned Marshall Keeble, emerged as the premier song leader in black Churches of Christ in California. Lee so impressed one white visitor that she asked: "Were you trained in music at the University of Southern California?" Lee never studied music formally, but he and his brother Floyd laid the groundwork for group singing in southern California. According to Bowers, Floyd Lee developed the first Radio Chorus at the McKinley Avenue Church of Christ (now Figueroa Church of Christ).[50] After Floyd Lee's group sang on a program at a predominantly white congregation in Los Angeles, he "then moved to the center of the stage in choral music in Southern California, a position he would not relinquish for the next fifty years of his life." Lee composed songs, assisted struggling congregations, and produced such albums as *In That City* and *Let's Work Together*.[51]

As more black immigrants arrived in southern California,[52] other black congregations grew, flourished, and developed their own song groups. In 1946, the Compton Avenue Church of Christ formed a musical chorus; a decade later, the West Adams Church of Christ assembled a chorus "to glorify God in song." Around the same time, the Figueroa Church of Christ launched its youth chorus with fifty members. Under the direction of Harold Hogan and Zenobia Minor, the group staged musical productions at Pepperdine College (now Pepperdine University) to "teach the love God through music, to introduce nonmembers to the Lord's church, and to assist in the improvement of congregational singing."[53]

African American newcomers from the South profoundly affected music in black Churches of Christ in Log Angeles. Carl Baccus, a native Texan, and Willie Norwood and Curtis McCollum, both former Mississippians, left lasting imprints on the hymnological practices of African American Churches of Christ in the Golden State. In 1961, the Southside Church of Christ in Los Angeles under the ministerial leadership of Baccus founded its first choral group. Willie Norwood's relocation from Mississippi to southern California marked a turning point in the story of music on the West Coast. Norwood organized an all-male singing group, "Brother Brother," at the Southside congregation. Norwood's children, Brandy and Ray J., have achieved national fame as both theatrical and musical performers. Curtis McCollum, a talented preacher and singer from the Magnolia State, brought the Sing-o-Rama to southern California. McCollum, along with Donald Harris, Wilene Knox, Willie Norwood, and Sampson Wiley Jr., meticulously planned the

Sing-o-Rama which attracted singing groups from across California and the nation. A special chorus also developed under the auspices of the Figueroa Church of Christ, growing out of preparation for the Sing-o-Rama.[54]

Bowers acknowledged the Imperial Singers, a group consisting of members of the Imperial and San Pedro Street Church of Christ in Los Angeles, as the oldest black chorus to perform without interruption. Well known and well received across southern California, the Imperial Singers showcased their musical talent on both radio and television, while in 1976 they produced two albums, *Blessed Good News* and *Blessed Assurance*. "They certainly have been a blessing," observed Bowers, "to the city of Los Angeles."[55]

Additionally, Bethel Smith, a diligent champion of Christian youth and education, formed a choral group of approximately forty young people, the "Little Angels." The children produced such quality music that a local couple purchased a bus which allowed them to travel southern California. Frequent touring and impressive performances enabled the Little Angels to record an album, *Out of the Mouth of Babes*. From the Little Angels emerged the Girls' Glee, ten to twelve girls who performed locally, nationally, and globally. Kenneth Hahn, a white Christian politician and friend of R. N. Hogan, invited the girls to sing at many city events in downtown Los Angeles. Mayor Tom Bradley then invited the group to represent the city by traveling abroad to Auckland, New Zealand, in a cultural exchange program.[56] After providing a historical sketch of the significance of a cappella music in black Churches of Christ in Los Angeles, Bowers aptly concluded that "singing has played a large role in church life."[57]

What proved true for African American Churches of Christ in Los Angeles stood equally the case for black Christians in Georgia. Minister and researcher Leroy Butler Jr. has highlighted several remarkable song leaders in black congregations in Georgia, including John O. Williams, W. F. Washington, Cornelius Mobley, and Wonderful Small Richardson. More significantly, Butler has offered a more current assessment of musical trends in this tradition, pointing out that song leading has undergone "major transitions" in contemporary times. "There are song leaders in our brotherhood," observed Butler, "whose singing abilities rival that of famous celebrities like Andraé Crouch, Marvin Sapp, and the legendary Sam Cooke." Butler placed the late Curtis McCollum, Harold Robinson, and Chris Turner in the same category as the aforementioned entertainers, adding, "for better or worse, song leading has undergone a transition in terms of what members appreciate and have grown to expect from song leaders."[58]

In their embryonic stages, African American Churches of Christ expected song leaders to be "able to carry a tune and to keep time," even though some did not possess "extraordinary voices or improvisational skills." Butler further explained: "Very few of them were formally trained as musicians; neither could most of them read music." In the modern era, black worshippers in Churches of Christ want song directors with melodious voices and "spontaneous improvisations" who can "take the church up to the heights of emotional ecstasy and spiritual delight" while praising and extolling the name of Jesus.[59]

Division has naturally occurred among African Americans in Churches of Christ over singing preferences. Eddie L. Briggs, a leader from Houston, Texas, opposed all forms of group singing, insisting instead that all congregants join in the singing. Cornelius Mobley, a trained musician and the first song leader at the West Adair Church of Christ (now Woodlawn Forest Church of Christ) in Valdosta, Georgia, appropriated Acts 16:25 to argue in favor of group singing. "Whether the singing was spontaneous or with outside force," averred Mobley, "the fact remains that two of God's children sang and persons heard them sing, so says the scriptures." Butler correctly noted that the Briggs-Mobley squabble reflects the growing tensions between so-called liberals and so-called conservatives in African American Churches of Christ.[60] Indeed, Briggs and Mobley viewed the role of music in the church differently, attesting that conflict was not only wide and far-reaching, but that it also mirrored other burgeoning struggles in black Churches of Christ.

Notwithstanding the disagreement over group singing, black people in Churches of Christ, like their black religious neighbors in Baptist, Methodist, and Pentecostal churches, have embraced music and have exerted great effort to praise God in "psalms, hymns, and spiritual songs." And, African American Churches of Christ drank from divergent religious and cultural streams in forming their own distinct hymnological tradition. The theology of their white spiritual forebears, the hymns of Anglo believers within and outside of the Stone-Campbell movement, and the compositions of African Americans in and beyond Churches of Christ creatively zig-zagged into the brotherhood of black Churches of Christ, creating a unique religious community. In 1962, a black contributor to the *Christian Echo* noted: "Hymn singing by the congregation was an important part of the worship service. Ably led, without musical instruments."[61]

—11—

"The Magic of Education"

African American Churches of Christ and the Pursuit of Knowledge

"There is one sin that slavery committed against me which
I will never forgive. It robbed me of my education."
—A former slave, *The Education of Blacks in the South, 1860–1935*

"As I have stated, it was a whole race trying to go to school. Few were
too young, and none too old, to make the attempt to learn."
—Booker T. Washington, *Up from Slavery*

"The education of the Negroes, then, the most important thing
in the uplift of the Negroes, is almost entirely in the hands of those
who have enslaved them and now segregate them."
—Carter G. Woodson, *The Mis-Education of the Negro*

In 1826, Frederick Douglass, an enslaved African American from Maryland, had an epiphany. Douglass's owner, Thomas Auld, sent him to live with his brother, Hugh Auld, and his wife, Sophia. A kind and cordial Mrs. Auld began to teach young Douglass the fundamentals of literacy—until her husband discovered her misdeeds. Hugh vehemently prohibited his wife from giving Douglass further instruction, sternly warning her: "If you give a nigger an inch, he will take an ell. A nigger should know nothing but to obey his master—to do as he is told to do. Learning would *spoil* the best nigger in the world." In Auld's view, giving a black person knowledge meant "no good, but a great deal of harm. It would make him discontented and unhappy."[1]

What Hugh Auld deemed as dangerous, Frederick Douglass viewed as a grand prize. "These words sank deep into my heart," recalled Douglass, "stirred up sentiments within that lay slumbering, and called into existence an entirely new train of thought. It was a new and special revelation, explaining dark and mysterious things, with which my youthful understanding had struggled, but struggled in vain.... From that moment, I understood the pathway from slavery to freedom."[2] Just as Auld saw illiteracy as key to keeping black people in bondage, Douglass perceived literacy as essential to dismantling the shackles of enslavement.

Booker T. Washington, a formerly enslaved Virginian who rose to become a premier educator in Alabama, never forgot the "intense desire" African Americans exhibited in pursuing an education. "As fast as any kind of teachers could be secured," Washington remembered, "not only were day-schools filled, but night-schools as well. The great ambition of the older people was to try to learn to read the Bible before they died."[3]

Douglass's illumination during legal slavery and Washington's experience as a newly freed person illustrate a poignant truth undergirding this chapter. On the one hand, black people in ante- and postbellum America came to realize that knowledge helped to pave the way from bondage to freedom. On the other hand, many white Americans fought strenuously to keep their black neighbors ignorant and subservient. Notwithstanding this stiff opposition against learning, black Americans, convinced of what Swedish sociologist Gunnar Myrdal has called the "magic of education,"[4] toiled feverishly to obtain an education by creating their own schools and institutions of higher learning. Like Douglass and Washington, African Americans in Churches of Christ realized that education was indispensable to a better life. Even when racism and discrimination barred them from virtually all the white schools in the South as well as many in the North, black people in Churches of Christ found ways to educate themselves and created paths to the education of their own sons and daughters.

Many enslaved people received instruction from sympathetic white people during the antebellum period, even though the practice violated codes and customs across the South. In 1819, Thomas Campbell gathered enslaved African Americans in Burlington, Kentucky, and schooled them until his neighbors demanded he stop the practice.[5] Sarah Grimke gained "malicious satisfaction" from teaching her black maids in South Carolina to read and write.[6] Ida Van Zandt Jarvis delighted in her "first educational work" of teaching enslaved black children in Texas who worked in her parents' house.[7] S. R. Cassius's mother, Jane, developed a bond with her white mistresses in Prince

William County, Virginia, who taught her how to read. Jane bequeathed her knowledge to her young son, who, after acquiring more formal academic training in the nation's capital, later launched his Tohee Industrial School in the late nineteenth century.[8]

In the postbellum era, schools for freed black people sprouted up across the South. Driven largely by a religious impulse, white teachers from the North flooded southern communities as "soldiers of light and love"[9] and helped launch Atlanta University in Georgia, Hampton University in Virginia, Howard University in Washington, DC, and Fisk University in Tennessee. By 1869, 9,503 teachers labored in schools for formerly enslaved people across the South.[10] Historian W. E. B. Du Bois called this labor of love the "crusade of the sixties," adding that "the teachers in these institutions came not to keep the Negroes in their place, but to raise them out of the defilement of the places where slavery had wallowed them."[11]

African Americans in the Stone-Campbell Movement felt the reverberations generated by the creation of these schools, and they benefitted from what Du Bois called the "gift of New England."[12] S. R. Cassius, before he converted to the Stone-Campbell Movement, met and received training under the guidance of Frances W. Perkins, a white instructor supported by the New England Freedmen's Aid Society. Cassius's encounter with Perkins proved providential and he believed his education made it impossible for him to become anything but "a Christian only."[13]

Additionally, the love and sympathy of northern white educators inspired African Americans in the Stone-Campbell Movement to build their own institutions. In 1867, Peter Lowery, who had purchased his own freedom before the Civil War, established the Tennessee Manual Labor University in Nashville. Trained by white preacher Tolbert Fanning, founder of Franklin College near Nashville, Lowery and his son, Samuel, offered at their school a combination of liberal arts and manual labor courses. When white Christians learned, however, that Samuel had reportedly embezzeled funds, the school lost substantial monetary support and eventually collapsed in 1874.[14]

Undeterred by the failings of the Tennessee Manual Labor University, black and white members of the Stone-Campbell Movement collaborated to launch the Louisville Christian Bible School in 1873; the Southern Christian Institute in Hemingway, Mississippi, in 1881; the Christian Bible College in New Castle, Kentucky, in 1886; the Louisville Bible School in 1892; and the Lum Graded School in Alabama in 1894.[15] The Southern Christian Institute served as a model for the all-black Jarvis Christian College in Hawkins, Texas, and contributed to the growth and development of Tougaloo College in Jackson, Mississippi.[16]

By 1895, Booker T. Washington had emerged as one of the premier black leaders in America. His reputable Tuskegee Institute in Alabama and his impassioned speech at the Atlanta Exposition in the fall of that year catapulted Washington to national and international fame. S. R. Cassius, a black preacher and educator in Churches of Christ, emerged as the "Booker T. Washington of Oklahoma" in 1899, when he organized his Tohee Industrial School "for the lifting up of the colored race." Financial woes, however, eventually doomed the school, resulting in its demise. Cassius specifically noted that the rise of the Colored Agriculture and Normal University (now Langston University) overshadowed his educational enterprise, making it "useless."[17]

The Educational Legacy of G. P. Bowser

The failure of Cassius's Oklahoma project, however, did not deter other black leaders from pressing forward with their dreams of educating their own people. In 1907, G. P. Bowser, a former Methodist cleric, converted to the Stone-Campbell Movement and organized a school at the Jackson Street Church of Christ in Nashville; two years later, he relocated the school to Silver Point, named it the Silver Point Christian Institute, and offered classes in Bible, algebra, Latin, English, and history, until it closed in 1918.[18]

After a two-decade hiatus, a determined Bowser made his way to Fort Smith, Arkansas, and founded the Bowser Christian Institute (BCI) in 1938. Bowser called the school his "old age project," but black leaders in Churches of Christ in Tennessee questioned the wisdom of his enterprise. The same year Bowser started the school, black and white leaders in Nashville, Tennessee, formed the Nashville Christian Institute (NCI) to educate black youth. Several black leaders in middle Tennessee urged Bowser to abandon his Institute in Arkansas. The renowned Marshall Keeble pled with Bowser to "drop the Fort Smith movement and come to Nashville and be supported by the churches." P. H. Black, a black leader in the Jefferson Street Church of Christ in Nashville, advised Bowser that since the property in Fort Smith had debt, he should "give up the Fort Smith movement and come to Nashville. We all think it best for you." Black, expressing concern for the sixty-five-year-old Bowser's physical and financial well-being, explained: "I want to see you get a

"The Magic of Education"

UNDYING DEDICATION

G. P. Bowser standing before one of his preaching charts and his wife, Francis (Fannie) Rebecca, holding the Bible.

G. P. Bowser (1874–1950) and his wife, Fannie, toiled to educate African Americans in Churches of Christ. Their collaboration led to the establishment of Southwestern Christian College (SwCC) in Terrell, Texas. Courtesy of Abilene Christian University.

salary and sit down and rest once before the end comes."[19] B. M. Woods and James M. Cannon joined the chorus of black leaders in Nashville, calling on Bowser to return east of the Mississippi River and help build NCI. "The brethren here are 100% in favor of helping you," assured Woods and Cannon. "We are asking you to please consider dropping the work where you are and make plans to come to Nashville and help us all here to put this school work in operation."[20]

Bowser nevertheless refused to give in and listed several reasons why the BCI should be continued. In Bowser's view, the Fort Smith effort had a promising future because there was no competition from neighboring black schools, unlike NCI with nearby Fisk University. The BCI, in Bowser's opinion, was beautifully located and had a promising start. More importantly, Bowser sensed that the white establishment in Nashville questioned his ability to "run a school" and handle money. "I cannot afford to be used as a tool," Bowser argued, "when they are afraid to trust my judgment in the use of money." Bowser further believed that he was "too old" to be peripatetic: "Old men are soon kicked aside as a relic of the past, to make room for younger men. I discover this tendency in the Nashville movement, hence suggest that a younger man be considered."[21]

Bowser possessed financial, practical, and racial concerns about the Nashville Movement. He declined to relocate to middle Tennessee because the NCI Board made him no solid offer of sustained monetary support. Furthermore, Bowser's aging body and declining health made it impractical for him to leave Fort Smith. More significantly, Bowser never forgot how C. E. W. Dorris and the Nashville white establishment mistreated his black students at the Southern Practical Institute in 1920, when white leaders required African Americans to enter their own school through the back door.[22] Bowser harbored deep animosity against white leaders in Nashville, and this animosity prompted him to spurn the Nashville project. Black and white leaders alike knew of Bowser's talent and realized their need for his ability; but Bowser did not trust them. And white leaders, who controlled NCI's resources which black people themselves had actually amassed, did not fully trust Bowser.

Notwithstanding Bowser's zeal and productive efforts, the Bowser Christian Institute had to close in 1946, just as the Silver Point Christian Institute had faded twenty-eight years earlier. Four of his spiritual sons, however, as we have seen—Levi Kennedy, G. E. Steward, R. N. Hogan, and J. S. Winston—picked up the torch of leadership and in 1948 carried Bowser's dream to Fort Worth, Texas, where they launched the Southern Bible Institute (SBI). The following year, the quartet relocated the school to Terrell, Texas, and formed what is now Southwestern Christian College (SwCC).[23]

The Story of Southwestern Christian College

The story of SwCC has been told in other places which may be consulted by those who wish a fuller discussion of the school's history.[24] Four major turning points have marked the school's rich yet difficult history—the emergence of Jack Evans Sr., the achievement of full accreditation, the addition

"The Magic of Education" 153

Two of the "Big Four," J. S. Winston (1906–2002) and R. N. Hogan (1902–1997) exerted great influence on younger leaders in African American Churches of Christ. Left to right: Jack Evans Sr., James Maxwell, Winston, and Hogan in an undated photograph. Courtesy of James Maxwell.

of a four-year Bible program, and the training of future leaders of black Churches of Christ. In 1967, Jack Evans Sr. became the fourth president of SwCC, marking the first major transition in the school's history. The previous three presidents—E. W. McMillan, H. L. Barber, and A. V. Isbell—had been white leaders. McMillan, a renowned preacher and missionary in Churches of Christ, worked as SwCC's first president from 1950 to 1953, and Barber led the fledgling institution for the next three years. Isbell succeeded Barber, and during his nine-year tenure, helped to reduce the school's six-figure debt.[25]

SwCC's student body seemed to hold Isbell in high regard, dedicating the 1962 yearbook to him. The volume's editors called Isbell "our dearly beloved president" who has "blazed a trail of glory which will serve as a beacon to success for the oncoming students."[26] These effusive remarks about Isbell, however, masked deep-seated racial conflict brewing on the campus. Isbell, for example, took exception with Columbus Grimsley, a black preacher in Churches of Christ from Fort Lauderdale, Florida, who during an annual lectureship at SwCC, lifted his text from Acts 10:34–35, which highlights God's interest in all races, and denounced racial discrimination in American society. Around the same time, Arthur L. Smith, a student from Valdosta, Georgia, publicly contested Isbell's racially insensitive remarks during a chapel assembly. The white president sought to expel the black student, but Roosevelt Sams, SwCC's academic dean, intervened and quelled the dispute.[27] The friction between Isbell, Grimsley, and Smith attests that the racial strife swirling in the Lone Star State and across the nation during the 1950s and 1960s had infiltrated the Terrell campus.

To address the racial animus in American society in general and at SwCC in particular, black board members, who by 1967 outnumbered their white counterparts, usurped their authority and appointed Jack Evans Sr. as the school's fourth president. Historian Wes Crawford has correctly observed that the year 1967 marked African American Churches of Christ's transition "from segregation to independence." That year SwCC's annual lectureship focused on the earlier mentioned demise of NCI and other racial matters, along with their hopes for their struggling college. Evans remarked that "1967 was the beginning of a new definition for the school." Crawford added that "Until Evans's presidency in 1967, white school presidents had forced the school to conform into the mold of many other southern institutions."[28] Evans broke the mold of his white predecessors not only by becoming the college's first black president, but also by making black people and their concerns about race pride and social justice a priority. Additional pivotal events in SwCC's history also occurred during Evans's tenure. In 1973, Evans and his devoted Vice President, James Maxwell, led the school to full accreditation. Nine years later, SwCC implemented a four-year Bible and Religious Education Program.[29]

Regrettably, the paucity of sources hampers historians' efforts to chronicle SwCC's enrollment over the years as well as the school's other innerworkings. Notwithstanding this scarcity of information, clearly SwCC's enduring legacy has been that of preparing preachers to fill pulpits for black Churches of Christ, preachers who often led the same congregations for decades.[30] Billy Curl, a native of Nacogdoches, Texas, completed his studies at SwCC in 1962, before becoming one of the first black students at Abilene Christian College (now Abilene Christian University). Curl then worked as a missionary in Ethiopia for six years before preaching four decades at the Crenshaw Church of Christ in Los Angeles, California.[31] Daniel Harrison, an Alabama native, completed his studies at SwCC in the 1950s, before settling in Chicago, Illinois, where he has served the Chatham-Avalon congregation for almost five decades.[32] In the Northeast, two black southerners each with SwCC affiliation have served for more than fifty years. Roosevelt Wells, a native of Waco, Texas, matriculated at SwCC in the 1950s before moving to New York where he has enjoyed a lengthy preaching tenure at the Harlem Church of Christ. Eugene Lawton, from St. Petersburg, Florida, enrolled at SwCC, where he began his preaching career. Since earning advanced degrees, Lawton has preached for almost fifty years across the Hudson River from Wells at the Newark Church of Christ and has exerted tremendous influence across the brotherhood of African American Churches of Christ.[33] In 1955, Andrew Hairston, from Winston-Salem, North Carolina, earned his associate of arts degree at SwCC and preached for congregations in Waco and Fort Worth, Texas, before settling for more than fifty years with the Simpson Street Church of Christ in Atlanta, Georgia.[34] Shelton Gibbs III, an alumnus of SwCC, has preached for almost three decades for the largest black Church of Christ in the United States—the Greenville Avenue Church of Christ in Richardson, Texas.[35] The preaching careers of Curl, Harrison, Wells, Lawton, Hairston, and Gibbs illustrate the role that SwCC has played and the contribution the school has made to the strengthening and development of African American Churches of Christ. The efforts of many other SwCC trained preachers in black Churches of Christ with shorter tenures and in different geographical locations have been documented in other sources.[36]

Currently, SwCC's future hangs in the balance, as its leaders grapple with declining enrollments, waning monetary support, and often unproductive administrative decisions. In consequence, SwCC's board secured the services of Ervin Seamster, a skillful administrator and dynamic preacher for the Light of the World Church of Christ in Dallas, Texas, to save the school from complete collapse.

Subsidiary Schools among African American Churches of Christ

While SwCC presently stands as the only accredited college under the guidance of members of African Americans in Churches of Christ, other lesser known schools train and instruct those who seek to serve local congregations.

In the 1960s, many white leaders in Churches of Christ feared that some of their liberal arts colleges were becoming unorthodox in their teachings or were failing to prepare preachers appropriately. Therefore, several congregations established their own "schools of preaching," including the Bear Valley School of Preaching in Denver, the Brown Trail School of Preaching in Fort Worth, the Memphis School of Preaching in Tennessee, the Sunset School of Preaching in Lubbock, and the White's Ferry Road School of Preaching in West Monroe, Louisiana.[37]

The urge for theological orthodoxy and better preacher preparation provided the impetus for these white preaching schools. Economics, however, along with the dire need for skilled leaders, apparently prompted African Americans in Churches of Christ to launch their own "schools of preaching." In the fall of 1970, the Figueroa Church of Christ in Los Angeles, California, hosted a meeting of area ministers and leaders. Four preachers presented a plan for launching a Bible school in southern California. G. P. Holt addressed the topic "The Need for Trained Preachers." Calvin H. Bowers then explained why there was a need for a school of preaching. John Green, a recent graduate of the Sunset School of Preaching in Lubbock, Texas, spoke on "How to Develop a Preacher Training School." R. N. Hogan, Figueroa's pulpit minister, closed the meeting by urging the attendees to move forward in launching a school to train leaders and preachers.[38]

Hogan and the Figueroa leadership agreed to house the new enterprise, and they called it the Los Angeles School of Preaching. The first group of fifty-six students met on January 4, 1971, to acquire a "sound knowledge of the Bible and the skills to communicate both the Word and their personal faith in an effective manner." Through the subsequent years, the Los Angeles School of Preaching has engendered many distinguished students. Upon completing his studies there, William Harper went on to minister for several years for the Southside Church of Christ in Seattle, Washington. Vincent Hawkins, a gifted communicator, studied at the preaching school before becoming the minister of the Inglewood Church of Christ in southern California. Fate Hagood III, a charismatic leader in black Churches of Christ, matriculated at the Los Angeles School of Preaching as well as SwCC before planting the Metropolitan Church of Christ in the same city.[39]

Loyd Clay Harris, a powerful African American preacher in Churches of Christ, received training under Earnest Carter, N. L. Evans, and Mac H. Wright, and he ministered in Louisiana and Texas before becoming the pulpit minister for the Highway 82 Church of Christ in Greenville, Mississippi.

"The Magic of Education" 157

In 1978, Loyd Clay Harris, a prominent preacher in Little Rock, Arkansas, launched the School of Religious Studies in the Mississippi Delta. Harris's school has exerted profound influence on many young black preachers and leaders in African American Churches of Christ (Courtesy of Loyd Clay Harris).

Harris attended several schools: Jarvis Christian College, Stephen F. Austin University, Texas A & M University in Commerce, Texas, International Bible Institute in Orlando, Florida, and Harding School of Theology. Just as older preachers mentored Harris, he assumed the responsibility of training other young men by founding the School of Religious Studies in the Mississippi Delta in 1978. Nine years later, Harris moved his school from Greenville to Moss Point, on the Mississippi Gulf Coast, where he also assumed duties as minister for the Meridian Street Church of Christ.

After eleven fruitful years in this area, Harris in 1999 became the pulpit minister for the McAlmont Church of Christ in Little Rock, Arkansas. The School of Religious Studies continues to thrive in Arkansas, proven training for career men and women who also desire instruction in Bible, Music, and Church Leadership.[40] The School of Religious Studies, explained Harris, aims "to train preachers, elders, deacons, Bible Class teachers, and other special workers including Personal Workers; to expand our Christian work force by soul-winning, edification, and the work of the church." Harris's institution offers the following degrees and certificates: Associate of Bible Ministry, Associate of Religious Studies, Associate of Christian Counseling, Certificate of Church Leadership, Certificate of Music, Youth Ministry Certificate, and Certificate of Teacher Training.[44]

Several outstanding young preachers came under Harris's influence at the School of Religious Studies and have emerged as effective leaders in African American Churches of Christ. Willie McCord, a preacher for the 10th Avenue Church of Christ in Columbus, Mississippi; Milton Hopkins, minister to the Atlanta Street Church of Christ in Texarkana, Texas; and Kenneth Jackson, evangelist at the West Valley congregation in Little Rock, Arkansas all studied at Harris's preaching school.[42] Darrell Holt, a native of Greenville, Mississippi, received baptism at the hands of Harris in 1978, and the new convert excelled at the School of Religious Studies, graduating cum laude. Holt went on to preach for black Churches of Christ in Mississippi, Tennessee, and Michigan before settling at the historic Figueroa Church of Christ in Los Angeles, California. On October 25, 2015, the passionate and energetic evangelist died of a heart attack after preaching a sermon called "Being Happy in the Midst of a Storm." His personal motto, "The Lord's help," and his favorite song, "Hard-Fighting Soldier," attest to the zeal, passion, energy, and earnestness Holt and many other African American preachers in Churches of Christ often poured into their sermons and services.[43]

What Loyd Clay Harris had accomplished in the Magnolia State, James E. Thompson achieved in Detroit, Michigan. A Tennessee native, Thompson became a member of the Church of Christ at an early age and began his preaching career in Florida. James and his wife, Marva, relocated from the Sunshine State to the Motor City in 1967, when race riots rocked the city, killing forty-three people.[44] Thompson purposely moved to the Detroit area in order to "establish a framework for peace," and he has skillfully served and shepherded a black flock in Mt. Clemens, Michigan, for more than fifty years. In 1991, Thompson launched the Midwestern Christian Institute as part of his plan to "offer students spiritual and professional guidance in reaching their long or short-term goals in Christian education."[45]

The rise of the Los Angeles School of Preaching in southern California, the School of Religious Studies in Mississippi, and the Midwestern Christian Institute in Michigan all underscore the belief of African Americans in Churches of Christ in the "magic" of Christian education. Black Christians sought to control not only their own congregations, but also their own educational institutions. Black leaders in Churches of Christ, knowing that many of their members had no ready access to SwCC and other institutions of higher learning because of distance and limited finances, focused on developing preachers and leaders to serve and minister to congregations in local, regional, and national contexts. They produced such servants as Darrell Holt, who was taught, baptized, and trained by Loyd Clay Harris in the Mississippi Delta, and he then traversed the United States and beyond, advancing the message of "the Lord's help."

— 12 —

Brothers in Arms

African American Churches of Christ in the Global Experience

"Men, you're the first Negro tankers to ever fight in the American Army. I would never have asked for you if you weren't good. I have nothing but the best in my Army. I don't care what color you are, so long as you go up there and kill those kraut sonsabitches. Everyone has their eyes on you and is expecting great things from you. Most of all, your race is looking forward to your success. Don't let them down, and, damn you, don't let me down!"
—General George Patton, addressing the 761st Tank Battalion

"Go ye therefore, and teach all nations, baptizing them in the name of the Father, and of the Son, and of the Holy Ghost: Teaching them to observe all things whatsoever I have commanded you: and, lo, I am with you always, even unto the end of the world. Amen.
—Matthew 28:19–20

Even though born on American soil, members of black Churches of Christ branched out beyond the borders of the United States. Two global currents moved these Christians beyond the confines of America. First, the duty of military participation in the wars of the twentieth century drew young black men out of their communities and into foreign countries. One such young man was Roosevelt Sams. Born in Dime Box, Texas, in 1923, Sams was one of ten children. After graduating from Dime Box High School for black students at age twenty, Sams entered the U. S. Army. One of more than one million African Americans who served in World War II, Sams followed General George Patton into the European theater of the war. There he earned four prestigious

Roosevelt Sams (1923–2003) served in the U. S. military during World War II before returning home and aligning with African American Churches of Christ. Sams left an indelible mark on his faith tradition as an educator and evangelist. Courtesy of Izetta Sams.

medals and an honorable discharge at war's end. As part of what journalist Tom Brokaw has called "the greatest generation," Sams returned to the Lone Star State and earned a bachelor's degree in education at Paul Quinn College, using the benefits under the G.I. Bill. Sams then married his high school sweetheart, Izetta Christman. In 1953, he received a master's degree in administration from Texas Southern University in Houston; two years later, Sams became academic dean at Southwestern Christian College in Terrell, serving at that post for eight years. In 1969, Sams became minister of what is now the Dell Crest Church of Christ in San Antonio, retiring twenty-one years later.

Roosevelt Sams's story provides a microcosmic view of African American Churches of Christ in the global experience. Pulled by military service into a foreign country, Sams labored as an American soldier on the battlefield, but returned home to wage war on the religious error of black religious groups—a soldier two times over—physically and spiritually.

A second, more voluntary, desire to evangelize peoples in other lands compelled other blacks in Churches of Christ to work on foreign fields. Young men and women, stirred by a passion to serve and please God, a passion driven by evangelistic fervor and a world awareness prompted by war, crossed the Atlantic and Pacific Oceans to disseminate the "pure gospel" to others.

This chapter examines the global experiences of African Americans in Churches of Christ who fought spiritual battles at home and literal battles abroad.

Hard Fighting Soldiers in World War I

Historians John Hope Franklin and Evelyn Brooks Higginbotham, in their seminal work, *From Slavery to Freedom*, pointed out that even though more than two million African Americans registered for service in World War I, only 367,000 were actually called into action.[2] In 1918, S. R. Cassius reported giving two of his offspring to the First World War. He proudly announced that one son, William M. Cassius, served in the Philippines, while the other, John F. Rowe Cassius, was stationed in France. At a time when pacifism was rife in Churches of Christ,[3] Cassius, buoyed by a sense of black pride, boasted about his sons' participation in the war, exclaiming that the "negro is no slacker."[4]

In her autobiography, *Another World Wonder*, Annie C. Tuggle noted that her brother Dewey H. Tuggle fought in World War I.[5] As the first unofficial historian of African American Churches of Christ, Tuggle also provided biographical sketches of three men who served in World War I. C. L. Caperton, born in Alabama in 1897, saw action in the First World War in Europe. Seventeen year old, Joe N. Mitchell, left his home in Caldwell, Texas, joined the Army, and served twenty-two months abroad. A. J. Rodgers, a Chicago native, enlisted in the Navy during World War I. His travels to foreign countries allowed him to mingle with "great peoples of the earth" and learn "many useful trades."[6]

Regrettably, we do not know the specific tasks or roles the aforementioned men filled when stationed overseas. Yet, significantly three of the foregoing men—Caperton, Mitchell, and Rodgers—converted to African American Churches of Christ and entered the preaching ministry after World War I. Perhaps wartime experiences softened their hearts and forced them to ponder their own mortality. Regardless of the reasons for their conversions, Caperton and Rodgers received baptism under the preaching of Marshall Keeble.[7]

Hard Fighting Soldiers in World War II

The bombing of Pearl Harbor thrust the United States into World War II, and sources reveal that some three million African Americans registered for service in that conflict. Of this number, approximately one million blacks saw action in the Army, 165,000 in the Navy, and seventeen thousand in the Marine Corps, and five thousand in the Coast Guard.[8] Of these numbers, it remains unclear how many claimed membership in African American Churches of Christ.

A few African American soldiers affiliated with Churches of Christ wrote to the *Christian Echo* to express themselves. In 1943, Elbert Hudson, who converted to a Church of Christ in Kilgore, Texas, reported: "I am still overseas, but holding onto the one faith." He acknowledged sending $5.00 to G. P. Bowser for the "fine work that he is doing, adding that he hoped "we meet again."[9] A month later, Kermit Nixon, a native of Midway, Texas, informed *Christian Echo* readers that he was stationed at Camp Gordon, Georgia. In his brief report, Nixon revealed his rigid exclusivistic theology by delineating the "five steps" one must take to become a member of "Christ's church." Displaying his deep desire to evangelize others even while away from home, Nixon also admitted that he was a soldier guided by dual loyalties, asserting: "Though I am in the U. S. Army, I am determined to fight for Christ."[10] Unsurprisingly, when he returned home from war, Nixon poured his life into teaching and preaching the "pure gospel." He spent several years ministering to the Sinclair Street Church of Christ in Gladewater, Texas.[11]

In the summer of 1943, Lloyd L. Watkins provided the *Christian Echo* audience with a glimpse into the horrors of war. "We are now engaged in a war, a great war, and a long war, and a fighting war. A war where there is no peace, and a war that makes man think of the promise God made to those of the body of Christ, that he 'shall wipe away all tears.'" Watkins felt that the brutality of war compelled soldiers to contemplate their own mortality and their eternal destiny. Unfortunately, we know nothing of Watkins's background or his location during World War II, but we do know that he was an African American Christian who desired to see men turn away from "war machines" and draw "closer to God."[12]

Tyree G. Wells: A Hard Fighting Soldier in the Korean War

A young man who experienced firsthand the excruciating pain of war was Tyree G. Wells, a native of Neches, Texas. Wells's mother reared her young family seventeen miles east, in Jacksonville. There, Wells attended the segregated schools, but fell short of completing his high school diploma. A member of African American Churches of Christ since age thirteen, Wells described himself as a "working boy" with little academic acumen and no interest in sports. Thus, when he enlisted in the U. S. Army after World War II, he exclaimed, "I have found a home."[13]

But his military "home" proved dangerous. Sent to Korea shortly after the outbreak of conflict, in November 1950, the day after Thanksgiving, Wells and his all-black 24th Infantry came under attack from North Korean soldiers. Wells recalled that the Koreans "were everywhere. I raised my rifle to fire and then I was shot in my jaw." The wound left a permanent scar that "looks like a dimple." After nine hours of grueling fighting, forty-five out of his fifty-three platoon members had been killed; Wells was one of the eight Americans captured.[14]

Over a three-year period of brutal captivity, Wells and his fellow prisoners of war ate two meals each day—breakfast and supper—consisting of barley, cracked corn, and rice. Their captors forced the prisoners to work for eight hours each day building mud huts, leveling hills, and working on drill fields. Korea's short hot summers did not trouble Wells, but the bitterly cold winters were a different matter. "It was so cold the fog turned to ice; the air was full of ice." Wells's ordeal ended only in July 1953, when he was among the contingent of prisoners freed during the prisoner exchange in Panmunjon.[15]

Notwithstanding Wells's trying experiences in the Korean War, he gave more than twenty years to the U. S. military, serving a government that, while it had desegregated the military forces in 1948, remained complicit in the denial of civil rights to African Americans. But Wells maintained his faith in God; and upon leaving the Army, he aligned with the all-black Border Street Church of Christ (now the Seminary Heights Church of Christ) in Jacksonville, Texas, where he has served dutifully as a song leader and Bible class teacher for many years.[16]

Regrettably, the paucity of sources makes it difficult to produce a complete portrait of the military experience of African Americans in Churches of Christ. Yet the testimony of Wells confirms that black men in Churches of Christ at times found a place in the U. S. military, contributing to peace and security both at home and abroad.

Hard Fighting Spiritual Soldiers on Foreign Soil

Evangelization efforts abroad actually predate the Civil War. Alexander Cross was the first known black missionary associated with the Stone-Campbell Movement who traveled abroad. In 1854, white Disciples sent Cross and his wife to Liberia to preach to the people there, but the mission failed when Cross contracted "immigrant's fever" and died prematurely.[17] In the twentieth century, S. R. Cassius published articles in a Canadian newspaper, *Bible Student*, calling the publication "full of good things" and hoping it gained enough support to establish it as "a permanent factor among the churches."[18] But Cassius did more than merely publish in a Canadian journal; he also traveled to that land and preached there on at least two occasions.[19]

In 1960, white benefactors financed Marshall Keeble's travels abroad to Africa, Asia, and Europe. Lucien Palmer, a white missionary, accompanied Keeble on this trip. When preaching in Nigeria, Keeble marveled that some Africans, after hearing the message of salvation, literally ran "into the water to be baptized. They ran. After getting into the water, they ran. That is the gospel that is so powerful and quick that it saves. That is the word of God." While in Nigeria, Keeble taught classes in the Nigerian Christian Village Schools and received many honors, including a robe and a "cane of authority." By 1960, when the civil rights movement in the United States was gaining ground, Keeble had become a global evangelist, observing: "A Christian can't go to Africa without being reminded of our Lord's commission."[20]

Black Churches of Christ in Nigeria

After World War II, as black Churches of Christ increased numerically and prospered financially, a growing concern arose about impoverished and unevangelized peoples beyond American shores. In the early 1960s, when many black Americans participated in sit-ins, freedom rides, and other nonviolent protests, certain African American leaders in Churches of Christ turned their attention abroad. In 1961, F. F. Carson, a leading proponent of global evangelism in African American Churches of Christ, sought to prod *Christian Echo* readers out of their complacency. When urging black congregations to support Myles T. Tune, a white Christian missionary to Hong Kong and alumnus of David Lipscomb College (now Lipscomb University), Carson challenged black Christians to remember the less fortunate. "It is hard for us who live in America with so many modern conveniences, ways and means to take care of those who are sick, food and lodging for those who are in need to realize what it means to be without food, clothing, medical care and the only roof over their heads, the canopy of heaven."[21]

Following his own convictions, in 1964, Carson traveled with Levi Kennedy to Nigeria and baptized 650 people in twenty days. R. N. Hogan called the feat "a record breaking event."²² While in Nigeria, Kennedy and Carson stayed with white Christians Glenn Martin and his wife; Carson also found housing with other white missionaries. "To me," Kennedy asserted, "they are real Christians." Even though he believed that whites accomplished good work among Nigerians, Kennedy insisted that American blacks could achieve much more, "since the color of their skin is as ours and they look upon us as their native sons returning to home shore to assist our fathers in this struggle for independence." "My affirmation," added Kennedy, "needs no qualifying for our recent visit there with its results prove without a doubt that Negro preachers can do a great job if they can be encouraged to go over there and work. I want you to *underscore* the word *WORK*."²³

Carson and Kennedy certainly were not afraid of hard work. Carson ministered to the North Richmond Church of Christ in northern California; Kennedy served black people living at Chicago's Southside at the Michigan Avenue Church of Christ (now Sheldon Heights Church of Christ). But reaching beyond their local concerns, these two men challenged their entire brotherhood of African American Churches of Christ to raise funds for the "Nigerian work."²⁴ R. N. Hogan, a diligent and highly successful minister at the Figueroa Church of Christ in Los Angeles, California, urged his *Christian Echo* audience to help Mrs. Carson accompany her husband to Nigeria. "She is worthy of all that can be done to help and encourage her to go. The women in Nigeria need teaching in many ways and Sister Carson is qualified to do it."²⁵

A decade later, the *Christian Echo* reported that there were eighty thousand Nigerians affiliated with Churches of Christ. The Avalon Church of Christ in Los Angeles and the Schrader Lane Church of Christ in Nashville, Tennessee, had joined the cause in lending their moral and financial support to mission work in Nigeria.²⁶

Black Churches of Christ in Ethiopia

By the spring of 1964, Billy Curl, a native of Nacogdoches, Texas, had completed two degrees: one in Bible at Southwestern Christian College and the other in Speech Therapy at Abilene Christian College (now Abilene Christian University). He then answered the call to do missionary work in Ethiopia among deaf children. John C. Stevens, then Abilene Christian's Vice-President, highly recommended Curl as a competent "Christian gentleman." His new bride, Mary, who had recently earned her nursing degree at ACC, planned to accompany him to East Africa "to provide simple medical care" for those living near the compound where they would work. The Curls received sufficient funds to move to Africa, most of their support coming from the Uptown Church of Christ in San Francisco, California.[27]

Two months after arriving in Ethiopia, Curl reported that the church work in Addis Ababa was progressing nicely. The "plan of salvation" astonished many Ethiopians who said: "I have not heard this before." One man, after hearing Curl's teaching, exclaimed: "I want to be baptized now—I don't want to wait." The believer's enthusiasm impressed Curl, who wrote: "It was a cold and rainy evening and we were encouraged by the stand he took. Many more have desired to be baptized during the evenings, although it was cold and raining." Curl expressed particular interest in the deaf population of Ethiopia, noting that a Deaf School would open with twenty-six students, part of an estimated 35,000 handicapped people in the country. He then warned *Christian Echo* readers: "Should we neglect these because they have a problem, then remember they will have to be judged in the Last Days just as we."[28]

The following spring, Curl reported greater interest and progress concerning the Ethiopian mission. Seven students had enrolled in a sewing class, while five students worked in an umbrella factory. Weekly Bible classes increased, creating a shortage of space and exhausting Curl's printed teaching material. "There is such an eagerness to learn on the part of the students and their desire for the Bible material keep our stock of lessons low. We can hardly get new printed lessons fast enough." Impassioned students wanted their friends to learn biblical truths. In light of such receptiveness, Curl was eager to "capitalize on the many opportunities that are being presented to us here."[29]

Eleven years later, R. N. Hogan again rallied African American Churches of Christ to reach out to starving Ethiopians, then suffering a severe famine. Calling starvation "one of the worst deaths that a person can die," he urged black Christians to support financially Calvin H. Bowers and his wife, Mozell, and Billy Curl and his wife, Mary, to serve on this "mission of mercy." Hogan entreated his *Christian Echo* readers to consider famished Ethiopians when frivolously spending money on entertainment, soft drinks, chewing gum, and cigarettes. "May God help us to open our hearts," pled Hogan, "and share our blessings with poverty stricken and starving people."[30] Presently, the diligent efforts of Curl, Hogan, Bowers, and others resulted in the establishment of thirty congregations in Ethiopia with 30,000 members.[31]

Black Churches of Christ in Liberia, West Africa

In the winter of 1966, a curious letter came across the desk of Roosevelt C. Wells, minister of the Washington Heights Church of Christ in New York City. A native of Waco, Texas, and graduate of Southwestern Christian College, Wells found his way to New York after serving black congregations in Texas and Oklahoma. The letter Wells received came from "a Rev. Gibson from Monrovia, Liberia," who was disgruntled with the theology of area churches; consequently, he established his own church, but sought an American bishop to help him organize it. Wells replied to the letter and then sent Gibson a copy of his book, *Ye Shall Know the Truth*. "I knew this would be the turning point," Wells concluded, "for if they replied after reading my book, they could be converted." After receiving a response from a still-dissatisfied Gibson, Wells left for Liberia on June 7, 1966. Upon arrival, Wells encountered people willing to listen and learn. Wells's powerful preaching yielded forty-eight baptisms, including the preacher, Gibson. Wells then reported: "We greatly rejoice that for the first time, the truth of the Gospel has been planted in the nation of Liberia, city of Monrovia, a city of over one and one-half million people."[32]

In the winter of 1967, Wells returned to Liberia and recorded thirty-five responses, as well as a new church plant in nearby Painesville. One of Wells's new converts was Paul Williams, who came to the United States and enrolled at Southwestern Christian College to prepare himself for the preaching ministry.[33]

In the spring of 1968 just before the assassination of Martin Luther King Jr., Wells reported to the *Christian Echo* readership that many "wonderful things" had been achieved through the missionary endeavors of the Washington Heights Church of Christ. First, electricity had been installed in the house of worship in Monrovia. Second, Paul Williams, a native Liberian, had been baptized and was now studying at Southwestern Christian College. Third, an elementary school had been established. Fourth, "Project Complete" had been launched to furnish Bibles, communion trays, and tracts for black Christians in Liberia. Fifth, plans for a citywide campaign—"Operate Saturate Monrovia—had been made to "turn the city of Monrovia upside-down." Wells then pled with the brotherhood of African American Churches of Christ: "Now is the time TO ACT NOT TALK."[34]

Black Churches of Christ in the West Indies

In 1963, O. L. Trone, a black Church of Christ minister in Detroit, Michigan, expressed interest in planting the "pure gospel" in Nassau, Bahamas. His prospects for evangelism there heightened when William Miller, a native of Nassau and former Anglican, converted to Churches of Christ. Generous Christians helped fund Miller's education at Southwestern Christian College; he then returned to Nassau, where he ministered to a congregation of forty people. In dire need of a house of worship and monetary support, Trone appealed: "The Bahamas field is ripe and ready to be harvested. About 85 percent of the people there have never heard of the Church of Christ, much less the gospel of Christ. What are we going to do about it?"[35]

In answer to this appeal, the following year Trone, his wife, Jeanette and Annie C. Tuggle arranged to travel with the latter's husband O. L. Trone to Jamaica to save souls. Trone had sent out an additional appeal to his fellowship: "The Churches of Christ here in America have a great door of opportunity open to them to send labourers to the islands scattered in the Caribbean Sea. Many in these ports are hungering and thirsting for the true gospel of the Lord Jesus Christ, but the labourers are few."[36]

In 1967, Tuggle, after garnering financial resources from black believers across the country, returned and spent three weeks in the Bahamas, Jamaica, and Haiti. In Kingston, Jamaica, she addressed a group of nurses and encouraged them in their efforts. Upon returning to her home congregation, the Vance Avenue Church of Christ in Memphis, Tennessee, Tuggle sought out a Gospel preacher to go to Jamaica to see the "great opportunities there." She found one of her "sons in the faith," Woodie W. Morrison, a black evangelist for the Collegiate Heights Church of Christ in Dayton, Ohio. The young preacher heeded Tuggle's prodding, traveled abroad, and ministered in Jamaica. Morrison acknowledged Tuggle's influence, noting that, "after hearing this humble, God-fearing, battle-scarred Christian soldier speak, I knew I had to go to Jamaica...."[37]

Black Churches of Christ in Guyana, South America

At times an individual conversion in the United States opened doors for African Americans in Churches of Christ to evangelize globally. In 1964, Alfred and Gloria McCurchin relocated from Guyana to Southern California. While studying at Pepperdine University to earn an engineering degree,

Alfred met Carroll Pitts, minister at the black Normandie Church of Christ in Los Angeles, California, who taught the immigrant the "Bible plan of salvation." Enthusiastic about knowing "the right way," McCurchin became impassioned about carrying the truth back to his people in South America. The Normandie congregation furnished McCurchin with full financial support as he studied two years at the Sunset School of Preaching in Lubbock, Texas, equipping him to serve effectively in his homeland.[38]

In 1968, the Normandie church cast its full moral and monetary support behind the McCurchins, sending them on a survey trip to determine a "suitable place" to establish a congregation in their homeland. The next year, the McCurchins returned and won their first convert, George McCurchin, Alfred's brother. In 1970, ministers and members in African American Churches of Christ in southern California joined with Pitts and others from the Normandie congregation and conducted a Vacation Bible School in Guyana, baptizing sixteen people. By 1973, six small congregations totaling two hundred members had been established in Guyana, and native ministers served these local churches. One minister, William Pantlitz, had formerly preached for two decades for the Roman Catholic Church; upon learning "the truth," Pantlitz received baptism into Churches of Christ and persuaded sixty out of his sixty-two congregants to join him. Pantlitz's decision cost him his house, however, as Catholic officials evicted him from the parsonage that he himself had erected.[39]

In 1974, the *Christian Echo* announced plans to send two full time missionaries to Guyana for two years. African American Churches of Christ in Southern California and beyond pooled their resources to send Willie and Samuella Lockert to Guyana. The husband had received baptism into the Church of Christ in Tennessee, but preached briefly in Detroit, Michigan, before ministering thirty years in California. After having traveled and served successfully in Guyana a year earlier, the Lockerts eagerly anticipated their return to Guyana. "After our two-week campaign there this summer we see, more than ever before," Willie Lockert wrote, "the real need for black Americans to go into full-time mission work."[40] Lockert's comment reflected a growing sentiment of many African American ministers in Churches of Christ in the second half of the twentieth century.

The missionary activity of African American Churches of Christ in Guyana is instructive for three reasons. First, a conversion of one person on American soil created openings for evangelism abroad, as the baptism of Alfred McCurchin led to inroads into South America. Second, by the late 1960s and

1970s, some African American Churches of Christ had become financially stable enough to support their own ministers as well as missionaries both at home and abroad. Third, and perhaps most importantly, during the upheavals of the civil rights era, African American Churches of Christ found a way to channel their energy and resources beyond the United States. Constantly dogged by the issues of race and racism in their homeland, African Americans in Churches of Christ gained a degree of relief for themselves by helping foreigners find peace with God. In this fashion, African American Churches of Christ in a sense lived double lives, straddling two complex worlds.

The lives of the leaders described above exemplify a fundamental shift in the activities of black Churches of Christ. S. R. Cassius, Marshall Keeble, F. F. Carson, Levi Kennedy, R. N. Hogan, Billy Curl, O. L. Trone, R. C. Wells, and Annie C. Tuggle—all native southerners with enslaved people in their ancestry—possessed an intense desire to help, to serve, and to save peoples abroad. All took their exclusivistic theology to foreign soil. While they knew about the civil rights movement at home and deeply felt the sting of racial discrimination, all chose to turn outward to unsaved outsiders. In the 1950s and 1960s, African Americans in Churches of Christ, fortified and emboldened by newfound numerical and monetary strength, turned primarily to their own people for financial support to fulfill in foreign lands what they viewed as their own duties under Christ's Great Commission.

EPILOGUE

From the Outhouse to the White House

The Paradox of Black Churches of Christ During the Obama Presidency

"Injustice anywhere is a threat to justice everywhere."
—Martin Luther King Jr., *Letter from Birmingham Jail*

"If there is anyone out there who still doubts that America is a place where all things are possible; who still wonders if the dream of our founders is alive in our time; who still questions the power of our democracy, tonight is your answer."
—Barack Obama, November 4, 2008

Mirroring the pilgrimage of black people in the United States, pain and paradox, as well as progress, permeates the story of African American Churches of Christ. Born in the shadow of chattel enslavement and rising in a culture of segregation stained by lynch law, African Americans in Churches of Christ formed their own distinct identity in the Jim Crow Era. Black founders resisted racism and discrimination, even while appealing to white Christians for monetary support; black leaders possessed the spiritual fortitude to contest what they believed to be religious error, but they lacked financial resources. At the same time, many white believers across the South yearned to have their black neighbors hear and obey the "pure gospel," but they dared not welcome them into their own congregations, plagued as they were by an overmastering fear of miscegenation. S. R. Cassius, like a prophet in the American wilderness, paved the way for his spiritual successors, as he fought against such racist attitudes prevalent in white churches as well as the broader society in which he lived.

Unlike Cassius, who railed constantly against antiblack literature and racist cinematic presentations, the most eminent black evangelist in Churches of Christ, Marshall Keeble, kept silent about such matters; he focused, rather, on saving souls. G. P. Bowser and his protégés—Levi Kennedy, G. E. Steward, R. N. Hogan, and J. S. Winston—would move down the same path as that of Cassius by openly castigating racism in white schools and churches. Women such as Annie C. Tuggle and Thelma Holt, for the most part, stood apart from such controversies yet still contributed significantly to the rise and expansion of African American Churches of Christ as teachers, missionaries, songsters, counselors, and nurturers.

Still other African Americans in Churches of Christ displayed concern for their people in the United States but focused their interest on those beyond their homeland. Drawn from their own country by the Second World War, many young black men urged their churches to follow the divine mandate to evangelize "all nations," and black Churches of Christ slowly gained sufficient strength in numbers and funds to send their missionaries to foreign lands. Aid for the poor beyond American borders also touched the hearts of many in black churches. R. N. Hogan often pled with *Christian Echo* readers to share their God-given blessings with impoverished peoples abroad. African Americans in Churches of Christ—collectively and individually—responded to Hogan's call and increased the charitable work and foreign membership rolls.

"Face to Face" with President Bill Clinton

In the last decade of the twentieth century, African American Churches of Christ showed interest in political issues. In the fall of 1993, W. F. Washington, a prominent black preacher for a three-thousand-member congregation in Fort Lauderdale, Florida, had a thrilling experience when he met President Bill Clinton and Hillary Clinton. The Clintons were in southern Florida to thank their supporters for helping with the 1992 victorious presidential campaign. The black preacher and white president shared similarities as fellow southerners and as children born to single mothers in impoverished backgrounds. "To be able to speak face to face with the President of the United States," the black Church of Christ evangelist testified, "if only for a moment, given where I've come from, speaks volumes." Upon his encounter with the chief executive, Washington told the Clintons that he was praying for them, and he expressed delight over Clinton's educational proposal to aid college students repay their school loans by doing community service in cities facing extreme poverty.[1]

When asked about social and political issues that were crucial to black advancement, Washington explained that the three E's—education, economics, and empowerment—were paramount. "When African Americans get their economic priorities straight," he elaborated, "any number of us can rise up and make a difference." Washington, while acknowledging the demoralizing and lingering effects of racism, challenged fellow blacks to prepare themselves to withstand racial discrimination. "Racism," the black minister added, "is like the weather; it will always be there, but if we fail to put on proper clothes, we will catch our death of cold." When asked if he was a politician, Washington affirmed: "No, I'm saved and a Christian. That's sufficient."[2]

Even though Washington never openly disclosed his political affiliation, he, like most African Americans, was aligned with the Democratic party. Washington's testimony further attests that while he was primarily preoccupied with preaching God's Gospel, he felt compelled to step beyond the pulpit to address the educational, racial, social, and political needs of African Americans. Indeed, for most African American preachers deeply concerned about meeting the spiritual and physical needs of their flock, being a Christian uninvolved in social and political issues was never enough.

African American Churches of Christ in the Twenty-First Century

The twenty-first century opened with conflict, fear, and controversy. The year 2000, often known simply as Y2K, was projected by some to create havoc in computer networks around the world. This prompted a widespread fear, stirring many families in America to purchase generators and to stockpile food and water supplies. The 2000 presidential contest between Republican George W. Bush and Democrat Al Gore resulted in political turmoil as the former won the disputed electoral college while the latter earned more popular votes. A Republican-dominated U. S. Supreme Court endorsed the election of George W. Bush, driving a deeper political wedge between American people in different political parties.

Amid this political controversy, theological conflict ensnared many African American Churches of Christ. In 2000, Jerry A. Taylor, a skilled African American preacher in Churches of Christ, launched the New Wineskins

Movement which urged Christians to strive for "honest evaluation and critique of Churches of Christ." Five years later, Taylor and his colaborers organized an "Undoing Racism in Churches of Christ and Beyond" conference which convened at the North Richland Hills Church of Christ in Texas. The gathering, attended by both black and white preachers from across the United States, addressed issues of poverty, racism, crime, and struggling black families.[3] That same year, Rick Hunter, an erudite preacher in southern California, presented a position paper at an annual lectureship in California, arguing in substance that "God saves, and God has children everywhere, God has saved them and not where a particular faith tradition says a person is saved or by their particular exclusive practice."[4] Hunter's bold stance ignited controversy among leaders in black Churches of Christ.

Such theological turmoil in African American Churches of Christ coincided with the political shifting in American society. In 2008, the citizenry of the United States elected the first African American president, Barack H. Obama. In earlier times, descendants of enslaved Africans would have never imagined a black president. As historians John Hope Franklin and Evelyn Brooks Higginbotham put it succinctly, "for the vast majority of those standing in the cold winter chill of Inauguration Day, the sight of a black president of the United States and a black First Lady, Michelle Obama, would once have been inconceivable. They may have also watched the president's swearing in, while simultaneously marveling at the idea of a black First Family as the occupants of the White House."[5] Barack Obama won 95% of the black vote, most likely reflecting the percentage of blacks in Churches of Christ who supported him; Bernice Watts, an African American woman in the East Capitol Street Church of Christ in Washington, DC, no doubt reflected the sentiment of most of her coreligionists: "It means so much to me see an African-American man become president of the United States. I hoped for this day, but I never thought that I would see it."[6]

Black barbershops, black schools, and black colleges and universities were replete with posters celebrating Obama's rise. Most black preachers in Churches of Christ, although eschewing some of his political pronouncements, placed portraits of President Obama on their office walls. The black chief executive acknowledged that "the folks in African American neighborhoods . . . identify with me even if they disagree with my policies."[7] Yet the killing of unarmed black men—Trayvon Martin in Florida, Michael Brown in Missouri, Eric Garner in New York, Dontre Hamilton in Wisconsin, Tamir Rice in Ohio, Walter Scott in South Carolina, and Freddie Gray in

From the Outhouse to the White House 177

Many African Americans expressed great pride when Barack Obama was elected President of the United States in 2008 and re-elected in 2012. This photograph reflects the excitement many African Americans felt when Obama ascended to the presidency. Courtesy of Thomas and Sons Funeral Home in Kaufman, Texas.

Maryland, among others—revealed the still-deep racial animosities infecting the nation. These events ignited storms of protests across the country while inspiring the rise of the "Black Lives Matter" movement in 2013 during President Obama's second term. The swirling of racial tension across America tempered the enthusiasm and optimism many African Americans had held for the country and her first black president.

Black Churches of Christ could not, of course, remain untouched by these affairs. On August 9, 2014, a white police officer, Darren Wilson, fatally shot a young black man, Michael Brown, in Ferguson, Missouri. After a grand jury refused to indict Wilson for killing Brown, the Ferguson Heights Church of Christ in Ferguson found itself engulfed in racial and social chaos. Brian Owens, a resident of Ferguson and member of the Ferguson Heights congregation, affirmed that "Worship is our protest." In Owens's view, "Christ's righteous revolution" involved fighting for hearts and souls—not in taking to the streets and staging protests. Conversely, Tanya Smith Brice, a member of the Church of Christ and professor at Benedict College in Columbia, South Carolina, has insisted that Christians have a divine and moral obligation to disrupt unjust systems.[8] Owens reflects the Marshall Keeble tradition of standing apart from social issues and refusing to contest racial discrimination and racial violence against African Americans openly, while Brice represents the stance reaching back to Cassius and Bowser, who fought racial injustice in American society.

On June 17, 2015, Dylann Roof, a twenty-one-year-old white supremacist, calmly walked into the all-black Emanuel African Methodist Episcopal Church in Charleston, South Carolina, and, after sitting quietly in a Bible class, rose and gunned down nine black parishioners. Roof proclaimed he intended to spark a "race war." In the wake of this tragedy, Bobby Green Jr., a black Church of Christ preacher in Charleston, struggled to heal members of his congregation. "One thing we struggle with is self-hatred . . . because of the conditions," maintained Green. "We need to appreciate our cultural contributions to our community—even if they're not appreciated by others. As a church, our vision is to produce a community that loves God, loves our neighbors and loves ourselves. Nothing else matters."[9]

While racial tension engulfed the nation, theological conflict continued to roil African American Churches of Christ. In August 2015, in Houston, Texas, Tommy Brooks, minister of the Highland Heights Church of Christ, invited H. Clay Williams and several other black ministers to a meeting designed to organize a "new national lectureship." Brooks and Williams, among others, insisted that some African American preachers in Churches of Christ had become unsound and unspiritual by allowing rhythmic handclapping, praise dancing, sexual immorality, and permitting preachers to wear the title "Dr."[10] Notwithstanding the earnest pleas of Jack Evans Sr. and other preachers from Terrell and Southwestern Christian College, Williams and his cohorts launched their inaugural lectureship from March 12–16, 2017—the National Church of Christ Lectureship—in DeSoto, Texas.[11] The lectureship's long-term effects remain to be seen, but the movement could possibly signal a fragmentation in black Churches of Christ.

Eight months before these ultraconservative African Americans in Churches of Christ launched their "new lectureship," however, more tragedy touched the era of the Obama presidency; on July 7, 2016, a black sniper, Micah Johnson, opened fire in Dallas, Texas, killing five white police officers.

Instead of averting their eyes from the upheaval, several black preachers in Churches of Christ immediately stepped forward to help heal the city of Dallas. J. K. Hamilton, minister of the Mountain View Church of Christ, walked across the street from the church and prayed with the officers of the Dallas Police Department. The Sunday morning after the violence, Jon W. Morrison, pulpit preacher for the Cedar Crest Church of Christ, the oldest black congregation in Dallas, delivered a stirring sermon entitled, "Holding On to Hope in a Hostile Country." Morrison told his audience: "You may feel discouraged personally. You may feel discriminated against racially. But God is still with us, and God is still with you." On Sunday night, the predominantly black Southern Hills Church of Christ in Dallas hosted a citywide prayer service. Carl Sherman, an African American Church of Christ preacher and mayor of the Dallas suburb of DeSoto, led a special prayer for law enforcement officers. In his opening remarks, Sherman affirmed: "Good will always reign over evil," adding: "Now, blue lives matter, and so do black lives matter. If Paul were here today, he would say Christian lives matter."[12] The words and works of Hamilton, Morrison, and Sherman illustrate a shifting of many African American preachers in Churches of Christ. Many black preachers in Churches of Christ in years past had remained virtually silent on issues of racial discrimination and social injustice. But today many young ministers in black Churches of Christ stand ready to voice concern about the social as well as the spiritual salvation of their followers.

The tragic episodes of racial violence and the killing of innocent black people in an era of America's first black president remain deeply troubling. The rise of Barack Obama clearly did not signal the demise of racism, and Americans, black and white, still face an uncertain journey ahead. Yet the founding fathers and mothers of black Churches of Christ, after spending years of toiling, scratching, clawing, and fighting to secure social justice and spiritual salvation for black people, would surely stand amazed at the progress many African American Churches of Christ and their members enjoy today. And the extraordinary strides made by black Churches of Christ in the years since slavery's end presage great things for these churches in the future. The path ahead may not resemble that taken in the past, but black leaders stand on the shoulders of spiritual giants, and their road will surely lead to even greater accomplishments in years to come.

NOTES

PROLOGUE

1. African American Churches of Christ trace their spiritual heritage back to the Stone-Campbell Movement or Restoration Movement, a religious group organized by Barton W. Stone (1772–1844) and Alexander Campbell (1788–1866), white Christian preachers who sought to "restore" New Testament Christianity in nineteenth-century America. For scholarly works on the history of the Stone-Campbell Movement, see David Edwin Harrell's two volumes, *Quest for a Christian America: The Disciples of Christ and American Society to 1866* (Tuscaloosa: University of Alabama Press, 2003 [1966]); vols. 1 and 2 of *A Social History of the Disciples of Christ* and *The Social Sources of Division of the Disciples of Christ, 1865–1900* (Tuscaloosa: University of Alabama Press, 2003 [1973]); Richard T. Hughes, *Reviving the Ancient Faith: The Story of Churches of Christ in America* (Grand Rapids, MI: Eerdmans Publishing, 1996); and Douglas A. Foster and others, eds., *The Encyclopedia of the Stone-Campbell Movement* (Grand Rapids, MI: Eerdmans Publishing, 2004).

2. The author concurs with George M. Frederickson's definition of racism, namely, the "hostile or negative feelings of one ethnic group or 'people' toward another and the actions resulting from such attitudes." Frederickson adds, "Racism exists when one ethnic group or historical collectively dominates, excludes, or seeks to eliminate another on the basis of differences that it believes are hereditary and unalterable." See Frederickson, *Racism: A Short History* (Princeton: Princeton University Press, 2002), 1, 170. According to theologians Gayraud S. Wilmore and James H. Cone, racism means the "conscious or unconscious belief in the inherent superiority of persons of European ancestry, especially those of northern European origin, which entitled these persons and all white persons to a position of power, dominance, and special privilege. The white racists believe that all black people, especially those of African ancestry, are innately inferior and this justifies the subordination and exploitation of the black man by the white man." See Gayraud S. Wilmore and James H. Cone, editors, *Black Theology: A Documentary History, 1966–1979* (Maryknoll, NY: Orbis Books, 1979), 280.

3. "Meet Our Ministers," *Christian Echo 35* (Aug. 20, 1940): 2.

4. Edward J. Robinson, *The Fight Is On in Texas: A History of African American Churches of Christ in the Lone Star State, 1865–2000* (Abilene, TX: Abilene Christian University Press, 2008), 137–43.

5. Francis Frank Carson and Francis Perry Carson, *A Matter of Faith* (Houston, TX: Whitley's Publishing and Printing, 1991), 27.

6. Ibid., 29.

7. K. C. Thomas helped launched the oldest African American Church of Christ in Dallas, Texas: the Cedar Crest Church of Christ. Thomas served the Cedar Crest congregation from 1924 to 1928 before moving on to plant what is now the Lawrence and Marder Church of Christ in 1928. See Robinson, *The Fight Is On in Texas*, 40–44.

8. Carson and Carson, *A Matter of Faith*, 29–30.

9. Ibid.

10. Ibid.

11. Ibid., 135–36.

12. Ibid., 33–37, 97.

13. W. E. B. Du Bois, *The Souls of Black Folk* (Boston: Bedford/St. Martin's, 1997 [1903]), 38.

14. Carson, *A Matter of Faith*, 39.

15. Earl I. West, *The Search for the Ancient Order: A History of the Restoration Movement, 1900–1918* (Indianapolis: Religious Book Service, 1979); Leroy Garrett, The Stone-Campbell Movement: An Anecdotal History of Three Churches (Joplin: College Press, 1987); Richard T. Hughes, *Reviving the Ancient Faith*; Robert Hooper, *A Distinct People: A History of Churches of Christ in the 20th Century* (West Monroe, LA: Howard Publishing, 1993), 255–80.

16. Edward J. Robinson, *To Save My Race from Abuse: The Life of Samuel Robert Cassius* (Tuscaloosa: University of Alabama Press, 2007); Edward J. Robinson, *Show Us How You Do It: Marshall Keeble and the Rise of Black Churches of Christ in the United States, 1914–1968* (Tuscaloosa: University of Alabama Press, 2008).

17. Calvin H. Bowers, *Realizing the California Dream: The Story of Black Churches of Christ in Los Angeles* (Calvin Bowers, 2001); Edward J. Robinson, *The Fight Is On in Texas: A History of African American Churches of Christ in the Lone Star State, 1865–2000* (Abilene, TX: Abilene Christian University Press, 2008).

18. J. S. Winston, "Work among the Colored People in the U.S.," in Howard L. Schug and Jesse P. Sewell, eds., *The Harvest Field* (Athens, AL: Bible School Bookstore, 1947).

19. Annie C. Tuggle, *Another World Wonder* (n.p., n.d.).

20. James Maxwell, *Let's Go Back . . . Way Back: Black Presence in the Restoration Movement* (Terrell, TX: James Maxwell, 2013).

21. W. W. Morrison, *The Shaping of a Brotherhood: Historical Reflections*, vol. 1 (W. W. Morrison, 2015).

22. LeRoy Butler Jr., *A New Citizenry in an Old South: The Story of the First Black Church of Christ in Georgia* (LeRoy Butler Jr., 2015).

23. Hughes, *Reviving the Ancient Faith*, 176.

24. S. W. Womack, "Mission Work among Colored People in Tennessee," *Gospel Advocate* 46 (Feb. 4, 1904): 80.

25. Marshall Keeble, "Among the Colored People," *Gospel Advocate* 59 (Jan. 25, 1917): 93.

26. Russell H. Moore, "The Outlook," *Christian Echo* 37 (Oct. 20, 1942): 4.
27. Joe Cryer, "The Outlook," *Christian Echo* 38 (June 20, 1943): 4.
28. Truly Cathey, "The Outlook," *Christian Echo* 38 (Apr. 5, 1943): 4.
29. John R. Vaughner, "The Outlook," *Christian Echo* 42 (Oct. 20, 1947): 5.
30. Carson, *A Matter of Faith*, 136.

1. BROTHERS IN BLACK

1. James R. Rogers, *The Cane Ridge Meetinghouse* (Cincinnati: Standard Publishing, 1910), 40–42; D. Newell Williams, *Barton Stone: A Spiritual Biography* (St. Louis: Chalice Press, 2000); Leroy Garrett, *The Stone-Campbell Movement: An Anecdotal History of Three Churches* (Joplin: College Press Publishing, 1987 [1981]), 102–6; and Sydney Ahlstrom, *A Religious History of the American People* (New Haven: Yale University Press, 2004 [1972]), 434–35.
2. Rogers, 45.
3. Ibid., 44.
4. Olaudah Equiano, *The Interesting Narrative of the Life of Olaudah Equiano, Written by Himself (Boston: Bedford Books, 1995 [1791])183-4* ; Carter G. Woodson, *The History of the Negro Church* 3rd ed. (Washington, DC: Associated Publishers, 1985 [1921]), 1; Albert J. Raboteau, *Slave Religion: The "Invisible Institution" in the Antebellum South* (New York: Oxford University Press, 1980 [1978]). Thomas Kidd, *The Great Awakening: A Brief History with Documents* (Boston: Bedford/St. Martin's, 2008), 17–19.
5. Anne E. Pinn and Anthony B. Pinn, *Fortress Introduction to Black Church History* (Minneapolis: Fortress Press, 2002), 27–30; Raboteau, *Slave Religion*, 131–39; Mechal Sobel, *Trabelin' On: The Slave Journey to an Afro-Baptist Faith* (Westport, CT: Greenwood Press, 1979), xvii–xxiv, 100–3; Richard S. Newman, *Freedom's Prophet: Bishop Richard Allen, the AME Church, and the Black Founding Fathers* (New York: New York University Press, 2008), 39–40 ; Nathan O. Hatch, *The Democratization of American Christianity* (New Haven: Yale University Press, 1989), 102–10.
6. Rogers, 45.
7. Robert L. Jordan, *Two Races in One Fellowship* (Detroit: United Christian Church, 1944), 23; Robert O. Fife, *Teeth on Edge* (Grand Rapids: Baker Book House, 1971), 67; Hap Lyda, "Black Disciples in the Nineteenth Century," in *The Untold Story: A Short History of Black Disciples* (St. Louis: Christian Board of Publication, 1976), 11; Peter A. Verkruyse, "African-American Preachers in the Restoration Tradition," *Christian Standard* (June 30, 1996): 6; D. Newell Williams, Douglas A. Foster, and Paul M. Blowers, eds., *The Stone-Campbell Movement: A. Global History* (St. Louis: Chalice Press, 2013), 39.
8. David Edwin Harrell, Jr., *Quest for a Christian America, 1800–1865: A Social History of the Disciples of Christ* (Tuscaloosa: University of Alabama Press, 2003 [1966]), 98; D. Newell Williams, *The Stone-Campbell Movement: A Global History (St. Louis: Chalice Press, 2013)*, 17-27.

9. Clement Eaton, *A History of the Old South: The Emergence of a Reluctant Nation* 3rd ed. (Prospect Heights, IL: Waveland Press, 1975), 198–200. Quotation is on p. 200.

10. Robert Richardson, *Memoirs of Alexander Campbell, Embracing a View of the Origin, Progress and Principle of the Religious Reformation Which He Advocated* (Indianapolis: Religious Book Service, 1897): 1:495.

11. David Walker, *Appeal, in Four Articles; Together with a Preamble, to the Coloured Citizens of the World, But in Particular, and Very Expressly, to Those of the United States of America* (New York: Hill and Wang, 1969 [1829]), 25.

12. Leroy Garrett, *The Stone-Campbell Movement: An Anecdotal History*, 226–27; Richardson, *Memoirs of Alexander Campbell*, 2:322–23.

13. Richardson, *Memoirs of Alexander Campbell*, 2:367.

14. Selina Huntington Campbell, *Home Life and Reminiscences of Alexander Campbell* (St. Louis: John Burns Publisher, 1882), 454–55. For an insightful study of Campbell's home life, Loretta M. Long, *The Life of Selina Campbell: A Fellow Soldier in the Cause of Restoration* (Tuscaloosa: University of Alabama Press, 2001).

15. John W. Blassingame, *The Slave Community: Plantation Life in the Antebellum South* (New York: Oxford University Press, 1979 [1972]), 224–25.

16. Deborah Gray White, *Ar'n't I a Woman?: Female Slaves in the Plantation South* (New York: W. W. Norton, 1985), 29, 49.

17. Stephen B. Oates, *The Fires of Jubilee: Nat Turner's Fierce Rebellion* (New York: Harper & Row, 1975), 105.

18. Richardson, *Memoirs of Alexander Campbell*, 2:367.

19. Woodson, *The History of the Negro Church*, 99-100; Raboteau, 189–90; Andrew Billingsley, *Mighty Like a River: The Black Church and Social Reform* (New York: Oxford University Press, 1999), 20.

20. Alexander Campbell, "Incidents on a Tour to the South," *Millennial Harbinger* (Apr. 1839): 188.

21. Campbell, "Our Position to American Slavery, No. VIII," *Millennial Harbinger* (June 1845): 263. See also Williams, Foster, and Blowers, *A Global History*, 36.

22. Campbell, "Our Position to American Slavery, No. V," *Millennial Harbinger* (May 1845): 234. See also, Harrell, *A Quest for a Christian America*, 1:97.

23. Eaton, *A History of the Old South: The Emergence of a Reluctant Nation* (Prospect Heights, IL: Waveland Press, 1987 [1975]), 366–67.

24. Frederick Douglass, *Narrative of the Life of Frederick Douglass, An American Slave, Written by Himself* (New York: W. W. Norton, 1997 [1845]), 75.

25. Ahlstrom, *Religious History*, 659–65.

26. Eaton, *Old South*, 462–86.

27. Harrell, *A Quest for a Christian America*, 1:93; Williams, Foster, and Blowers, *A Global History*, 38.

28. Fife, *Teeth on Edge*, 7-17;, and Williams, Foster, and Blowers, *A Global History*, 37.

29. Robinson, *To Save My Race*, 11–13; Robinson, *Show Us How You Do It*, 47–55; Williams, Foster, and Blowers *A Global History*, 76–77.

30. John Hope Franklin and Evelyn Brooks Higginbotham, *From Slavery to Freedom: A History of African Americans*, 9th edition (New York: McGraw-Hill, 2011), 220; John Hope Franklin, *The Emancipation Proclamation* (Garden City, NY: Doubleday and Company, 1963), 114; Michael Perman, *Emancipation and Reconstruction, 1862–1879* (Wheeling, IL: Harlan Davidson, 1987), 21; James M. McPherson, *Battle Cry of Freedom: The Civil War Era* (New York: Ballantine Books, 1988), 497 (quotation on page 565).

31. Robinson, *To Save My Race*, 14; Todd W. Simmons, "Preston Taylor: Seeker of Dignity for Black Disciples," *Discipliana* 60 (Winter 2000): 100; Annie C. Tuggle, *Another World Wonder* (n.p., n.d.), 54–55; Janet B. Hewett, ed., *The Roster of Union Soldiers, 1861–1865* (Wilmington, NC: Broadfoot Publishing, 1997), 207–8, lists approximately 256 black men named "Henry Clay" who served in various Union regiments composed of African American soldiers.

32. Campbell, "Our Position to American Slavery, No. V," *Millennial Harbinger* (May 1845): 234.

33. S. R. Cassius, *Negro Evangelization and the Tohee Industrial School* (Cincinnati: Christian Leader Print., 1898), 10.

34. G. P. Bowser, "Gems for Thought," *Christian Echo* (Oct. 1974): 10. This article, it seems, first appeared in 1946. See G. P. Bowser, "As the Editor Sees It," *Christian Echo* (Jan. 1988): 6–7.

2. MOTHER CHURCHES

1. William E. Montgomery, *Under Their Own Vine and Fig Tree: The African-American Church in the South, 1865–1900* (Baton Rouge: Louisiana State University Press, 1993), 106.

2. "Keeble to Be Here," *Gospel Advocate* 83 (Dec. 25, 1941): 1242.

3. "Oldest Churches of Christ in the U.S.," *Christian Chronicle* 70 (Oct. 2013): 13.

4. Leroy Garrett, *The Stone-Campbell Movement: An Anecdotal History of Three Churches* (Joplin: College Press Publishing, 1987 [1981]), 186.

5. "Oldest Churches of Christ in the U.S.," *Christian Chronicle* 70 (Oct. 2013): 13.

6. *Clay County Tennessee 1986* (n.p., n.d.), 55; Tasneem Ansariyah-Grace, "Home on the Hill," *Citizen-Statesman* (Nov. 2, 1999): 10-A; Jill Thomas, "Keeping Free Hill Alive," *Herald-Citizen* (Oct. 29, 2000): C-1; author interview with Sandy Norris (Oct. 5, 2015). Many thanks to both Sandy Norris and Judith Cutright for pointing me to this pertinent information.

7. G. P. Bowser, "Work among the Colored People," *Gospel Advocate* 50 (Feb. 20, 1908): 125; G. P. Bowser, "Work among the Colored People in Tennessee," *Gospel Advocate* 50 (Nov. 5, 1908): 717.

8. John T. Ramsey, "Work among the Colored People," *Gospel Advocate* 53 (Nov. 30, 1911): 1405.

9. Gilbert A. Johnson, "Among the Colored Folks," *Gospel Advocate* 63 (Nov. 17, 1921): 1130.

10. Earl I. West, *The Search for the Ancient Order: A History of the Restoration Movement, 1900–1918* (Indianapolis: Religious Book Service, 1979), 3:164.

11. Frank Richey, "'Parson' George Ricks—From Slave to Servant of God," (unpublished manuscript in author's possession). Many thanks to Frank Richey for sharing this information with the author. See also Ervin C. Jackson, "George Ricks," in *The Encyclopedia of the Stone-Campbell Movement*, ed. Douglas A. Foster, Paul M. Blowers, Anthony L. Dunnavant, and D. Newell Williams (Grand Rapids: Eerdmans, 2004), 652. For other examples of whites in the antebellum South who violated the code of prohibiting black people from acquiring literacy, see Robinson, *The Fight Is On in Texas*, 140. Ida Van Zandt Jarvis, encouraged by her mother, taught young enslaved African Americans on their Texas plantation how to read and write. See also Robinson, *To Save My Race*, 13. In Prince William County, Virginia, Amanda, and Susan Macrae helped the mother of S. R. Cassius become literate.

12. Jackson, "George Ricks," 652. Loren Schweninger, *Black Property Owners in the South, 1790-1915* (Urbana: University of Illinois Press, 1990), 146, has documented that 1,752 black people in Alabama owned land in 1870.

13. George Ricks, "Letter from a Colored Brother—Help Wanted," *Gospel Advocate* 10 (Jan. 2, 1868): 23-24.

14. "Items and Personal" *Gospel Advocate* 72 (Apr. 29, 1885): 263.

15. Richey, "'Parson' George Ricks."

16. Lynn A. McMillon, "A History of the Churches of Christ in Tate County, Mississippi, 1836-1965" (master's thesis, Harding College Graduate School of Religion, 1966), 29.

17. Ibid., 51-52.

18. "Ministerial License," in *71st Annual National Lectureship Booklet* (n.p., 2015), 34-35; Tuggle, *Another World Wonder*, 64; Robinson, *The Fight Is On in Texas*, 120.

19. Robinson, *The Fight Is On in Texas*, 42-44.

20. F. F. Carson, *A Matter of Faith* (Houston, Texas: Carol Carson, 1991), 24.

21. Robinson, *The Fight Is On in Texas*, 22-23.

22. Ibid., 21-24.

23. Ibid., 22.

24. Ibid., 23-24.

25. S. R. Cassius, "Among Our Colored Disciples," *Christian Companion* 22 (Oct. 7, 1915): 4-5. Robinson, *Show Us How You Do It*, 47-55, has made this point elsewhere.

26. McMillon, "A History of the Churches of Christ," 51-52.

27. Robinson, *The Fight Is On in Texas*, 20-21; Richey, "'Parson' George Ricks."

28. David Lipscomb, "Race Prejudice," *Gospel Advocate* 20 (Feb. 21, 1878): 120-21.

3. FOUNDING FATHERS

1. Franklin and Higginbotham, *From Slavery to Freedom* (New York: McGraw-Hill, 2011), 235-59; McPherson, *Battle Cry of Freedom*, 848-49.

2. Richard S. Newman, *Freedom's Prophet: Bishop Richard Allen, the AME Church, and the Black Founding Fathers* (New York: New York University Press, 2008), 16.

3. This information was extracted from *71st Annual National Lectureship:*

"Celebrating the Covenant" (n.p., 2015), 34–35. Many thanks to David C. Penn, Minister for the Robbins Church of Christ in Robbins, Illinois, for alerting me to this information.

4. Quotation is from S. W. Womack, "Among the Colored People," *Gospel Advocate* 57 (Dec. 30, 1915): 1326. See Edward J. Robinson, "The Two Old Heroes," *Discipliana* 65 (Spring 2005): 3–20.

5. S. W. Womack, "Our Colored Brethren," *Christian Standard* (Dec. 27, 1879): 413.

6. S. W. Womack, "Church News," *Gospel Advocate* 44 (Apr. 10, 1902): 237.

7. S. W. Womack, "Church News," *Gospel Advocate* 44 (July 10, 1902): 445.

8. David Lipscomb, "The Church—Its Work," *Gospel Advocate* 27 (Apr. 15, 1885): 225–26. See also David Edwin Harrell Jr., *Sources of Divisions in the Disciples of Christ, 1865–1900: A Social History of the Disciples of Christ*, vol. 2 (Tuscaloosa: University of Alabama Press, 2003 [1973]), 52.

9. Edward J. Robinson, *Show Us How You Do It*, 11–21.

10. Alexander Campbell, "Among the Colored People," *Gospel Advocate* 56 (Apr. 9, 1914): 414.

11. Alexander Campbell, "Work among the Colored People," *Gospel Advocate* 51 (Dec. 2, 1909): 1523.

12. Alexander Campbell, "Among the Colored People," *Gospel Advocate* 57 (Dec. 16, 1915): 1277. See also Robinson, "The Two Old Heroes," 7–8, 11.

13. Quoted in J. E. Choate, *Roll Jordan Roll: A Biography of Marshall Keeble* (Nashville: Gospel Advocate Company, 1974), 7.

14. T. G. M'Lean, "Among the Colored Folks," *Gospel Advocate* 62 (Feb. 19, 1920): 183. See also, Robinson, "The Two Old Heroes," 13.

15. T. G. M'Lean, "Among the Colored Folks," *Gospel Advocate* 62 (Apr. 15, 1920): 389. See also, Robinson, "The Two Old Heroes," 13.

16. Richard T. Hughes, *Reviving the Ancient Faith: The Story of Churches of Christ* (Grand Rapids: Eerdmans, 1996), 47–63.

17. Robinson, *To Save My Race*, 11–21, 116.

18. Ibid., 41.

19. Ibid., 41–42.

20. Ibid., 14–19.

21. Ibid., 18.

22. Ibid., 95–110, 117.

23. Cassius, *The Third Birth of a Nation* 2nd ed. (Cincinnati: F. L. Rowe, 1925), 34, 85, 91; Robinson, *To Save My Race*, 143. Here Cassius mirrored the testimony of other enslaved African Americans. Frederick Douglass called the enslavement of black people "the hell of slavery." Douglass, *Narrative of the Life of Frederick Douglass, An American Slave, Written by Himself* (New York: W. W. Norton, 1997 [1845]), 15. Solomon Northup, a free black man kidnapped and enslaved in Louisiana, referred to chattel enslavement as the "bitter cup of slavery," the "weight of slavery," and a "cruel, unjust, and barbarous" institution. Northup, *Twelve Years a Slave* (Mineola, New York: Dover Publications, 1970 [1853]), 121, 125, 206.

24. Robinson, *To Save My Race*, 11–12, 28–29.

25. Cassius, "The Race Problem," *Christian Leader and the Way* 18 (Mar. 15, 1904): 2; J. S. DeJarnette, "An Oklahoma Protest," *Christian Leader and the Way* 18 (Apr. 12, 1904): 12. See also Robinson, *To Save My Race*, 29.

26. For a scholarly and insightful treatment of the controversial career of Henry McNeal Turner, see Stephen Ward Angell, *Bishop Henry McNeal Turner and African-American Religion in the South* (Knoxville: University of Tennessee Press, 1992), 81–107.

27. Leon F. Litwack, *Been in the Storm So Long: The Aftermath of Slavery* (New York: Vintage Books, 1979), 470. Dennis C. Dickerson, *African American Preachers and Politics: The Careys of Chicago* (Jackson: University Press of Mississippi, 2010), 4, brilliantly shows that African Methodist Episcopal clergymen Archibald J. Carey Sr. and his son Archibald J. Carey Jr. "pursued politics as intrinsic elements to their clerical responsibilities, moving easily from proclamations in the pulpit to public pronouncements, on issues crucial to African American advancement." Dickerson then adds, "from Richard Allen, Absalom Jones, Henry Highland Garnet, and others in the late eighteenth and nineteenth centuries to Martin Luther King, Jr., Jesse Jackson, Al Sharpton, and their contemporaries in the twentieth and twenty-first centuries, black clergy have long condemned the racial subjugation of African Americans and offered theological commentaries on civic justice and equality for this oppressed minority. Similarly, women such as Harriet Tubman, Sojourner Truth, Anna Arnold Hedgeman, Fanny Lou Hamer, among others, without the benefit of ordination but motivated by the same spiritual fervor as their male counterparts, pushed their religiously based activism to the forefront of the black freedom struggle. Black liberation was integral to the theology of these religious leaders and provided a core element of their civic consciousness."

28. Angell, *Bishop Henry McNeal Turner*, 261.

29. The first quotation is from Cassius, "Among Our Colored Disciples," *Christian Companion* 22 (Oct. 7, 1915): 4–5. The second quotation is from Cassius in Robinson, ed., *To Lift Up My Race: The Essential Writings of Samuel Robert Cassius* (Knoxville: University of Tennessee Press, 2008), 103.

30. Edward J. Blum and Paul Harvey, *The Color of Christ: The Son of God and the Saga of Race in America* (Chapel Hill: University of North Carolina Press, 2012), 150–54.

31. Cassius, "The Race Problem," *Christian Leader* 15 (Feb. 12, 1901): 9. Robinson, ed., *To Lift Up My Race*, 45.

32. Cassius, "Among Our Colored Disciples," *Gospel Advocate* 37 (Aug. 19, 1915): 838–839; Cassius, "Among Our Colored Disciples," *Christian Companion* 22 (Oct. 7, 1915): 4–5; Robinson, ed., *To Lift Up My Race*, 12, 80.

33. Cassius, "I Have the Faith," *Christian Leader* 36 (Jan. 31, 1922): 3; Robinson, ed., *To Lift Up My Race*, 86.

4. "MAKING LOVE TO OUR DAUGHTERS"

1. Thomas P. Bailey, "Race Orthodoxy in the South," *Neale's Monthly Magazine* (1913); quoted in C. Vann Woodward, *Origins of the New South* (Baton Rouge: Louisiana State University Press, 1971 [1951]), 355–56.
2. David Edwin Harrell Jr., *Sources of Division in the Disciples of Christ, 1865-1900: A Social History of the Disciples of Christ*, vol. 2 (Tuscaloosa: University of Alabama Press, 2003 [1973]), 24.
3. H. W. Brands, T. H. Breen, R. Hal. Williams, and Ariela J. Gross, *American Stories: A History of the United States* (Boston: Pearson Education, 2012 [2009]), 490.
4. Richard Hofstadter, *Social Darwinism in American Thought* (New York: George Braziller, 1959), 180; Brands et al., *American Stories* 534–45.
5. *Rudyard Kipling's Verse* (New York: Doubleday, Doran, 1945), 321–23.
6. G. P. O., "The Negro's Future," *Christian Leader* 16 (Nov. 11, 1902): 3.
7. "Negro Evangelization," *Gospel Advocate* 47 (July 20, 1905): 452.
8. John M. McCaleb, "The Japan Letter," *Christian Leader* 21 (Jan. 1, 1907): 2.
9. Price Billingsley, "Our Obligation to the Negro," *Gospel Advocate* 54 (Dec. 5, 1912): 1308.
10. Ibid., 1309. Here, Billingsley echoed the sentiment of Cassius, who indicted the white South for the moral flaws of American blacks. He also rebuked white Christians for their preoccupation with foreign missions while neglecting the black man at home. See Robinson, *To Save My Race*, 28-29, 157–59.
11. G. F. Gibbs, "A Plea for the Carolina Negro," *Christian Leader* 37 (Dec. 11, 1923): 3.
12. H. C. Denson, "Bro. Gibbs' Plea," *Christian Leader* 37 (Dec. 18, 1923): 7.
13. G. A. Klingman, "Query Department," *Christian Leader* 34 (Mar. 23, 1920): 5.
14. W. U. Benton, "North Georgia Negro Mission," *Christian Leader* 36 (Aug. 8, 1922): 11.
15. W. U. Benton, "Among the Colored Folks," *Gospel Advocate* 63 (Nov. 3, 1921): 1084. See also Robinson, *Show Us How You Do It*, 50.
16. W. U. Benton, "North Georgia Negro Mission," *Christian Leader* 36 (Aug. 8, 1922): 11.
17. David Edwin Harrell Jr., *Sources of Division*, 16-22, has correctly pointed out that journals published by white Christians helped to develop and direct the minds of whites in the Disciples of Christ and whites in Churches of Christ. Robinson, *Show Us How You Do It*, 47–55, has argued elsewhere that white journals published by white Churches of Christ shaped the theological formation of black Churches of Christ.
18. W. U. Benton, "North Georgia Negro Mission," *Christian Leader* 36 (Aug. 8, 1922): 11.
19. Frederick L. Rowe, "Doesn't Like the Negro," *Christian Leader* 36 (Sept. 5, 1922): 6.
20. Harrell, *Sources of Division*, 207.
21. David Chalmers, *Hooded Americanism: The First Century of the Ku Klux Klan*,

1865-1965 (New York: Doubleday, 1965), 28–38; Kathleen M. Blee, *Women of the Klan: Racism and Gender in the 1920s* (Berkeley: University of California Press, 1991), 2; and Nancy Maclean, *Behind the Mask of Chivalry: The Making of the Second Ku Klux Klan* (New York: Oxford University Press, 1994), 3–22. In 1913, Leo Frank, a Jewish businessman, was charged with raping a white teenage girl, Mary Phagan, in Atlanta, Georgia. Two years later, a white mob lynched Frank.

22. "Can a Christian Join the Klan?" *Christian Leader* 37 (Oct. 23, 1923): 2–3.

23. "Can a Christian Join the Klan? II" *Christian Leader* 37 (Nov. 6, 1923): 6–7.

24. "No More at Present," *Christian Leader* 38 (Jan. 1, 1924): 7.

25. H. Leo Boles, "Query Department," *Gospel Advocate* (Mar. 10, 1927): 232.

26. Joel Williamson, *New People: Miscegenation and Mulattoes in the United States (Baton Rouge: Louisiana State University Press, 1995)*; Joshua D. Rothman, *Notorious in the Neighborhood: Sex and Families across the Color Line in Virginia, 1787-1861* (Chapel Hill: University of North Carolina Press, 2003).

27. Wilbur J. Cash, *The Mind of the South* (New York: Alfred A. Knopf, 1941), 114–17.

28. *Richmond Times* (1901); quoted in H. W. Brands, *T. R.: The Last Romantic* (New York: Basic Books, 1997), 423.

29. "Niggers in the White House," *Greenwood Commonwealth* (Jan. 31, 1903): 1. See also Willard B. Gatewood Jr., *Theodore Roosevelt and the Art of Controversy: Episodes of the White House Years* (Baton Rouge: Louisiana State University Press, 1970), 32–61.

30. This was especially true for most white members of the Stone-Campbell Movement. See Harrell, *Sources of Division*, 179, 206; Robinson, ed., *To Lift Up My Race*, 95–110; Robinson, *The Fight Is On in Texas*, 137–53.

31. McCaleb, "Japan Letter—How to Reach the Colored Man," *Christian Leader and the Way* 21 (Sept. 3, 1907): 2–3.

32. Ibid. For useful biographical information on McCaleb, see Gary Owen Turner, "Pioneer to Japan: A Biography of J. M. McCaleb" (master's thesis, Abilene Christian College, 1972); Ed Matthews, "John Moody McCaleb," in Douglas A. Foster, Paul M. Blowers, Anthony L. Dunnavant, and D. Newell Williams, eds., *The Encyclopedia of the Stone-Campbell Movement* (Grand Rapids: Eerdmans, 2004), 505–6.

33. Pete Daniel, *Lost Revolutions: The South in the 1950s* (Chapel Hill: University of North Carolina Press, 2000), 189–90, 274.

34. Robinson, *Show Us How You Do It*, 73–98.

35. Quoted in Robinson, *The Fight Is On in Texas*.

5. "IN A CLASS BY HIMSELF"

1. Philip Dray, *At the Hands of Persons Unknown: The Lynching of Black America* (New York: The Modern Library, 2003), 3–5. Mary Louise Ellis, "'Rain Down Fire:' The Lynching of Sam Hose" (Ph.D. diss., Florida State University, 1992).

2. Quoted in Dray, *Hands of Persons Unknown*, 4, 13, 14; W. E. B. Du Bois, *The Souls of Black Folk* (Boston: Bedford/St. Martin's, 1997 [1903]), 103; David Levering Lewis,

Notes to Pages 45–49   191

W. E. B. Du Bois: *The Fight for Equality and the American Century, 1919–1963* (New York: Henry Holt, 2000), 374.

3. S. R. Cassius, "Acknowledgments," *Christian Leader* 13 (May 16, 1899): 5. See also Robinson, *To Save My Race*, 67; Robinson, ed., *To Lift Up My Race*, 75–76.

4. Reinhold Niebuhr, *Moral Man and Immoral Society: A Study in Ethics and Politics* (New York: Scribner's Sons, 1932) 277, 281. See also James H. Cone, *The Cross and the Lynching Tree* (Maryknoll, NY: Orbis Books, 2011), 56.

5. Harrell, *Sources of Division*, 207. Richard T. Hughes, *Reviving the Ancient Faith: The Story of Churches of Christ in America* (Grand Rapids: Eerdmans, 1996), 108–133, has brilliantly traced the social justice impulse from Barton W. Stone to David Lipscomb.

6. Robinson, ed., *To Lift Up My Race*, xxi.

7. Edward J. Blum, *Forging the White Republic: Race, Religion, and American Nationalism, 18651898* (Baton Rouge: Louisiana State University Press, 2005 [2015]), 18.

8. Joel Williamson, *Miscegenation and Mulattoes in the United States* (Baton Rouge: Louisiana State University Press, 1995), xii, 63, defines "mulattoes" or "new people" as "half black and half white." See also Joshua D. Rothman, *Notorious in the Neighborhood: Sex and Families across the Color Line in Virginia, 1787–1861* (Chapel Hill: University of North Carolina Press, 2003.

9. S. R. Cassius, "Behold, I Make All Things New" *Christian Leader* 33 (Jan. 7, 1919): 8; Robinson, *To Save My Race from Abuse*, 14–19.

10. Robinson, *To Save My Race from Abuse*, 20–21.

11. Harrell, *Sources of Division*, 180.

12. S. R. Cassius, "A Colored Brother's Protest," *Christian Evangelist* (Nov. 14, 1889): 726; Robinson, *To Save My Race*, 61–62.

13. James H. Garrison, "A Colored Brother's Protest," *Christian Evangelist* (Nov. 14, 1889): 726.

14. Hughes, *Reviving the Ancient Faith*, 85–86; Robinson, *Show Us How You Do It*, 11–21.

15. C. C. Smith, "Our Colored Disciples," *Christian Leader* 10 (Jan. 21, 1896): 13; Robinson, *To Save My Race*, 64–65.

16. S. R. Cassius, "Our Colored Disciples," *Christian Leader* 10 (Jan. 21, 1896): 13; Robinson, *To Save My Race*, 69.

17. S. R. Cassius, "Among Our Colored Disciples," *Christian Leader* 16 (Nov. 25, 1902): 3.

18. S. R. Cassius, "Adrift," *Christian Leader* 16 (Dec. 30, 1902): 4–5.

19. S. R. Cassius, "Negro Evangelization," *Christian Standard* (Jan. 15, 1916): 30–31.

20. S. R. Cassius, "The Right Man in the Right Place," *Christian Companion* 23 (Sept. 14, 1916): 2.

21. Cassius, "Negro Evangelization," 30–31.

22. S. R. Cassius, "The Race Problem," *Christian Leader and the Way* 18 (Mar. 15, 1904): 2; Robinson, *To Save My Race*, 28–29.

23. J. S. De Jarnette, "An Oklahoma Protest," *Christian Leader and the Way* 18 (Apr. 12, 1904): 12.

24. S. R. Cassius, "The Great Commission," *Christian Leader* 44 (Dec. 2, 1930): 3. David Edwin Harrell Jr., *Sources of Division*, 204-205, has noted that white leaders in the Stone-Campbell Movement—North and South—generally opposed "social equality."

25. Robinson, *To Save My Race*, 135–55.

26. Quoted in Dick Lehr, The Birth of a Nation: *How a Legendary Filmmaker and a Crusading Editor Reignited America's Civil War* (New York: Public Affairs, 2014), 226.

27. Ibid., 135, 156 (Wilson's quotation), 272.

28. Ibid., 107–9, 175.

29. Ibid., 191 (quotations), 258–60.

30. Dennis C. Dickerson, *African American Preachers and Politics: The Careys of Chicago* (Jackson: University Press of Mississippi, 2010), 42.

31. Robinson, *To Save My Race*, 141.

32. S. R. Cassius, "Among Our Colored Disciples," *Gospel Advocate* 37 (Aug. 19, 1915): 838–39; Robinson, ed., *To Lift Up My Race*, 80.

33. S. R. Cassius, "The American Negro," *Christian Leader* 34 (Feb. 24, 1920): 6; Robinson, *To Save My Race*, 7.

34. S. R. Cassius, "Field Reports," *Christian Leader* 43 (Apr. 23, 1929): 13; Robinson, *To Save My Race*, 156–57.

35. S. R. Cassius, "My Trip to the East," *Christian Leader* 36 (June 20, 1922): 12; Robinson, *To Save My Race*, 164.

36. Frederick L. Rowe called S. R. Cassius the "Booker T. Washington of Oklahoma," in S. R. Cassius, "The Tohee Industrial School," *Christian Leader* 13 (Aug. 15, 1899): 13; Robinson, *To Save My Race*, 95–110.

37. S. R. Cassius, "I Have Kept the Faith," *Christian Leader* 36 (Jan. 31, 1922): 3; Robinson, *To Save My Race*, 91–92.

38. S. R. Cassius, "The Condenser," *Christian Leader* 15 (Oct. 15, 1901): 5. See also R. Vernon Boyd, *A History of the Stone-Campbell Churches in Michigan, with Emphasis on the A Cappella Churches of Christ* (R. Vernon Boyd, 2009), 274–310.

39. S. R. Cassius, "The Characteristics of the Man," *Christian Leader and the Way* 18 (May 31, 1904): 5.

40. S. R. Cassius, "Bro. Cain is Dead," *Christian Leader* 32 (Aug. 27, 1918): 5; Robinson, ed., *To Lift Up My Race*, 27–28.

41. White supporters from Illinois, Henry Atkins Deusen and Mary E. Van Deusen, greatly admired Cassius; the latter wrote to Cassius after her husband's death: "Brother, my husband loved you." John W. Harris, when comparing Frederick Douglass and S. R. Cassius, called the former "a moon," the latter, "a sun." Robinson, *To Save My Race*, 104, 115; 163.

42. S. R. Cassius, "Looking Backward," *Christian Leader* 29 (Dec. 14, 1915): 4;

S. R. Cassius, "An Appreciation of Booker T. Washington," *Gospel Advocate* 29 (Dec. 23, 1915): 1302; Robinson, ed., *To Lift Up My Race*, 24–26.

6. SETTING THE HOUSE ON FIRE

1. Choate, *Roll Jordan Roll*, 65.
2. In this regard, Marshall Keeble was strikingly similar to S. R. Cassius, who preached to show that "I am right and they are wrong." See Cassius, "My Trip to the East," 12; Robinson, *To Save My Race*, 164; Edward J. Robinson, ed., *A Godsend to His People: The Essential Writings and Speeches of Marshall Keeble* (Knoxville: University of Tennessee Press, 2008), xvi. Keeble once confessed that "the Negro didn't like my religion, and the white man didn't like the color of my skin." See Willie Cato, *His Hand and Heart: The Wit and Wisdom of Marshall Keeble* (Winona, MS: J. C. Choate, 1990), 18.
3. Marshall Keeble, "Among the Colored Folks," *Gospel Advocate* 59 (Oct. 11, 1917): 996.
4. Choate, *Roll Jordan Roll*, 35; Robinson, *Show Us How You Do It*, 2.
5. Marshall Keeble, "Among the Colored Folks," *Gospel Advocate* 63 (Sept. 15, 1921): 911; Robinson, *Show Us How You Do It*, 15–16.
6. Marshall Keeble, "Among the Colored Folks," *Gospel Advocate* (Mar. 4, 1920): 235; Marshall Keeble, "An Interesting Report," *Gospel Advocate* 61 (June 12, 1919): 573; Robinson, *Show Us How You Do It*, 47–55.
7. B. C. Goodpasture, ed., *Marshall Keeble: Biography and Sermons* (Nashville, Tennessee: Gospel Advocate Company, 1966 [1931]), 38.
8. Albert J. Raboteau, *A Fire in the Bones: Reflections on African-American Religious History* (Boston: Beacon Press, 1995), 146.
9. Ibid., 171–72.
10. Ibid., 69.
11. Joe H. Morris, "News and Notes," *Gospel Advocate* 81 (Aug. 31, 1939): 828.
12. Robinson, *Show Us How You Do It*, 38.
13. Hughes, *Reviving the Ancient Faith*, 59.
14. Choate, *Roll Jordan Roll*, 33, 97.
15. Choate, *Roll Jordan Roll*, 39–40; Robinson, *Show Us How You Do It*, 104.
16. Choate, *Roll Jordan Roll*, 53.
17. Ibid., 104.
18. Marshall Keeble, "Among the Colored Folks," *Gospel Advocate* 61 (Nov. 13, 1919): 1131; Robinson, *Show Us How You Do It*, 104.
19. Choate, *Roll Jordan Roll*, 43–44.
20. Ibid., 64.
21. Ibid., 66.
22. Cato, *His Hand and His Heart*.
23. Choate, *Roll Jordan Roll*, 94.

24. Ibid., 99, 104.
25. Goodpasture, ed., *Biography and Sermons*, 22.
26. B. F. Hall quoted in Hughes, *Reviving the Ancient Faith*, 100.
27. Goodpasture, ed., *Biography and Sermons*, 23.
28. Ibid., 23–24.
29. Ibid., 25–26.
30. Michael W. Casey, *Saddlebags, City Streets and Cyberspace: A History of Preaching in the Churches of Christ* (Abilene, TX: Abilene Christian University Press, 1995), 150–51.
31. Hughes, *Reviving the Ancient Faith*, 30-32; Robinson, *Show Us How You Do It*, 57–58.
32. Goodpasture, ed., *Biography and Sermons*, 37–38.
33. Ibid.
34. Ibid., 39–40.
35. C. Eric Lincoln and Lawrence H. Mamiya, *The Black Church in the African American Experience* (Durham: Duke University Press, 1990), 80–81; Anne H. Pinn and Anthony B. Pinn, *Fortress Introduction of Black Church History* (Minneapolis: Fortress Press, 2002), 112–13.
36. Goodpasture, ed., *Biography and Sermons*, 39–40.
37. Hughes, *Reviving the Ancient Faith*, 113–14, observes, "This notion became the linchpin in what Campbell increasingly would call the *ancient gospel*."
38. Goodpasture, ed., *Biography and Sermons*, 43–44.
39. Ibid., 47.
40. Ibid., 49–50.
41. Hughes, *Reviving the Ancient Faith*, 51–52.
42. Goodpasture, ed., *Biography and Sermons*, 53–54.
43. Ibid.
44. Ibid., 55.
45. Ibid., 58–59.
46. Robinson, ed., *A Godsend to His People*, 40.
47. Goodpasture, ed., *Biography and Sermons*, 77.
48. Ibid., 86–87.
49. Ibid., 88.
50. John Rogers, *The Biography of Eld. Barton Warren Stone, Written by Himself: With Additions and Reflections* (Cincinnati: J. A. & U. P. James, 1847), 51. Stone's cohorts included Robert Marshall, John Dunlavy, Richard M'Nemar, John Thompson, and David Purviance. See also D. Newell Williams, "Last Will and Testament of the Springfield Presbytery," in Foster et al., eds., *Encyclopedia of the Stone-Campbell Movement*, 453–55.
51. C. Leonard Allen and Richard T. Hughes, *Discovering Our Roots: The Ancestry of Churches of Christ* (Abilene, TX: Abilene Christian University Press, 1988), 7–9. See also Robinson, *Show Us How You Do It*, 64–67.

52. Goodpasture, ed., *Biography and Sermons*, 89.
53. Rogers, *Biography of Barton Stone*, 52.
54. Robinson, *Show Us How You Do It*, 120–22.
55. Choate, *Roll Jordan Roll*, 52.
56. Ibid., 64.
57. Robinson, *Show Us How You Do It*, 137–72, treats Keeble's spiritual sons and grandson.
58. Ibid., 47–55.
59. Marshall Keeble, "Among the Colored Brethren," *Gospel Advocate* 93 (May 17, 1951): 317–18. See also Robinson, ed., *A Godsend to His People*, 40–51. For Eugene Lawton's sermon on "moral purity," see his *Fasten Your Seatbelts: Turbulence May Be Ahead* (New Jersey: Lawton, 1983), 101. The subject of Lawton's sermon was "Will the Real Preacher Please Stand Up?"
60. Michael Eric Dyson, *I May Not Get There with You: The True Martin Luther King, Jr.* (New York: The Free Press, 2000), 134–35.

7. WARHORSES

1. Marshall Keeble, "Report of M. Keeble," *Gospel Advocate* 73 (Jan. 8, 1931): 44–45. See also Robinson, ed., *A Godsend to His People*, 28.
2. For an assessment of Keeble's "strategy," see Robinson, *Show Us How You Do It*, 68–69; Robinson, *The Fight Is On in Texas*, 55–58. After planting a black Church of Christ in Paris, Texas, Keeble sent Luke Miller and after establishing a black congregation in Waco, Texas, Keeble recommended O. L. Aker to serve there. Both Miller and Aker were spiritual "sons" of Marshall Keeble.
3. R. Vernon Boyd, *Undying Dedication: The Story of G. P. Bowser* (Nashville: Gospel Advocate Company, 1985), 29.
4. Rayford W. Logan, *The Betrayal of the Negro: From Rutherford B. Hayes to Woodrow Wilson* (New York: De Capo Press, 1997 [1954]), 83.
5. Franklin and Higginbotham, *From Slavery to Freedom*, 288, 290.
6. Boyd, *Undying Dedication*, 18–22.
7. Gunnar Myrdal, *An American Dilemma: The Negro Problem and Modern Democracy* (New York: Harper, 1944), 884. David L. Chappell, *A Stone of Hope: Prophetic Religion and the Death of Jim Crow* (Chapel Hill: University of North Carolina Press, 2004), 44, has pointed out that black Americans' thirst for education helped to expose them to a "prophetic tradition," which in turn empowered them to topple Jim Crow.
8. G. P. Bowser, "As Ye Find Christ, Walk in Him," *Gospel Advocate* 46 (Mar. 24, 1904): 190; Boyd, *Undying Dedication*, 26–27.
9. Boyd, *Undying Dedication*, 86.
10. F. B. Shepherd, "Work among the Negroes," *Gospel Advocate* 72 (Dec. 18, 1930): 1226; Robinson, *Show Us How You Do It*, 40.
11. Boyd, *Undying Dedication*, 49.

12. Ibid., 31, 82, 100–101.
13. Choate, *Roll Jordan Roll*, 97.
14. Boyd, *Undying Dedication*, 49.
15. Ibid., 66. Robinson, *The Fight Is On in Texas*, 126–27.
16. Boyd, *Undying Dedication*, 69.
17. Franklin and Higginbotham, *From Slavery to Freedom*, 370–71.
18. "A Paper for the Colored Brethren," *Gospel Advocate* 44 (Feb. 6, 1902): 92.
19. G. P. Bowser, "Questions," *Christian Echo* 40 (Oct. 20, 1945): 3.
20. Ibid.
21. Robinson, *The Fight Is On in Texas*, 99–105.
22. "Questions," *Christian Echo* 37 (Sept. 5, 1942): 3; "Questions," *Christian Echo* 37 (Nov. 5, 1942): 7.
23. Annie C. Tuggle, *Our Ministers and Song Leaders* (Detroit: Annie C. Tuggle, 1945), 84. See also Robinson, *Show Us How You Do It*, 25–26.
24. T. H. Busby, "The Wages of Sin Is Death," *Christian Echo* 68 (Apr. 1970): 7; "Brother T. H. Busby Passes," *Christian Echo* 68 (Sept. 1970): 1; Tuggle, *Our Ministers*, 28; Boyd, *Undying Dedication*, 58.
25. Tuggle, *Another World Wonder*, 61; Edward J. Robinson, *I Was Under a Heavy Burden: The Life of Annie C. Tuggle* (Abilene, TX: Abilene Christian University Press, 2011), 42.
26. Boyd, *Undying Dedication*, 82, 91–96.
27. Franklin and Higginbotham, *From Slavery to Freedom*, 456–58. Isabel Wilkerson, *The Warmth of Other Suns: The Epic Story of America's Great Migration* (New York: Vintage Books, 2010), 9.
28. R. Vernon Boyd, "Organizational Difference Between the Black and White Church of Christ," *Firm Foundation* (Jan. 8, 1974): 19, 27. See also R. Vernon Boyd, "An Interpretive Analysis of the Integration of Two Churches" (DMin thesis, Harding Graduate School of Religion, 1986), 113.
29. Tuggle, *Our Ministers*, 94; Boyd, *Undying Dedication*, 81–82; Robinson, *Show Us How You Do It*, 122.
30. Maxwell, *Let's Go Back*, 56; Boyd, *Undying Dedication*, 82.
31. Robinson, *Show Us How You Do It*, 122–23.
32. G. E. Steward, *Our Pulpit* (Fort Worth, TX: Steward, 1965), 195; Boyd, *Undying Dedication*, 78; Robinson, *I Was under a Heavy Burden*, 74.
33. G. P. Holt, "Purpose of the Lectureship in 1977," *Christian Echo* 76 (Apr. 1977): 4. See also Tuggle, *Our Ministers*, 140.
34. Holt, "Purpose of the Lectureships," 4.
35. Boyd, *Undying Dedication*, 79.
36. Robinson, *The Fight Is On in* Texas, 105–18.
37. J. S. Winston, "A Greater Southern Bible Institute," *Christian Echo* 45 (Feb. 20, 1949): 7.
38. Winston, "Work among the Colored People," 72–73.
39. J. S. Winston, "Hindering Causes," *Christian Echo* 50 (Apr. 1954): 3.

40. J. S. Winston, "The Need of Leadership," *Christian Echo* 51 (Mar. 1995): 6.
41. J. S. Winston, "Elders: The Problem of Ordination," *Christian Echo* 71 (Nov.-Dec. 1973): 1, 8.
42. Ibid.
43. J. S. Winston, "A Day to be Remembered: Ordination of Elders and Deacons," *Christian Echo* (Apr. 1992): 9. See also *40 Years of Leadership: Charlie and Ida McClendon Appreciation Booklet* (n. p., 2013), in author's possession.
44. Robinson, *The Fight Is On in Texas*, 120.
45. Calvin H. Bowers, *Realizing the California Dream*; Maxwell, *Let's Go Back*, 54–55.
46. Robinson, *Show Us How You Do It*, 128-133; Robinson, *The Fight Is On in Texas*, 119–24.
47. R. N. Hogan, "Southwestern Is Producing," *Christian Echo* 51 (Nov. 1955): 2.
48. Marion V. Holt, "What Are They Doing Now?" *Christian Echo* 51 (Nov. 1955): 3. A more detailed list of these young Southwestern Christian College graduates appears in Robinson, *The Fight Is On in Texas*, 124–25.
49. Maxwell, *Let's Go Back*, 191–93.
50. Robinson, *Show Us How You Do It*, 131.
51. "Echo Staffer Appointed to Art Institute Board of Governors," *Christian Echo* 63 (June 1963): 6–7.
52. Nancy Weiss, *Farewell to the Party of Lincoln: Black Politics in the Age of FDR* (Princeton: Princeton University Press, 1983), 13–33; R. N. Hogan, "Christians and Their Right to Vote," *Christian Echo* (Jan. 1977): 4. In this article, there is a picture of Hogan standing beside the president-elect.
53. R. N. Hogan, "Brother David Lipscomb Stood with God on the Race Prejudice in the Church of Christ," *Christian Echo* (June 1960): 3.
54. Robinson, *The Fight Is On in Texas*, 129.
55. R. N. Hogan, "The Grab of the Century," *Christian Echo* 63 (Dec. 1968): 1–2.
56. Hughes, *Reviving the Ancient Faith*, 292-295. See also Wes Crawford, *Shattering the Illusion: How African American Churches of Christ Moved from Segregation to Independence* (Abilene, TX: Abilene Christian University Press, 2013).
57. R. N. Hogan, "The Relationship between the Evangelist and Elder," *Christian Echo* (Mar. 1990): 2.
58. Boyd, *Undying Dedication*, 34.
59. R. Vernon Boyd, "Organizational Difference," *Firm Foundation* 91 (Jan. 8, 1974): 19, 27.
60. See Robinson, *Show Us How You Do It*, 137–72.
61. Bowser, "The Colored School at Silver Point, Tenn.," *Gospel Advocate* 58 (May 4, 1916): 458.

8. "NONVIOLENT GADFLIES"

1. Ralph Ellison, *Invisible Man* (New York: Random House, 1995 [1952]), 3, 95.
2. James Maxwell, ed., "Orum Lee Trone," in *God's Declaration of Independence:*

Southwestern Christian College 38th Annual Lectureship Series (Terrell, TX: Southwestern Christian College, 1975), 81.

3. *50th Annual National Youth Conference of Churches of Christ* (July 23-29, 2001), 5-6. This event was held on the campus of the University of South Carolina in Columbia. Many thanks to Philip and Delbra Wade for sharing this booklet with me.

4. Ibid.

5. Patricia (Jenkins) Armstrong, in discussion with the author, June 3, 2014.

6. Patricia (Jenkins) Armstrong, in discussion with the author, July 30, 2015.

7. Patricia (Jenkins) Armstrong, in discussion with the author, June 3, 2014.

8. Ibid.

9. Raymond Arsenault, *Freedom Riders: 1961 and the Struggle for Racial Justice* (New York: Oxford University Press, 2006), 8. Patricia (Jenkins) Armstrong is referenced on pages 291, 538, and 620. See also John Lewis and Michael D'orso, *Walking with the Wind: A Memoir of the Movement* (San Diego: Harcourt Brace, 1998), 58–59, 71–72.

10. Martin Luther King Jr., "Letter from Birmingham Jail" in Jonathan Rieder, ed., *Gospel of Freedom: Martin Luther King, Jr.'s Letter from Birmingham Jail and the Struggle That Changed a Nation* (New York: Bloomsbury Press, 2013), 172.

11. Barclay Key, "Race and Restoration: Churches of Christ and the African American Freedom Struggle" (PhD diss., University of Florida, 2007), 217.

12. Ethel (Carr) Crowder, in discussion with the author, Dec. 28, 2015.

13. Terri Jo Ryan, "Breaking Waco's Color Barriers," *Waco-Tribune Herald* (Feb. 22, 2014): 4-B.

14. Ibid.

15. Mahalia Jackson, "Traveling Jim Crow" [1966], in Gerda Lerner, ed., *Black Women in White America: A Documentary History* (New York: Vintage Books, 1973), 384.

16. Norman Anderson, "Reflections . . . on Selma and Montgomery," *Christian Echo* 60 (June 1965): 1; "Restless in Retirement, Former Postal Official Will Write Column in 'News,'" *Nashville News* (May 14, 1992): 4; Maxwell, *Let's Go Back*, 225.

17. Adamson, "Reflections," 1. See also Franklin and Higginbotham, *From Slavery to Freedom*, 526.

18. Adamson, "Reflections," 1.

19. Fred Gray, *Bus Ride to Justice: Changing the System by the System* (Montgomery: Black Belt Press, 1995), 19.

20. Kelyne M. Provitt (daughter of the late K. K. Mitchell), in discussion with the author, Aug. 1, 2014. Gray, *Bus Ride to Justice*, 28, 256.

21. Ibid., 94, 97.

22. Ibid., 110-32, 281-90. Lynn McMillon, "On Ferguson, Faith and the Fight for Equality," *Christian Chronicle* 72 (July 2015): 12.

23. Hughes, *Reviving the Ancient Faith*, 292-93.

24. Gray, *Bus Ride to Justice*, 257.

25. Hughes, *Reviving the Ancient Faith*, 304-305.

26. Carroll Pitts Jr., "Politics and the Negro Revolution," *Mission* (June 1968): 373.
27. O. L. Trone, "Overcoming Racial Prejudice—Its Remedy," *Christian Echo* 52 (Sept. 1956): 4.
28. Ibid.
29. R. N. Hogan, "Enemies of Righteousness," *Christian Echo* (Aug. 1956): 2.
30. Ibid.
31. King, "Letter from Birmingham Jail," 173.
32. Hogan, "Enemies of Righteousness," *Christian Echo* (Aug. 1959): 2.
33. Hogan, "Tradition Versus God's Commandments," *Christian Echo* 58 (July 1963): 1.
34. Hogan, "My Personal Observations," *Christian Echo* 58 (Aug. 1963): 1.
35. Robinson, *The Fight Is On in Texas*, 124–34.
36. Hogan, "My Personal Observations," 5.
37. Ibid.
38. Ibid. See also, Hughes, *Reviving the Ancient Faith*, 290; Robinson, *The Fight Is On in Texas*, 166.
39. Barclay Key, "Race and Restoration: Churches of Christ and the African American Freedom Struggle" (PhD diss., University of Florida, 2007), 126.
40. Andrew J. Hairston, "Color Lines in the Church of Christ," *Christian Echo* 59 (Apr. 1964): 7.
41. Hairston, "The Same Confession, but a Different Baptistry," *Christian Echo* 60 (Jan. 1965): 6.
42. Ibid.
43. Hairston, "Is the Race Issue Social?" *Christian Echo* 59 (June 1964): 5.
44. James Maxwell, "The Sociological Impact of the Race Issue," *Christian Echo* 59 (July 1964): 1; James Maxwell, "The Sociological Impact of the Race Issue" *Christian Echo* 59 (Sept. 1964): 2.
45. Franklin and Higginbotham, *From Slavery to Freedom*, 545.
46. Alvin S. Simmons, "The Church of Christ and Race Relations," *Christian Echo* 59 (Oct. 1964): 3. See also Robinson, *Show Us How You Do It*, 162–63.
47. Humphrey Foutz, "When Rendering Unto Caesar," *Christian Echo* 59 (Nov. 1964): 5; Maxwell, *Let's Go Back*, 196–97.
48. Calvin Bowers, "Reflections on the Death of Martin Luther King," *Christian Chronicle* 25 (Apr. 19, 1968): 2.
49. G. P. Holt, "Cool Summers on a Hot Eternity," *Christian Echo* (June 1968): 1.
50. *The 38th Annual Lauderdale Lectures and Ministers' Institute Conference* (Jan. 19–23, 2014) www.thekingcenter.org/archive/document/letter-w-f-washington-mlk (Jan. 1, 2015).
51. James Kennedy, "Silent Church in Turbulent World," *Carolina Christian* 10 (June 1968): 8, 10.
52. Andrew J. Hairston, "Spiritual Equality in Christ," *Christian Echo* (Oct. 1969): 5.
53. Ibid.
54. Eugene Lawton, *Let Me Sound My Trumpet* (Newark, NJ: Lawton, 1975), 15–16.

55. Ibid., 79–80. The statement "white people are blue eyed devils" echoes the pronouncement of black nationalist leader, Malcolm X, who often attached the label to white people. See *The Autobiography of Malcolm X as Told to Alex Haley* (New York: Random House, 1964), 226, 229.
56. Maxwell, *Let's Go Back*, 191–92.
57. R. C. Wells, *I Shall Not Be Moved* (New York: Dr. R. C. Wells, 1979), 174–75, 181.
58. Ibid., 184–85.
59. Ibid., 185.

9. MAKING SOMETHING OUT OF NOTHING

1. J. S. Winston, "George Phillip Bowser: An Outstanding Pioneer, Educator and Gospel Preacher," *Christian Echo* 84 (Nov.-Dec. 1992): 2.
2. Mary McLeod Bethune, "A College on a Garbage Dump" [1941], in Gerda Lerner, *Black Women in White America: A Documentary History* (New York: Vintage Books, 1973), 138.
3. Tuggle, *Another World Wonder* (n.p., n.d.), 46.
4. Jacqueline Jones, *Labor of Love, Labor of Sorrow: Black Women, Work and the Family, from Slavery to the Present* (New York: Vintage Books, 1985), 23, 102.
5. Anthea D. Butler, *Women in the Church of God in Christ: Making a Sanctified World* (Chapel Hill: University of North Carolina Press, 2007), 12.
6. Bettye Collier-Thomas, *Jesus, Jobs, and Justice: African American Women and Religion* (New York: Alfred A. Knopf, 2010), xxx.
7. Robinson, *Show Us How You Do It*, 2.
8. Tuggle, *Another World Wonder*, 10. See also Robinson, *I Was under a Heavy Burden*, 20–22.
9. Tuggle, *Another World Wonder*, 45.
10. Ibid., 45–46.
11. Ibid., 112.
12. Robinson, *I Was under a Heavy Burden*, 56–61.
13. Tuggle, *Another World Wonder*, 113.
14. Ibid., 114–15.
15. Ibid. Phoebe and Lydia were encouragers and supporters of Paul and his ministerial companions (see Acts 16:14-15, 40; Romans 16:1-2).
16. Gray, *Bus Ride to Justice*, 10–11. See also Robinson, *I Was under a Heavy Burden*, 75, 81.
17. Annie C. Tuggle, "The Bowser Christian Institute," *Christian Echo* (1942): 2.
18. Tuggle, *Our Ministers and Song Leaders*, 5.
19. Tuggle, *Another World Wonder*, 201–202.
20. Thelma M. Holt, *My Task* (Indianapolis: Holt, 1978), 101, 103.
21. Thelma M. Holt, *Reach Out and Touch: A Book of Remembrances, Favorite Poems and Thoughts from the Book of Psalms* (Indianapolis: Holt, n.d.), 75.

22. Ibid., 75–76.
23. Ibid., 77.
24. Robinson, *I Was under a Heavy Burden*, 63–81.
25. Holt, *Reach Out*, 81.
26. Ibid.
27. Ibid., 80.
28. Thelma Holt, "Learning to Live," *Christian Echo* 52 (Dec. 1957): 3.
29. Holt, *Reach Out*, 74.
30. Holt, *My Task*, preface.
31. Ibid., 12.
32. Phyllis Davis (instructor at Southwestern Christian College and granddaughter of Thelma Holt), in discussion with the author, March 22, 2016, has confirmed that her grandmother and grandfather divorced after several years of marriage. The details of the divorce are unclear.
33. Holt, My Task, 15–16, 21.
34. Ibid., 28.
35. Ibid., 31, 39.
36. Tuggle, *Another World Wonder*, 11; Robinson, *I Was under a Heavy Burden*, 86.
37. Holt, *My Task*, 41–42.
38. Ibid.
39. Ibid., 43.
40. Collier-Thomas, *Jesus, Jobs, and Justice*, xxv.
41. Ibid., 86.
42. Deborah Gray White, *Too Heavy a Load: Black Women in Defense of Themselves, 1894–1994* (New York: W. W. Norton, 1999), 16.
43. Pinn and Pinn, *Fortress Introduction*, 36, 41, 81–91; Angell, *Bishop Henry McNeal Turner*, 181–83.
44. Maxwell, *Let's Go Back*, 61–72.
45. Ezekiel Z. Webster, "The Outlook," *Christian Echo* 38 (Aug. 1943): 5.
46. Robinson, *The Fight Is On in Texas*, 120–21.
47. Maybelline Griffin, "Maggie Hogan," *Christian Echo* (Jan.-Feb. 1997): 9; "Women at Work," *Christian Echo* (Oct. 1974): 5; Maxwell, *Let's Go Back*, 67.
48. Holt, *Reach Out and Touch*, 78.

10. "I'M COMING UP LORD"

1. James H. Cone, *The Spirituals and the Blues: An Interpretation* (New York: Seabury Press, 1972), 32.
2. Andrew Ward, *Dark Midnight When I Rise: The Story of the Jubilee Singers Who Introduced the World to the Music of Black America* (New York: Farrar, Straus and Giroux, 2000), 112.
3. C. Eric Lincoln and Lawrence H. Mamiya, *The Black Church in the African*

American Experience (Durham: Duke University Press, 1999 [1990]), 350. See also *Slave Songs of the United States* (Bedford, MA: Applewood Books, 1867).

4. Solomon Northup, *Twelve Years a Slave* (New York: Dover Publications, 1970 [1853]), 216.

5. Selina Huntington Campbell, *Home Life and Reminiscences of Alexander Campbell* (St. Louis: John Burns, 1882), 455.

6. Quoted in Edward J. Blum, *Reforging the White Republic: Race, Religion, and American Nationalism, 1865–1898* (Baton Rouge: Louisiana State University Press, 2015 [2005]), 67.

7. Frederick Douglass, Narrative of the Life of Frederick Douglass, An American Slave, Written by Himself (New York: W. W. Norton, 1997 [1845]), 19.

8. Booker T. Washington, *Up from Slavery* (New York: Oxford University Press, 1995 [1901]), 11.

9. S. R. Cassius, "Lord, I Done Done," *Christian Leader* 43 (Nov. 19, 1929): 16; Robinson, *To Save My Race*, 34–35; see also Jon Michael Spencer, *Black Hymnody: A Hymnological History of the African-American Church* (Knoxville: University of Tennessee Press, 1992).

10. W. E. B. Du Bois, *The Souls of Black Folk* (Boston: Bedford/St. Martin's 1997 [1903]), 185, 187. Ward, *Dark Midnight*, 122, 180–81, 398–400; Eileen Southern, *The Music of Black Americans: A History* (New York: W. W. Norton, 1997 [1971]), 227–29.

11. Choate, *Roll Jordan Roll*, 18.

12. Tuggle, *Another World Wonder*, 50.

13. Goodpasture, ed., *Biography and Sermons of Marshall Keeble*, 43–44.

14. Choate, *Roll Jordan Roll*, 48. Robinson, *Show Us How You Do It*, 80.

15. Choate, *Roll Jordan Roll*, 67.

16. Robinson, *The Fight Is On in Texas*, 67–77; Robinson, *Show Us How You Do It*, 137–39.

17. Choate, *Roll Jordan Roll*, 60.

18. Ibid., 75, 78, 86.

19. Edith L. Blumhofer, *Her Heart Can See: The Life and Hymns of Fanny J. Crosby* (Grand Rapids: Eerdmans, 2005), 239; Bruce J. Evensen, *God's Man for the Gilded Age: D. L. Moody and the Rise of Modern Mass Evangelism* (New York: Oxford University Press, 2003), 7–9.

20. Choate, *Roll Jordan Roll*, 79.

21. Ethel Thompson, "The Outlook," *Christian Echo* (Oct. 1941): 5.

22. Roberta Lucas, "The Outlook," *Christian Echo* (Dec. 20, 1941): 5.

23. Leroy Butler Jr., *A New Citizenry in an Old South: The Story of the First Black Church of Christ in Georgia* (Leroy Butler Jr., 2015), 158.

24. Tuggle, *Our Ministers and Song Leaders*, 5.

25. Moses Lard, "Instrumental Music in Churches and Dancing," *Lard's Quarterly* 1 (1864): 330-331; Leroy Garrett, *The Stone-Campbell Movement: An Anecdotal History of*

Three Churches (Joplin: College Press, 1987 [1981]), 466. See also Hughes, *Reviving the Ancient Faith*, 15, 86–88.

26. G. E. Steward, *Our Pulpit* (Fort Worth: Steward, 1965), 182.

27. Spencer, *Black Hymnody*, 4–5; Lincoln and Mamiya, *Black Church*, 373–76.

28. Calvin H. Bowers, *Realizing the California Dream*, 197.

29. Forrest M. McCann, "A History of Great Songs of the Church," *Restoration Quarterly* (Fourth Quarter, 1996): 219.

30. Ibid., 222.

31. Alfred L. Brophy, *Reconstructing the Dreamland: The Tulsa Race Riot of 1921, Race, Reparations, and Reconciliation* (New York: Oxford University Press, 2002).

32. Boyd, *Undying Dedication*, 53, 69-72. Regrettably, I have not been able to find copies of Bowser's hymnal, *Choice Selections*.

33. Southern, *Music of Black Americans*, 263. See also Dennis C. Dickerson, "Heritage and Hymnody: Richard Allen and the Making of African Methodism," in Mark A. Noll and Edith L. Blumhofer, eds., *Sing Them Over Again to Me: Hymns and Hymnbooks in America* (Tuscaloosa: University of Alabama Press, 2006), 178–79.

34. Robinson, ed., *A Godsend to His People*, xxi.

35. Gene C. Finley, ed., *Our Garden of Song: A Book of Biography of Song Writers of the Church of Christ and Articles and Other Items of Interest of Our Worship in Song* (West Monroe, LA: Howard, 1980), 30, 93, 175, 242, 471.

36. Ibid., 157, 167, 191, 480.

37. Robinson, *To Save My Race*, 34; Spencer, *Black Hymnody*, 65–66.

38. Spencer, *Black Hymnody*, 86, 151.

39. Quoted in Nick Salvatore, *Singing in a Strange Land: C. L. Franklin, the Black Church, and the Transformation of America* (New York: Little, Brown, 2005), 69–70.

40. Finley, *Our Garden of Song*, 152.

41. Willie Eva Burnett's testimony appears in *My Southwestern Story: A Collection of Memories, Submitted by Alumni, Faculty, and Friends of Southwestern Christian College* (Southwestern Christian College Alumni Association, 2009), in author's possession.

42. Barry Graham, in discussion with the author, Aug. 25, 2011, and May 28, 2014.

43. Robinson, *The Fight Is On in Texas*, 169–70.

44. Sylvia Rose, *Songs of Faith* (Detroit: Srose Publishing Company, 1985), 9, 16, 17.

45. Veronica Williams, in discussion with the author, Nov. 24, 2014.

46. Thomas Fitzgerald, in discussion with the author, July 16, 2015; Veronica Williams, in discussion with the author, Nov. 24, 2014.

47. Chris Turner, in discussion with the author, July 21, 2015. For the widespread influence of Sam Cooke on American music, see Anthony Heilbut, *The Gospel Sound: Good News and Bad Times* (New York: Limelight, 1989 [1971]), xviii, 87–93; Greg Kot, *I'll Take You There: Mavis Staples, the Staple Singers, and the March up Freedom's Highway* (New York: Scribner, 2014), 66–72. Peter Guralnick, *Sweet Soul Music: Rhythm and Blues and the Southern Dream of Freedom* (New York: Harper & Row,

1986), 13, has correctly observed: "Not surprisingly nearly every Southern soul singer, almost without exception, took Sam Cooke, the urbane former gospel Soul Stirrer, for a model."

48. Butler, *A New Citizenry*, 157.
49. Joi Carr, in discussion with the author, Mar. 29, 2016.
50. Bowers, *Realizing the California Dream*, 190.
51. Ibid., 190–91.
52. Robinson, *Show Us How You Do It*, 126–27; Quintard Taylor, *In Search of the Racial Frontier: African Americans in the American West, 1528-1900* (New York: W. W. Norton, 1998), 223.
53. Bowers, *Realizing the California Dream*, 191–92.
54. Ibid., 193, 195, 200.
55. Ibid., 197–98.
56. Ibid.
57. Ibid.
58. Butler, *A New Citizenry*, 156.
59. Ibid.
60. Ibid., 162.
61. Albert E. Kirk, "The Outlook," *Christian Echo* (Nov. 1962): 9.
62. "The Outlook," *Christian Echo* (Feb. 1988): 9.

11. "THE MAGIC OF EDUCATION"

1. Frederick Douglass, *Narrative of the Life of Frederick Douglass, An American Slave, Written by Himself* (New York: W. W. Norton, 1997 [1845]), 29.
2. Ibid.
3. Washington, *Up from Slavery*, 18.
4. Myrdal, *An American Dilemma*, 884.
5. Harrell, *Quest for a Christian America*, 101.
6. Gerda Lerner, *The Grimke Sisters from South Carolina: Pioneers for Women's Rights* (New York: Oxford University Press, 1998), 19.
7. Robinson, *The Fight Is On in Texas*, 140–41. For an excellent study of African Americans' pursuit of their educational destiny in the Christian Church (the Disciples of Christ), see Lawrence A. Q. Burnley, *The Cost of Unity: African American Agency and Education in the Christian Church, 1865-1914* (Macon, GA: Mercer University Press, 2008).
8. Robinson, *To Save My Race*, 13, 104–110.
9. Jacqueline Jones, *Soldiers of Light and Love: Northern Teachers and Georgia Blacks, 1865-1873* (Athens: University of Georgia Press, 1992 [1980]).
10. Franklin and Higginbotham, *From Slavery to Freedom*, 250.
11. Du Bois, *The Souls of Black Folk*, 97.
12. Ibid.
13. Robinson, *To Save My Race*, 14–15, 19.

14. "Elder Peter Lowery," *Gospel Advocate* 30 (Feb. 1, 1888): 11; Harrell, *Sources of Division*, 2:163; Jesse Curtis Pope, "Tennessee Manual Labor University," in Foster et al., *Encyclopedia of the Stone-Campbell Movement*, 729–30; Bobby Lovett, "Tennessee Manual Labor University" *The Tennessee Encyclopedia of History and Culture*. www.tennesseeencyclopedia.net, accessed on Aug. 11, 2016.

15. Hap Lyda, "Black Disciples in the Nineteenth Century" in William K. Fox, ed., *The Untold Story: A Short History of Black Disciples* (St. Louis: Christian Board, 1976): 9–19.

16. Andrew R. Wood, "Southern Christian Institute (1875-1954)" in Foster et al., eds., *The Encyclopedia of the Stone-Campbell Movement*, 694–95.

17. Robinson, *To Save My Race*, 101-110. See also Robinson, ed., *To Lift up My Race*, 33–41.

18. Boyd, *Undying Dedication*, 37–63.

19. Marshall Keeble, "School Suggestions," *Christian Echo* (July 20, 1939): 6; P. H. Black, "School Suggestions," *Christian Echo* (Nov. 20, 1939): 6.

20. P. H. Black, B. M. Woods, and James M. Cannon, "School Suggestions," *Christian Echo* (Sept. 1939): 6.

21. Bowser, "My Views about the Matter," *Christian Echo* (Sept. 1939): 6.

22. Calvin H. Bowers, *Realizing the California Dream*, 277.

23. Robinson, *The Fight Is On in Texas*, 111–13.

24. Jack Evans, "The History of Southwestern Christian College, Terrell, Texas." (master's thesis, Texas Western College, 1963): 1–4; Robinson, *The Fight Is On in Texas*, 155–76.

25. Robert Hooper, *A Distinct People: A History of Churches of Christ in the 20th Century* (Eugene, Oregon: Wipf and Stock, 2001 [1993]), 270. For insightful information on the life and work of E. W. McMillan in Cleburne, Texas, and Abilene, Texas, before relocating to Terrell, see: John C. Stevens, *No Ordinary University: The History of a City Set on a Hill* (Abilene, TX: Abilene Christian University Press, 1998), 124, 125, 131, 132.

26. The Annual Staff, *The 1962 Ram* (Terrell, TX, 1962).

27. Robinson, *The Fight Is On in Texas*, 157.

28. Theodore Wes Crawford, "From Segregation to Independence: African Americans in Churches of Christ" (PhD diss., Vanderbilt University, 2008), 116. See also Wes Crawford, *Shattering the Illusion: How African American Churches of Christ Moved from Segregation to Independence* (Abilene, TX: Abilene Christian University Press, 2013), 24.

29. Robinson, *The Fight Is On in Texas*, 159.

30. Ibid., 124, 165–71, 179–80.

31. Ibid., 166; For an overview of the legacy of Billy Curl, see the website http://www.crenshawchurchofchrist.com,accessed on July 25, 2017.

32. For a biographical sketch of Daniel Harrison, see the website http://www.chathamavaloncoc.com, accessed on July 25, 2017.

33. For a biographical sketch of Eugene Lawton, see the website:http://www.newarkchurchofchrist.org, accessed on July 25, 2017.

34. Robinson, *The Fight Is On in Texas*, 124. For a biographical sketch of Andrew Hairston, see the website http://www.simpsonstreetchurchofchrist.org, accessed on July 25, 2017.

35. Robinson, *The Fight Is On in Texas*, 166–67.

36. Ibid., 155–76, 179–80.

37. Hughes, *Reviving the Ancient Faith*, 332.

38. Bowers, *Realizing the California Dream*, 299-300.

39. Ibid.

40. http://www.srs.org, accessed July 18, 2017.

41. Ibid.

42. Other men who received training at the School of Religious Studies include Anthony Powell; Jeff Bohanna of Memphis, Tennessee; Mario Carr; Marion Patterson; Willie Sanborn (preached for the Belzoni Church of Christ for his death); L. C. Griffin; Freddie Vaughans; Willie Williams of Cape Girardeau, Missouri; Adell Anderson, minister of the Wall Street Church of Christ in Carbondale, Illinois; Dwight Brownlee, preacher for the West End Church of Christ in Memphis, Tennessee; Keith Bryant, minister for the Main Street Church of Christ in Stuttgart, Arkansas; Royce Green of DeKalb, Texas; Chris Dillon of Atlanta, Georgia; Markius Ingram, minister of the Ninth Street Church of Christ in Paducah, Kentucky; Ambrose LaCaze, minister of the Lake Street Church of Christ in Natchitoches, Louisiana; and Ricky Gordon, a deceased student with the Eastside Church of Christ in Garland, Texas. Many thanks to Loyd Clay Harris for sharing this information with me via email.

43. Hamil R. Harris and Erik Tryggestad, "Los Angeles Minister Dies after Delivering Sermon," last modified Nov. 4, 2015, accessed July 18, 2017, http:// www.christianchronicle.org.

44. Franklin and Higginbotham, *From Slavery to Freedom*, 579.

45. http://www.northbroadwaychurchofchrist.org (accessed on July 18, 2017).

12. BROTHERS IN ARMS

1. Roosevelt Sams, *My Experience Relevant to My Work at Southwestern Christian College, Terrell, Texas* (No publisher, 1989), 7, 12. See also Tom Brokaw, *The Greatest Generation* (New York: Random House, 1998).

2. Franklin and Higginbotham, *From Slavery to Freedom*, 329.

3. Earl I. West, *The Search for the Ancient Order*, 3:374–77; R. Vernon Boyd, *Undying Dedication: The Story of G. P. Bowser* (Nashville: Gospel Advocate Company, 1985); Michael Casey, *From Religious Outsiders to Insiders: The Rise and Fall of Pacifism in the Churches of Christ* (Waco: Baylor University Press, 2002), 12–21. Richard T. Hughes, *Reviving the Ancient Faith*, 153.

4. S. R. Cassius, "Among Our Colored Disciples," *Christian Leader* 32 (Aug. 13, 1918): 8. See also Robinson, *To Save My Race*, 84.

5. Tuggle, *Another World Wonder*, 5, 17, 19.
6. Tuggle, *Our Ministers and Song Leaders*, 36, 112, 128.
7. Ibid., 128.
8. Franklin and Higginbotham, *From Slavery to Freedom*, 457–58.
9. Elbert Hudson, "Overseas," *Christian Echo* 38 (Nov. 5, 1943): 4.
10. Kermit Nixon, "From a Soldier in the U. S. Army, and a Soldier in the Christian Army," *Christian Echo* 38 (Dec. 5, 1943): 2.
11. Robinson, *The Fight Is on in Texas*, 23.
12. Lloyd L. Watkins, "Present You Faultless before the Presence of His Glory and to Keep You from Falling," *Christian Echo* 38 (July 5, 1943): 2.
13. Tyree G. Wells, in discussion with the author, July 24, 2015.
14. Ted Thompson, "Ex-Pow Tells Amazing Tale of Survival," *Jacksonville Daily Progress* (Feb. 8, 1988): C-1.
15. Ibid.
16. Tyree G. Wells, in discussion with the author, July 24, 2015. See also Robinson, *The Fight Is on in Texas*, 74–75.
17. Harrell, *A Quest for a Christian America, 1800-1865: A Social History of the Disciples of Christ* (Tuscaloosa: University of Alabama Press, 2003 [1966]), 1:97–107.
18. S. R. Cassius, "Bible School Jottings," *Bible Student* 1 (Mar. 1904): 1.
19. Robinson, *To Save My Race*, 156.
20. Marshall Keeble, *From Mule Back to Super Jet* (Nashville: Gospel Advocate Company, 1962), 30, 33. Robinson, ed., *A Godsend to His People*, 98, 100.
21. "Negro Group Sets Precedent; Will Back White Preacher," *Christian Chronicle* 18 (Mar. 10, 1961): 1. See also "Richmond Negro Church to Send out White Missionary," *Singapore-Far East Newsletter* (Sept. 12, 1961): 10–11; and F. F. Carson, "The Outlook," *Christian Echo* (Aug. 1964): 9–10.
22. R. N. Hogan, "Let's Send Her with Him," *Christian Echo* 60 (Jan. 1965): 1.
23. Levi Kennedy, "Serving the Needs of the Nigerian," *Christian Echo* (Feb. 1963): 5.
24. F. F. Carson, "The Great Challenge," *Christian Echo* (Feb. 1964): 4; F. F. Carson, "The Great Challenge," *Christian Echo* (Apr. 1964): 4.
25. R. N. Hogan, "Lets Send Her with Him," *Christian Echo* (Jan. 1965): 1.
26. Eno Otoyo, "Four New Churches Established in Oron Division," *Christian Echo* (May 1964): 6–7.
27. "Billy Curl to Enter Ethiopia in July," *Christian Echo* (June 1964): 3.
28. Billy C. Curl, "From Ethiopia," *Christian Echo* 59 (Sept. 1964): 1–2.
29. Billy C. Curl, "Report from Ethiopia," *Christian Echo* (Apr. 1965): 10.
30. R. N. Hogan, "We Must Continue to Do Our Best," *Christian Echo* (June 1976): 3.
31. See http://www.crenshawchurchofchrist.com, accessed on July 26, 2017.
32. R. C. Wells, "History of the Liberia Works," *Christian Echo* (Apr. 1969): 4.
33. Ibid., 9.
34. R. C. Wells, "Monrovia Missionary Work Expands," *Christian Echo* 63 (Mar. 1968): 1.

35. O. L. Trone, "The Work in Nassau, Bahamas Pleads for Our Help—Do We Care?" *Christian Echo* (Mar. 1963): 7.

36. O. L. Trone, "Missionaries to Jamaica, West Indies," *Christian Echo* 59 (Apr. 1964): 1.

37. Tuggle, *Another World* Wonder, 156–57, 173, 176; see also Robinson, *I Was under a Heavy Burden: The Life of Annie C. Tuggle*, 79–80.

38. "Operation Outreach—Guyana," *Christian Echo* (Oct. 1967): 4; Alfred McCurchin, "Introducing My Country, Guyana," *Christian Echo* (Aug. 1968): 7.

39. "1971 Campaign for Christ in Guyana, South America," *Christian Echo* 69 (Sept. 1971): 4; Carroll Pitts, Jr., "30 Baptized in Guyana, South America Campaign," *Christian Echo* 71 (Oct. 1973): 1, 8.

40. Ibid., 8. "American Missionaries Going to Guyana, South America," *Christian Echo* (Feb. 1974): 7.

EPILOGUE

1. "Local Minister Speaks with President Clinton" *Christian Echo* (January-February 1994): 10.

2. Ibid.

3. Robinson, *The Fight Is On in Texas*, 174.

4. Rick Hunter, "First Century Grace for 21st Century Burdens" (in author's possession). Quotation is from an email message to author, Sept. 7, 2017.

5. Franklin and Higginbotham, *From Slavery to Freedom*, 638–39.

6. Hamil R. Harris, "D. C. Members Celebrate First Black President," *Christian Chronicle* (Feb. 2009): 1.

7. Michael Eric Dyson, *The Black Presidency: Barack Obama and the Politics of Race in America* (Boston: Houghton Mifflin Harcourt, 2016), xvi.

8. Bobby Ross, Jr., "Worship Is Our Protest," *Christian Chronicle* (Jan. 15, 2015):1; http://www.christianchronicle.org, accessed Aug. 22, 2017.

9. Ted Parks, "Fighting Injustice with Shared Silence," *Christian Chronicle* (July 2015): 10.

10. The author was present at the Aug. 1, 2015, meeting in Houston, Texas, and took notes of the exchange between Jack Evans, Sr., James Maxwell, Ben Foster, Sr., Jon Morrison, John C. Whitley, and Tommy Brooks. H. Clay Williams and other preachers in the Dallas, Texas, area conduct a weekly television program called, *According to the Scriptures*, based on Paul's assertion in 1 Corinthians 15:3–4.

11. http://www.ncocl.net, accessed on Aug. 28, 2017.

12. Bobby Ross, Jr., "In Dallas, A Somber Sunday," *Christian Chronicle* (Aug. 2016): 1, 13.

BIBLIOGRAPHY

NEWSPAPERS

Bible Student (Canada), 1904.
Christian Chronicle (Edmond, Oklahoma), 2013.
Christian Companion (Wichita, Kansas), 1915.
Christian Echo (Fort Smith, Arkansas; Los Angeles, California), 1935-1995.
Christian Evangelist (St. Louis, Missouri), 1889.
Christian Leader (Cincinnati, Ohio), 1895-1930
Firm Foundation (Austin, Texas), 1974.
Gospel Advocate (Nashville, Tennessee), 1855-1861, 1865-1995.
Greenwood Commonwealth (Greenwood, Mississippi), 1903.
Herald-Citizen (Cookeville, Tennessee), 2000.
Jacksonville Daily Progress (Jacksonville, Texas), 1988.
Lard's Quarterly. 1864.
Millennial Harbinger (Bethany, Virginia), 1845.
Singapore-Far East Newsletter. 1961.
Waco-Tribune (Waco, Texas), 2014.

ARTICLES AND BOOKS

Abdul-Jabbar, Kareem. *Brothers in Arms: The Epic Story of the 761st Tank Battalion, WWII's Forgotten Heroes*. New York: Broadway Books, 2004.
Ahlstrom, Sydney. *A Religious History of the American People*. New Haven: Yale University Press, 2004 [1971].
Allen, C. Leonard and Richard T. Hughes. *Discovering Our Roots: The Ancestry of Churches of Christ*. Abilene, Texas: Abilene Christian University Press, 1988.
Ansariyah-Grace, Tasneem. "Home on the Hill" *Citizen-Statesman* (Nov. 2, 1999): 10-A.
Arsenault, Raymond. *Freedom Riders: 1961 and the Struggle for Racial Justice*. New York: Oxford University Press, 2006.
Baldwin, James. *The Fire Next Time*. New York: Vintage Books, 1962.
Billingsley, Andrew. *Mighty Like a River: The Black Church and Social Reform*. New York: Oxford University Press, 1999.
Blassingame, John W. *The Slave Community: The Plantation Life in the Antebellum South*. New York: Oxford University Press, 1979 [1972].

Blee, Kathleen M. *Women of the Klan: Racism and Gender in 1920s*. Berkeley: University of California Press, 1991.

Blum, Edward J. *Reforging the White Republic: Race, Religion, and American Nationalism, 1865–1898*. Baton Rouge: Louisiana State University Press, 2005 [2015].

Blum, Edward J., and Paul Harvey. *The Color of Christ: The Son of God and the Saga of Race in America*. Chapel Hill: University of North Carolina Press, 2012.

Blumhofer, Edith L. *Her Heart Can See: The Life and Hymns of Fanny J. Crosby*. Grand Rapids, MI: Eerdmans, 2005.

Bowers, Calvin H. *Realizing the California Dream: The Story of Black Churches of Christ in Los Angeles*. Calvin H. Bowers, 2001.

Boyd, R. Vernon. *A History of Stone-Campbell Churches in Michigan, With Emphasis on the A Cappella Churches of Christ*. R. Vernon Boyd, 2009.

———. *Undying Dedication: The Story of G. P. Bowser*. Nashville: Gospel Advocate Company, 1985.

Brands, H. W. *T. R.: The Last Romantic*. New York: Basic Books, 1997.

Brands, H. W., T. H. Breen, R. Hal Williams, and Ariela J. Gross. *American Stories: A History of the United States*. Boston: Pearson Education, 2012 [2009].

Brokaw, Tom. *The Greatest Generation*. New York: Random House, 1998.

Brophy, Alfred L. *Reconstructing the Dreamland: The Tulsa Riot of 1921, Race, Reparations, and Reconciliation*. New York: Oxford University Press, 2002.

Burnley, Lawrence A. Q. *The Cost of Unity: African American Agency and Education in the Christian Church, 1865–1914*. Macon, Georgia: Mercer University Press, 2008.

Butler, Anthea D. *Women in the Church of God in Christ: Making a Sanctified World*. Chapel Hill: University of North Carolina Press, 2007.

Butler, LeRoy, Jr. *A New Citizenry in an Old South: The Story of the First Black Church of Christ in Georgia*. LeRoy Butler, Jr., 2015.

Campbell, Selina Huntington. *Home Life and Reminiscences of Alexander Campbell*. St. Louis: John Burns, 1882.

Carson, F. F., and Francis Perry Carson. *A Matter of Faith*. Houston, Texas: Whitley's, 1991.

Casey, Michael W. *Saddlebags, City Streets and Cyberspace: A History of Preaching in the Churches of Christ*. Abilene, TX: Abilene Christian University Press, 1995.

Cassius, S. R. *Negro Evangelization and the Tohee Industrial School*. Cincinnati: Christian Leader Print, 1898.

———. *The Third Birth of a Nation*. 2nd ed. Cincinnati: F. L. Rowe, 1925.

Cato, Willie. *His Hand and His Heart: The Wit and Wisdom of Marshall Keeble*. Winona, MS: J. C. Choate, 1990.

Chalmers, David. *Hooded Americanism: The First Century of the Ku Klux Klan, 1865–1965*. New York: Doubleday, 1965.

Chappell, David L. *A Stone of Hope: Prophetic Religion and the Death of Jim Crow*. Chapel Hill: University of North Carolina Press, 2004.

Choate, J. E. *Roll Jordan Roll: A Biography of Marshall Keeble*. Nashville: Gospel Advocate Company, 1974.

Collier-Thomas, Bettye. *Jesus, Jobs, and Justice: African American Women and Religion.* New York: Alfred A. Knopf, 2010.
Cone, James H. *The Cross and the Lynching Tree.* Maryknoll, NY: Orbis Books, 2011.
———. *The Spirituals and the Blues: An Interpretation.* New York: Seabury Press, 1972.
Crawford, Wes. *Shattering the Illusion: How African American Churches of Christ Moved from Segregation to Independence.* Abilene, TX: Abilene Christian University Press, 2013.
Daniels, Pete. *Lost Revolutions: The South in the 1950s.* Chapel Hill: University of North Carolina Press, 2000.
Dickerson, Dennis C. *African American Preachers and Politics: The Careys of Chicago.* Jackson: University Press of Mississippi, 2010.
Douglass, Frederick. *Narrative of the Life of Frederick Douglass, An American Slave Written by Himself.* New York: W. W. Norton, 1997 [1845].
Dray, Philip. *At the Hands of Persons Unknown: The Lynching of Black America.* New York: Modern Library, 2002.
Du Bois, W. E. B. *The Souls of Black Folk.* Boston: Bedford/St. Martin's, 1997 [1903].
Dyson, Michael Eric. *I May Not Get There with You: The True Martin Luther King, Jr.* New York: The Free Press, 2000.
———. *The Black Presidency: Barack Obama and the Politics of Race in America.* Boston: Houghton Mifflin Harcourt, 2016.
Eaton, Clement. *A History of the Old South: The Emergence of a Reluctant Nation.* 3rd ed. (Prospect Heights, IL: Waveland Press, 1975).
Ellison, Ralph. *Invisible Man.* New York: Random House, 1995 [1952].
Equiano, Olaudah. *The Interesting Narrative of the Life of Olaudah Equiano, Written by Himself.* Boston: Bedford Books, 1995 [1791].
Evensen, Bruce J. *God's Man for the Gilded Age: D. L. Moody and the Rise of Modern Mass Evangelism.* New York: Oxford University Press, 2003.
Fife, Robert O. *Teeth on Edge.* Grand Rapids, MI: Baker Book House, 1971.
Finley, Gene C. ed. *Our Garden of Song: A Book of Biography of Song Writers of the Church of Christ and Articles and Other Items of Interest of Our Worship in Song.* West Monroe, LA: Howard, 1980.
Foster, Douglas A., Paul M. Blowers, Anthony L. Dunnavant, and D. Newell Williams, eds., *The Encyclopedia of the Stone-Campbell Movement.* Grand Rapids, MI: Eerdmans, 2004.
Franklin, John Hope and Evelyn Brooks Higginbotham. *From Slavery to Freedom: A History of African Americans*, 9th edition. New York: McGraw-Hill, 2011.
Frederickson, George M. *Racism: A Short History.* Princeton: Princeton University Press, 2002.
Garrett, Leroy. *The Stone-Campbell: An Anecdotal History of Three Churches.* Joplin: College Press, 1987.
Gatewood, Willard B., Jr. *Theodore Roosevelt and the Art of Controversy: Episodes of the White House Years.* Baton Rouge: Louisiana State University Press, 1970.

Goodpasture, B. C., ed., *Biography and Sermons of Marshall Keeble, Evangelist.* Nashville: Gospel Advocate Company, 1966 [1931].
Gray, Fred D. *Bus Ride to Justice: Changing the System by the System.* Montgomery: Black Belt Press, 1995.
Gunnar, Myrdal. *An American Dilemma: The Negro Problem and Modern Democracy.* New York: Harper & Brothers, 1944.
Guralnick, Peter. *Sweet Soul Music: Rhythm and Blues and the Southern Dream of Freedom.* New York: Harper & Row, 1986.
Harrell, David Edwin, Jr. *Quest for a Christian America, 1800–1865: A Social History of the Disciples of Christ.* Tuscaloosa: University of Alabama Press, 2003 [1966].
———. *Sources of Division in the Disciples of Christ, 1865–1900: A Social History of the Disciples of Christ.* Vol. 2. Tuscaloosa: University of Alabama Press, 2003 [1973].
Hatch, Nathan O. *The Democratization of American Christianity.* New Haven, CT: Yale University Press, 1989.
Heilbut, Anthony. *The Gospel Sound: Good News and Bad Times.* New York: Limelight, 1989 [1971].
Hewett, Janet B., ed. *The Roster of Union Soldiers, 1861–1865.* Wilmington, NC: Broadfoot, 1997.
Hofstadter, Richard. *Social Darwinism in American Thought.* New York: George Braziller, 1959.
Holt, Thelma M. *My Task.* Indianapolis: Holt, 1978.
———. *Reach Out and Touch: A Book of Remembrances, Favorite Poems and Thoughts from the Book of Psalms.* Indianapolis: Holt, n. d.
Hooper, Robert. *A Distinct People: A History of Churches of Christ in the 20th Century.* Eugene, OR: Wipf and Stock, 2001 [1993].
Hughes, Richard T. *Reviving the Ancient Faith: The Story of Churches of Christ in America.* Grand Rapids, MI: Eerdmans, 1996.
Jones, Jacqueline. *Labor of Love, Labor of Sorrow: Black Women, Work and the Family, from Slavery to the Present.* New York: Vintage Books, 1985.
———. *Soldiers of Light and Love: Northern Teachers and Georgia Blacks, 1865–1873.* Athens: University of Georgia Press, 1992 [1980].
Jordan, Robert L. *Two Races in One Fellowship.* Detroit: United Christian Church, 1944.
Keeble, Marshall. *From Mule Back to Super Jet.* Nashville: Gospel Advocate Company, 1962.
Kidd, Colin. *The Forging of Races: Race and Scripture in the Protestant Atlantic World, 1600–2000.* New York: Cambridge University Press, 2006.
Kidd, Thomas. *The Great Awakening: A Brief History with Documents.* Boston: Bedford/St. Martin's, 2008.
Kot, Greg. *I'll Take You There: Mavis Staples, The Staple Singers, and the March up Freedom Highway.* New York: Scribner, 2014.
Lawton, Eugene. *Fasten Your Seatbelts: Turbulence May Be Ahead.* Newark, NJ: Lawton, 1983.

Lehr, Dick. *The Birth of a Nation: How a Legendary Filmmaker and a Crusading Editor Reignited America's Civil War*. New York: Public Affairs, 2014.
Lerner, Gerda. *The Grimke Sisters from South Carolina: Pioneers for Women's Rights*. NewYork: Oxford University Press, 1998.
———, ed. *Black Women in White America: A Documentary History*. New York: Vintage Books, 1973.
Lewis, David Levering. *W. E. B. Du Bois: The Fight for Equality and the American Century, 1919–1963*. New York: Henry Holt, 2000.
Lewis, John, and Michael D'orso. *Walking with the Wind: A Memoir of the Movement*. San Diego: Harcourt Brace, 1998.
Lincoln, C. Eric, and Lawrence H. Mamiya. *The Black Church in the African American Experience*. Durham: Duke University Press, 1990.
Litwack, Leon F. *Been in the Storm So Long: The Aftermath of Slavery*. New York: Vintage Books, 1979.
Logan, Rayford W. *The Betrayal of the Negro: From Rutherford B. Hayes to Woodrow Wilson*. New York: De Capo Press, 1997.
Long, Loretta M. *The Life of Selina Campbell: A Fellow Soldier in the Cause of Restoration*. Tuscaloosa: University of Alabama Press, 2001.
Lyda, Hap. "Black Disciples in the Nineteenth Century" in *The Untold Story: A Short History of Black Disciples*. St. Louis: Christian Board, 1976.
Maxwell, James. *God's Declaration of Independence: Southwestern Christian College 38th Annual Lectureship Series*. Terrell, TX: Southwestern Christian College, 1975.
———. *Let's Go Back . . . Way Back: Black Presence in the Restoration Movement*. Terrell, Texas: James Maxwell, 2013.
McPherson, James M. *Battle Cry of Freedom: The Civil War Era*. New York: Ballantine Books, 1988.
Montgomery, William E. *Under Their Own Vine and Fig Tree: The African-American Church in the South, 1865–1900*. Baton Rouge: Louisiana State University Press, 1993.
Morrison, W. W. *The Shaping of a Brotherhood: Historical Reflections, Volume 1*. Plano, TX: Cheudi, 2015.
My Southwestern Story: A Collection of Memories, Submitted by Alumni, Faculty, and Friends of Southwestern Christian College. Southwestern Christian College Alumni Association, 2009.
Myrdal, Gunnar. *An American Dilemma: The Negro Problem and Modern Democracy*. New York: Harper & Brothers, 1944.
Newman, Richard S. *Freedom's Prophet: Bishop Richard Allen, the AME Church, and the Black Founding Fathers*. New York: New York University Press, 2008.
Niebuhr, Reinhold. *Moral Man and Immoral Society: A Study in Ethics and Politics*. New York: Scribner's Sons, 1932.
Noll, Mark A., and Edith L. Blumhofer, eds., *Sing Them Over Again to Me: Hymns and Hymnbooks in America*. Tuscaloosa: University of Alabama Press, 2006.
Northup, Solomon. *Twelve Years a Slave*. New York: Dover Publications, 1970.

Oates, Stephen B. *The Fires of Jubilee: Nat Turner's Fierce Rebellion*. New York: Harper & Row, 1975.

Person, Michael. *Emancipation and Reconstruction, 1862–1879*. Wheeling, IL: Harlan Davidson, 1987.

Pinn, Anne E., and Anthony B. Pinn. *Fortress Introduction to Black Church History*. Minneapolis: Fortress Press, 2002.

Raboteau, Albert J. *A Fire in the Bones: Reflections on African-American Religious History*. Boston, Massachusetts: Beacon Press, 1995.

———. *Slave Religion: The "Invisible Institution" in the Antebellum South*. New York: Oxford University Press, 1980 [1978].

Rampersad, Arnold. *The Life of Langston Hughes: Volume 1: 1902-1941: I, Too, Sing America*. New York: Oxford University Press, 2002.

Richardson, Robert. *Memoirs of Alexander Campbell, Embracing a View of the Origin, Progress and Principles of the Religious Reformation Which He Advocated*. Indianapolis: Religious Book Service, 1897.

Richey, Frank. "'Parson' George Ricks—From Slave to Servant of God." Unpublished manuscript.

Rieder, Jonathan, ed. *Gospel of Freedom: Martin Luther King, Jr.'s Letter from Birmingham Jail and the Struggle That Changed a Nation*. New York: Bloomsbury Press, 2013.

Robinson, Edward J., ed. *A Godsend to His People: The Essential Writings and Speeches of Marshall Keeble*. Knoxville: University of Tennessee Press, 2008.

———. *I Was under a Heavy Burden: The Life of Annie C. Tuggle*. Abilene, TX: Abilene Christian University Press, 2011.

———. *The Fight Is On in Texas: A History of African American Churches of Christ in the Lone Star State, 1865–2000*. Abilene, TX: Abilene Christian University Press, 2008.

———. *Show Us How You Do It: Marshall Keeble and the Rise of Black Churches of Christ in the United States, 1914–1968*. Tuscaloosa: University of Alabama Press, 2008.

———, ed. *To Lift Up My Race: The Essential Writings of Samuel Robert Cassius*. Knoxville: University of Tennessee Press, 2008.

———. *To Save My Race from Abuse: The Life of Samuel Robert Cassius*. Tuscaloosa: University of Alabama Press, 2007.

Rogers, James R. *The Cane Ridge Meetinghouse*. Cincinnati: Standard, 1910.

Rogers, John. *The Biography of Eld. Barton Warren Stone, Written by Himself: With Additions and Reflections*. Cincinnati: J. A. & U. P. James, 1847.

Rothman, Joshua D. *Notorious in the Neighborhood: Sex and Families across the Color Line in Virginia, 1787–1861*. Chapel Hill: University of North Carolina Press, 2003.

Salvatore, Nick. *Singing in a Strange Land: C. L. Franklin, the Black Church, and the Transformation of America*. New York: Little, Brown, 2005.

Sams, Izetta. *My Life from A to Z.* (n.p., 2015).
Schweninger, Loren. *Black Property Owners in the South, 1790–1915.* Urbana: University of Illinois Press, 1990.
Simmons, Todd W. "Preston Taylor: Seeker of Dignity for Black Disciples." *Discipliana* 60 (Winter 2000): 99-109.
Slave Songs of the United States. Bedford, MA: Applewood Books, 1867.
Sobel, Mechal. *Trabelin' On: The Slave Journey to an Afro-Baptist Faith.* Westport, CT: Greenwood Press, 1979.
Southern, Eileen. *The Music of Black Americans: A History.* New York: W. W. Norton, 1997 [1971].
Spencer, Jon Michael. *Black Hymnody: A Hymnological History of the African-American Church.* Knoxville: University of Tennessee Press, 1992.
Stevens, John C. *No Ordinary University: The History of a City Set on a Hill.* Abilene, TX: Abilene Christian University Press, 1998.
Steward, G. E. *Our Pulpit.* Fort Worth, TX: Steward, 1965.
Taylor, Quintard. *In Search of the Racial Frontier: African Americans in the American West.* New York: W. W. Norton, 1998.
Tuggle, Annie C. *Another World Wonder.* N. p., n. d.
———. *Our Ministers and Song Leaders.* Detroit: Annie C. Tuggle, 1945.
Walker, David. *Appeal, in Four Articles; Together with a Preamble, to the Coloured Citizens of the United States of America.* New York: Hill and Wang, 1969.
Ward, Andrew. *Dark Midnight When I Rise: The Story of the Jubilee Singers Who Introduced the World to the Music of Black America.* New York: Farrar, Straus and Giroux, 2000.
Ward, Stephen Angell. *Bishop Henry McNeal Turner and African-American Religion in the South.* Knoxville: University of Tennessee Press, 1992.
Washington, Booker T. *Up from Slavery.* New York: Oxford University Press, 1995 [1901].
Weiss, Nancy J. *Farewell to the Party of Lincoln: Black Politics in the Age of FDR.* Princeton: Princeton University Press, 1983.
West, Earl I. *The Search for the Ancient Order: A History of the Restoration Movement, 1900–1918.* Indianapolis: Religious Book Service, 1979.
White, Deborah Gray. *Ar'nt I a Woman?: Female Slaves in the Plantation South.* New York: W. W. Norton, 1985.
———. *Too Heavy a Load: Black Women in Defense of Themselves, 1894–1994.* New York: W. W. Norton, 1999.
Wilkerson, Isabel. *The Warmth of Other Suns: The Epic Story of America's Great Migration.* New York: Vintage Books, 2010.
Williams, D. Newell. *Barton Stone: A Spiritual Biography.* St. Louis: Chalice Press, 2000.
Williams, D. Newell, Douglas A. Foster, and Paul M. Blowers, eds., *The Stone-Campbell Movement: A Global History.* St. Louis: Chalice Press, 2013.

Williamson, Joel. *New People: Miscegenation and Mulattoes in the United States.* Baton Rouge: Louisiana State University Press, 1995.
Wilmore, Gayraud S. and James H. Cone, eds., *Black Theology: A Documentary History, 1966–1979.* Maryknoll, NY: Orbis Books, 1979.
Winston, J. S. "Work among the Colored People in the United States." In *The Harvest Field*, edited by Howard L. Schug and Jesse P. Sewell, 71-76. Athens, AL: Bible School Bookstore, 1947.
Woodson, Carter G. *The History of the Negro Church.* Washington, DC: Associated Publishers, 1921.
―――. *The Mis-Education of the Negro.* Chicago: African American Images, 2000 [1933].
Woodward, C. Vann. *Origins of the New South.* Baton Rouge: Louisiana State University Press, 1971 [1951].
X, Malcolm, and Alex Haley. *The Autobiography of Malcolm X as Told to Alex Haley*, 1st edition New York: Grove Press, 1964.

UNPUBLISHED SOURCES

Boyd, R. Vernon. "An Interpretive Analysis of the Integration of Two Churches." DMin thesis, Harding Graduate School of Religion, 1986.
Crawford, Theodore Wesley. "From Segregation to Independence: African Americans in Churches of Christ." PhD diss., Vanderbilt University, 2008.
Ellis, Mary Louise. "'Rain Down Fire:' The Lynching of Sam Hose." PhD diss., Florida State University, 1992.
Evans, Jack, Sr. "A History of Southwestern Christian College." master's thesis, Texas Western College, 1963.
Key, Barclay. "Race and Restoration: Churches of Christ and the African American Freedom Struggle." PhD diss., University of Florida, 2007.
McMillon, Lynn A. "A History of Churches of Christ in Tate County, Mississippi, 1836–1965." master's thesis, Harding College Graduate School of Religion, 1966.
Turner, Gary Owen. "Pioneer to Japan: A Biography of J. M. McCaleb." master's thesis, Abilene Christian College, 1972.

INTERNET SOURCES

www.chathamavaloncoc.com
www.christianchronicle.org
www.crenshawchurchofchrist.com
www.newarkchurchofchrist.org
www.northbroadwaychurchofchrist.org
www.simpsonstreetchurchofchrist.org
www.srs.org
www.tennesseeencyclopedia.net

INDEX

Page numbers in **boldface** refer to illustrations.

Adamson, Norman, 101, 102
Adkisson, Alvin, 94
Aker, O. L., xxvi
Akers, Doris, 139
Alderman, Connie, 62
Allen, Richard, 22
American Colonization Society, 4
Anderson, Sarah Alice, 22
Another World Wonder, 122, 163
Arms, Alms, 137
Arnold, Robert S., 138
Atlanta Constitution, 45
Auld, Hugh, 147, 148
Auld, Sophia, 147

Baccus, Carl, 18, 19, 143
Baccus, Edna, 18
Bailey, Frederick Augustus Washington (Frederick Douglass), 8
Bailey, Mack Allen, 18
Bailey, Thomas Pearce, 33, 34
Baldwin, James, 93
Baldwin, W. C., 119
Barber, H. L., 153
Bates, D. H., 39
Bennentt, Jefferson, 22
Benton, W. U., 38, 39
Bethune, Mary McLeod, 117, 118
Bible Student, 166
Billingsley, Price, 36
"Birth of a Nation," 39, 50–52, 77
Black, P. H., 150
Blakeney, Warren, 142

Blassingame, John W., 7
Blum, Edward J., 46
Blumhofer, Edith, 136
Boatright, Otis H., 96
Boles, H. Leo, 41
Bonner, Larry, 107
Booth, J. B., 24, 25
Booth, John Wilkes, 21
Botome, Elizabeth, 134
Bowdre, Alvertice, 87
Bowers, Calvin, 94, 109, 142–44, 156, 168
Bowers, Mozell, 168
Bowser, Fannie, 118, 124, 131, 132, **151**
Bowser, G. P., xxv, xxvi, 11, 15, 73–91, 105, 117, 123, 124, 126, 129, 130, 136, 138, 139, 150, **151**, 156, 164, 174, 178
Bowser Christian Institute (BCI), 75, 122, 125, 129, 150, 151, 152
Boyd, R. Vernon, 75, 85
Bradley, L. C., 136
Bradley, Tom, 144
Brice, Tanya Smith, 178
Bridges, Ruby, 98
Briggs, Eddie L., 145
Brokaw, Tom, 162
Brooks, Tommy, 178
Brown, Michael, 176, 177
Brown v. Board of Education (1954), 43
Bruce, Blanche K., 27, 53
Brumley, Albert E., 138
Bunner, A. A., 38
Burnett, Willie Eva, 140
Burton, A. M., 76, 78, 123

Busby, T. H., 78, 79, 136
Bush, Elijah, 142
Bush, George W., 175
Butler, Anthea D., 118
Butler, J. Milton, 136
Butler, Leroy, Jr., xxv, 142, 144, 145

Cain, Joseph E., 53
Campbell, Alexander (coworker with S. W. Womack), 4, 22, 23, 24–30, 33, 52, 58
Campbell, Alexander (enslaved preacher), 4
Campbell, Alexander (white leader), 4, 6, 7, 8, 9, 10, 14, 40, 133, 137
Campbell, Selina, 6, 7, 133
Campbell, Stafford, 4
Campbell, Thomas, 5, 6, 8, 10, 14, 40, 107, 148
Candler, Allen D., 45
Cannon, James M., 151
Caperton, C. L., 163
Carey, Archibald J., 51
Carpenter, Mary, 131
Carr (Crowder), Ethel, 98, **99**
Carr, Joi, 142
Carr, Mary, 98, **99**
Carr, Virgil, 98
Carson, Anthony, 18
Carson, F. F., xxii, xxiii, xxiv, xxv, xxvi, xxvii, 17, 18, 166, 167, 171, 172
Carson, Perry, xxii, 18
Carson, Sarah, xxii, xxiii, 18
Carter, Earnest, 156
Carter, Jimmy, 88
Carter, Manuel, 17
Casey, Michael, 63
Cassius, A. L., xv, 27
Cassius, John F. Rowe, 163
Cassius, S. R., xxvi, 10, 13, 19, 22, 26–30, 45–54, 134, 139, 148–50, 163, 166, 171, 172, 173, 174, 178
Cassius, William M., 163

Cathey, Alexander, 16
Cathey, Ben, 17
Cathey, Edmond, 16
Cathey, Geneva, 17
Cathey, Isaac, 16
Cathey, Nathan, 17, 22
Cathey, Susie, 16
Cathey, T. G., 16
Cathey, Truly, xxvii
Cecil, Cloys, 87
Childress, Billy, xxii
Choice Selections, 138
Christian Baptist, 60, 137
Christian Echo, xxvi, xxvii, 60, 75, 77, 87, 88, 106, 109, 111, 117, 126, 131, 145, 164, 166–69, 171, 174
Christian Evangelist, 47, 77, 78
Christian Leader, 28, 30, 35, 38, 39, 40, 41, 53, 54
Christian Standard, xv, 23
Christman, A. C., 87
Clansman, 50, 51
Clarke, Grandma, 67
Clay, Henry, 10
Clay, John Henry, 136, 137
Clinton, Bill, 174
Clinton, Hillary, 174
Cole, Imogene, 131
Collection of Revival and Plantation Melodies, 138
Collier-Thomas, Bettye, 119
Colston, A. J., 122
Colvin, Claudette, 102
Cone, James H., 133
Congress of Racial Equality (CORE), 96
Cooke, Sam, 142, 144
Cranford, Alfred, 45
Crawford, Wes, 154
Crihfield, Arthur, 60
Crosby, Fanny J., 136, 137
Cross, Alexander, 165, 166
Crouch, Andrae, 144
Cryer, Joe, xxvi

Cuffee, Paul, 22
Curl, Billy, 107, 154, 155, 167, 168, 171, 172
Curl, Mary, 167, 168

Darwin, Charles, 34
Davis, G. W., 38, 39
Davis, Kenneth, 140
Davis, Sam, 74
De Jarnette, J. S., 28
Dean, Wayburn, 140
Dedrick, Isaac, 87
Dennis, J. W., 139
Denson, H. C., 37
Dickerson, Dennis C., 51
Dicus, A. W., 139
Dixon, Jr., Thomas, 50, 52
Dorris, C. E. W., 76, 152
Dorsey, Thomas A., 139
Douglass, Frederick, 3, 8, 9, 27, 45, 46, 52,
    53, 112, 134, 147, 148
Dred Scott Case, 9
Du Bois, W. E. B., xxiv, 45, 46, 51, 52, 135,
    149
Dudley, S. J., 111
Durley, Leroy R., xxiii, xxvii
Dyson, Michael Eric, 71

Edmerson, John, 142
Edwards, W. C., 142
Eiland, F. L., 138
Ellison, Ralph, 93
Elston, Ben J., 40
English, D. M., xxvi, 94
Equiano, Olaudah, 133
Errett, Isaac, 23
Evans, Jack, Sr., 131, 152–**153**, 154, 178
Evans, N. L., 142, 156
Evans, Patricia, 131

Fanning, Tolbert, 10, 62, 149
Farmer, James, 96
Ferrill, J. W., 139
Firm Foundation, 60

Fitzgerald, Ella, 142
Fitzgerald, Thomas, 142
Fitzhugh, T. W., xxvi
Florence, Franklin, 104
Forten, James, 22
Foutz, Humphrey, 109
Frank, Leo, 39
Franklin, Benjamin (church leader), 40
Franklin, Benjamin (political leader), 22
Franklin, John Hope, 74, 163, 176
From Slavery to Freedom, 163
Fugitive Slave Law, 9
Fulson, Arthur, 87

Gadsden Purchase, 9
Garfield, James A., 27
Garner, Eric, 176
Garrison, James H., 46–48
Garvey, Marcus, 77
Gibbs, G. F., 37
Gibbs, Shelton, III 155
Gibson, Rev., 170
Goldwater, Barry, 109
Gomillion v. Lightfoot (1960), 103
Gooden, Dalton, 98, 99
Goodpasture, B. C., 62, 71, 123
Gore, Al, 175
Gospel Advocate, 10, 16, 19, 29, 35, 38, 41,
    54, 58, 60, 62, 70, 73
Graham, A. Hugh, 139–**141**
Graham, Barry, 140
Granger, Gordon, 17
Grant, Ulysses S., 21, 27
Gray, Fred D., 89, 90, 102–4, 121
Gray, Freddie, 176
Great Songs of the Church, 138
Green, Bobby, Jr. 178
Green, John, 141
Greenwood Commonwealth, 42
Griffith, D. W., 50–52
Grimke, Sarah, 148
Grimsley, Columbus, 154
Guardian, 51

Hagood, III, Fate, 156
Hahn, Kenneth, 87, 88, 144
Hairston, Andrew, 87, 107, 108, 111, 155
Hall, B. F., 62
Hamilton, Dontre, 176
Hamilton, J. K., 179
"Hard Fighting Soldier" (song's origin), xxvi
Hardeman, N. B., 60, 123
Harding, James A., 38
Harper, William, 156
Harrell, David Edwin, 34, 39, 46
Harris, Donald, 143
Harris, Loyd Clay, 156–**157**, 158–59
Harris, Roy, 138
Harrison, Daniel, 155
Harrison, Frances, 131
Harrison, R. H., xxvi
Hawkins, Vincent, 156
Hayes, Hugh L., 17
Hayes, Rutherford B., 27
Hervey, G. B., xxvii
Higginbotham, Evelyn Brooks, 74, 163, 176
Hill, Virginia, 14
Hofstader, Richard, 34
Hogan, Harold, 143
Hogan, Maggie, 86, 131
Hogan, R. N., xxvi, 17, 43, 80, 81, 86–**88**, 90, 91, 105–9, 136, 137, 139, 144, 152, **153**, 156, 166–68, 171, 172, 174
Holt (Bowser), Thelma M., 117, 119, 124–32, 136, 174
Holt, Charlotte, 125
Holt, Darrell, 158, 159
Holt, G. P., 81, 82, 109, 110, 156
Holt, Marion F., Jr. 125
Holt, Marion F., Sr. 124, 125
Hopkins, Milton, 158
Hose, Sam, 45, 46
Howard, John R., 60
Hudson, Elbert, 164
Hughes, Langston, xxi, xxii

Hughes, Richard T., 26
Hughes, Sarah Ann, 130
Hunter, Rick, 176

Invisible Man, 93
Isbell, A. V., 153, 154
Ivory, Robert, 142

Jackson, Mahalia, 100, 101, 139
January, Samuel, 4
Jarvis, Ida Van Zandt, 148
Jarvis Christian College, xxii, 18, 150
Jefferson, Thomas, 5, 22
Jenkins, Andrew, 95
Jenkins, J. W., 47
Jenkins, Jennie, 95
Jenkins, Patricia, 95–**97**, 98
Jesus, Jobs, and Justice: African American Women and Religion, 119
John Brown's Raid, 9
Johnson, Andrew, 27
Johnson, Gilbert A., 15
Johnson, John T., 137
Johnson, Lyndon B., 109
Johnson, Micah, 178
Jones, Absalom, 22
Jones, Alonzo, 78
Jones, Jacqueline, 118
Jorgenson, E. L., 125, 138

Kansas-Nebraska Act, 9
Keeble, Laura, 131
Keeble, Marshall, xxv, xxvi, 13, 43, 54, 57–64, **65**, 66–71, 73, 79, 84, 90, 96, 104, 119, 121, 123, 135, 137, 140, 143, 166, 167, 172, 174, 178
Keeble, Minnie, 62, 119, 131, 135
Kennedy, Alberta, 131
Kennedy, James, 111
Kennedy, Levi, Jr. 80, 81, 82, 86, 91, 139, 152, 166, 167, 172, 174
Kennedy, Levi, Sr. 22, 29, 52
Key, Barclay, 98, 107

Kidd, Colin, 33
Killebrew, James F., 41
King, Carole, 142
King, Martin Luther, Jr. 60, 96, 97, 102, 104, 106, 108, 109–11, 169, 173
Kipling, Rudyard, 35
Kirk, John, 9
Klingman, G. A., 37
Knox, Wilene, 143

Langston, John M., 27, 54
Lard, Moses, 60
Larrieux, Amel, 142
"Last Will and Testament of the Springfield Presbytery," 69
Lawton, Eugene, 70, 71, 111–13, 155
Lee, Floyd, 143
Lee, Jarena, 130
Lee, Robert E., 17, 21
Lee, William, 121, 136, 143
Leonard, Frederick, 96
Leopard's Spots, 50
Letter from Birmingham Jail, 97, 106
Lewis, John, 96
Lincoln, Abraham, 10, 17, 21, 27
Lipscomb, David, 10, 16, 19, 22, 23, 29, 38, 40, 41, 46, 58, **59**, 123
Little, Fred M., 40
Litwack, Leon F., 28
Liuzzo, Viola, 101
Locke, C. C., 17
Locke, Herbert, 94
Locke, Rene, 17
Lockert, Samuella, 171
Lockert, Willie, 171
Lowery, Peter, 149
Lowery, Samuel, 149
Lyons, Wilma E. (F. F. Carson's wife), xxii

Macrae, James W. F., 28,
Malcolm X, 104
Manny, Betsy, 14
Marshall, Andrew, 7, 8

Martin, Glenn, 167
Martin, T. Q., 38
Martin, Trayvon, 176
Mason, Charles H., 64, 65
Maxwell, James, xxv, 108, 131, **153**, 154
McCaleb, John M., 35, 42, 43
McClendon, Charlie E., 86
McCollum, Curtis, 143, 144
McCord, Willie, 158
McCurchin, Alfred, 170, 171
McCurchin, Gloria, 170, 171
McGarvey, J. W., 40
McMillan, E. W., 153
McNeal, Andy, 142
McPherson, Joe, 58
Millenial Harbinger, 6
Miller, Luke, 57, 69, 125, 135, 136
Miller, William, 170
Minor, Zenobia, 143
Mitchell, Joe N., 163
Mitchell, K. K., 102, **103**, 121
M'Lean, T. G., 25
Mobley, Cornelius, 144, 145
Montgomery, William E., 13
Moody, Dwight L., 136
Moon, E. W., 37, 38, 39
Moore, Russell H., xxvi
Morris, Joe, 60
Morrison, Jon W., 179
Morrison, W. W., xxv, 122, 170
Murrah, Jeff, 142
My Task, 127, 129
Myers, J. C., 53
Myrdal, Gunnar, 148

Nashville Christian Institute (NCI), 102, 104, 121, 125, 151, 152
National Association for the Advancement of Colored People (NAACP), 77, 100
National Youth Conference, 93–95
Newman, Richard S., 22
Newton, John, 137
Niebuhr, Reinhold, 46

Nixon, Arlette, 102
Nixon, Edgar D., 102
Nixon, Kermit, 18, 164
Nixon, Richard M., 129
Nixon, Walter, 18
Northup, Solomon, 133
Norwood, Brandy, 143
Norwood, Ray J., 143
Norwood, Willie, 142, 143

Oates, Stephen B., 7
Obama, Barack, 173, 176, **177**, 179
Obama, Michelle, 176, **177**
O'Sullivan, John L., 8
Our Ministers and Song Leaders of the Church of Christ, 122, 137
Owens, Brian, 177
Owens, William H., 120, 121

Palmer, Lucien, 166
Pantlitz, William, 171
Parks, Rosa, 96, 102, 118
Patton, George, 161
Paul Quinn College, 99, 162
Pendergrass, George, 140
Pepperdine, George, 87
Perkins, Frances W., 47, 149
Pitts, Carroll, 104, 105, 171
Plessy v. Ferguson (1896), 119
Pool, Charley, 6
Pool, James, 6

Raboteau, Albert J., 59
Ramsey, Harrison, 124
Ramsey, John T., 15, 120
Reach Out and Touch: A Book of Remembrances, Favorite Poems, and Thoughts from the Book of Psalms, 126
Revels, Hiram, 27, 53
Rice, Tamir, 176
Richardson, Robert, 7
Richardson, Wonderful Small, 144

Richie, Lionel, 142
Richmond Times, 42
Ricks, Abraham, Jr., 15
Ricks, Abraham, Sr., 15
Ricks, Charlotte, 15
Ricks, George, xv, 15, 16, 52
Robinson, Harold, 140, 144
Robinson, Henry, 77
Robinson, Jackie, 100
Rodgers, A. J., 163
Roof, Dylan, 178
Roosevelt, Franklin D., 88
Roosevelt, Theodore, 42
Rose, Sylvia, 140
Rowe, Frederick, 27, 38, 39, 40
Rowe, John F., 38, 39, 47

Sams, Izetta, 131, 162
Sams, Roosevelt, 161, **162**
Sankey, Ira, 136
Sapp, Marvin, 144
Scott, Walter (unarmed black victim), 176
Scott, Walter (white leader), 66, 137
Seamster, Ervin, 155
Sensational Nightingales, xxxvi
"Sermon on the Law," 14, 137
Shakespeare, William, 50
Shaw, T. J., 23
Shepherd, F. B., 75
Sherman, Carl, 179
Shoffner, Zelma Estella, 15
Silver Point Christian Institute (SPCI), 75, 78, 79, 91, 124
Simmons, Alvin S., 109
Simmons, William J., 39
Singleton, Octavius, 48
Smith, Arthur L., 154
Smith, Bethel, 144
Smith, C. C., 48
Smith, John, 96
Snow, Phoebe, 142

Social Darwinism, 34
Socrates, 97
Southern Bible Institute (SBI), 75, 152
Southern Christian Leadership Conference (SCLC), 96, 100
Southwestern Christian College (SwCC), 75, 142, 152, 162, 169, 170
Spain, Carl, **89**, 107
Spencer, Charles, 4
Spencer, Herbert, 34
Srygley, James, 16
Stevens, John C., 167
Stevens, Thaddaeus, 21
Steward, Ella, 80, 121, 131
Steward, G. E., xxvi, 80, 81, 82, 86, 91, 121, 131, 137, 139, 152, 174
Stone, Barton W., 3, 4, 14, 40, 69, 137
Stowe, Harriet Beecher, 9
Straight Company, 142
Student Nonviolent Coordinating Committee (SNCC), 100
Sumner, Charles, 21
Swanigan, Carl, 94, 95
Swanson, Bishop, 61, 68

Tallmadge, Jr. James, 5
Taylor, Jerry, 175, 176
Taylor, Marshall, 138
Taylor, Preston, 10, 23, 52, 57, 58
Teddlie, T. S., 138
Teel, Gordon, 107
Thomas, K. C., xxii, 18
Thompson, Adoniram J., 48
Thompson, James E., 158
Thompson, W. L., 139
Tindley, Charles A., 139
Traitor, 50
Trone, Jeanette, 170
Trone, Orum L., Jr., 94, 95
Trone, Orum L., Sr., 93, 94, 105, 170, 172
Trotter, William Monroe, 51, 52
Truth, Sojourner, 118

Tuggle, Annie C., xxiv, xxv, 24, 79, 80, 117–**123**, 124–25, 129, 130, 135, 137, 163, 170, 172, 174
Tuggle, Dewey, 163
Tune, Myles T., 166
Turner, Chris, 142, 144
Turner, Henry McNeal, 28, 29, 130
Turner, Nat, 7, 8, 10

Uncle Tom's Cabin, 9
Universal Negro Improvement Association (UNIA), 77

Vardaman, James K., 28, 49
Vaughner, John R., xxvii, 136
Vincent, C. G., 40

Wagner, Frederick Augustus, 53
Walker, David, 6
Walker, Ronald, 141
Wallace, George, 101
Waller, John, 120
Ward, Andrew, 133
Warrick, Jessie, 18
Washington, Booker T., 27, 42, 52, 54, 134, 147, 148, 150, 174
Washington, George, 22
Washington, W. F., 110, 113, 144, 174, 175
Watkins, Lloyd L., 164
Watts, Bernice, 176
Watts, Isaac, 137
Webster, Ezekiel, 131
Wells, Ida B., 52, 118
Wells, R. C., 87, 112, 113, 155, 169, 172
Wells, Tyree, 164, 165
Wesley, Charles, 137
Wheatley, Phillis, 118
White, Deborah Gray, 7
White, George, 134
Wilder, Johnnie, Jr., 142
Wiley, Sampson, Jr., 143

Williams, H. Clay, 178
Williams, John O., 144
Williams, Paul, 169
Williams, Veronica, 140, 141
Wilson, Darren, 177
Wilson, David, 142
Wilson, Woodrow, 51
Winston, J. S., xxv, xxvi, 80–**84**, 85–86, 91, 117, 131, 136, 139, 152, **153**, 174
Winston, Mizetta, 131
Womack, Hattie, 23
Womack, Minnie, 23, 135

Womack, S. W., xxvi, 10, 22, 23, 24, 27, 29, 51, 58
Womack, Sallie, 23
Women's Army Corps (WAC), 79
Woods, B. M., 151
Woods, Hiram, 26
Woods, Robert, 121
Woodson, Carter G., 147
Wright, Mac H., 156
Wyrick, Ernest D., 94

Ye Shall Know the Truth, 169

www.ingramcontent.com/pod-product-compliance
Lightning Source LLC
Chambersburg PA
CBHW030516080526
44586CB00011B/206